DAVID:

HIS LIFE AND TIMES.

BY

REV. WILLIAM J. DEANE, M.A.,

RECTOR OF ASHEN, ESSEX

WIPF & STOCK · Eugene, Oregon

Wipf and Stock Publishers
199 W 8th Ave, Suite 3
Eugene, OR 97401

David
His Life and Times
By Deane, William J.
Softcover ISBN-13: 978-1-7252-9927-6
Hardcover ISBN-13: 978-1-7252-9928-3
eBook ISBN-13: 978-1-7252-9929-0
Publication date 2/1/2021
Previously published by Anson D. F. Randolph and Co., 1885

This edition is a scanned facsimile of
the original edition published in 1885.

PREFACE.

THE events of David's life are told in copious detail in the two Books of Samuel and in the beginning of the First Book of Kings; the Chronicler takes up his story after the death of Saul, and the Psalms afford glimpses of his inner life and may be regarded as a spiritual comment upon the outward circumstances of his career. Of his connection with the Psalter I have spoken in the concluding chapter; suffice it here to say, that taking his contributions at the lowest computation, enough remains to convey a very exalted idea of his powers and to show the working of his soul under very varied experiences. Without entering into vexed questions of authorship, I have felt justified in quoting passages from the Psalms which, whether written by David or not, illustrate his history and his feelings. I have not loaded my pages with formal refutations of the aspersions which have been cast upon his motives and his character. In a popular work of this kind such controversial matter would have been out of place. Virtually I have defended him from undeserved reproaches, and the reader will find in the explanations afforded by the text, what, I trust, is a just view of his failings and merits.

The biography of David has exercised many pens. I may mention the works of R. Chandler, Krummacher, Stahelin, and Weiss, and as most satisfactory, Dean Stanley's Lectures and his Article in "The Dictionary of the Bible." Outside Holy

Scripture there is no reliable information concerning David. Josephus and Eusebius add little worthy of credit, while Talmudic and Mohammedan legends are quite unhistorical

Since I have finished writing this little book, I find that I have entered into some details, especially in David's later years, which are also given in Archdeacon Farrar's volume, "Solomon · his Life and Times." I think it best to let the passages remain, as my story would not be complete without them, and readers would not thank me for referring them to another work for particulars which they naturally expect to find here.

CONTENTS.

CHAPTER I.

EARLY LIFE 1
Bethlehem—Family of Jesse—David's life as shepherd—Samuel's circuit—He arrives at Bethlehem, selects and anoints David—David's early training.

CHAPTER II.

INTRODUCED TO SAUL 10
Philistines invade the land—Elah—Goliath—David sent to the camp, is introduced to Saul, fights with and kills the giant—Defeat of the Philistines—David's interview with Saul—Friendship with Jonathan—David returns home, is summoned to Court to relieve Saul's melancholy madness.

CHAPTER III.

LIFE AT COURT 24
David's rapid advancement—Saul jealous of David, plans his death, offers him Merab as wife, substitutes Michal on certain conditions—David fulfils the conditions and marries Michal—Renewed schemes of Saul—Jonathan's expostulation leads to a temporary reconciliation—Saul again threatens David's life—David saved by Michal, flees to Rama—Futile attempts to arrest him there—David's interview with Jonathan—Saul's enmity proved irreconcilable—The friends' parting.

CHAPTER IV.

OUTLAW LIFE IN JUDÆA 40
David at Nob—Received by Ahimelech—Flees to Gath—Takes refuge in Adullam—Destruction of Nob—David relieves Keilah—At Ziph—Last interview with Jonathan—David at Hachilah and Maon—In imminent peril—Spares Saul's life at Engedi, and expostulates with him—Carmel—Nabal and Abigail—David marries Abigail—Spares Saul's life a second time—Saul regrets his persecution, and promises to cease from further pursuit.

CHAPTER V.

EXILE IN FOREIGN LAND 65
David takes refuge among the Philistines, dwells at Gath, removes to Ziklag—His expeditions—The Philistines invade the land of Israel—David marches with them, is sent back to Ziklag, which he finds plundered and burnt, pursues and defeats the Amalekites—Battle of Gilboa—Death of Saul and his sons reported to David—David's elegy.

CHAPTER VI.

KING AT HEBRON 81
David removes to Hebron, is anointed king of Judah—Ishbosheth, the rival king, at Mahanaim—Battle at the Pool of Gibeon—Defeat of Abner and death of Asahel—Abner makes overtures to David—Michal restored—Abner assassinated by Joab—David's feelings at this event—Ishbosheth murdered—David anointed king of Israel—Philistines make war—The Well of Bethlehem—Double defeat of the Philistines

CHAPTER VII.

KING AT JERUSALEM 99
Capture of Jerusalem—The seat of government established there—Removal of the Ark from Kirjath-Jearim—Perez-Uzzah—Ark brought to Jerusalem—Michal's insulting words—Organization of priests and Levites—Psalmody—Military organization—Civil administration—David proposes to build a temple, is forbidden to undertake it, but is promised a great future—Mephibosheth

CHAPTER VIII.

FOREIGN WARS 121
War with Philistines—Moabites defeated and punished—War with Ammonites—Aramæan league against Israel—Hadadezer—Rabbah—Defeat of Syrians—Further operations—Aramæan cities reduced—Edom conquered—Psalms of victory—Extent of David's kingdom—Rabbah taken—Ammonites severely treated

CHAPTER IX.

SIN AND ITS CONSEQUENCES 136
Polygamy—Adultery with Bathsheba—Vain attempts to implicate Uriah—Uriah virtually murdered by Joab's connivance—Nathan's parable—David's repentance—Death of his child—Solomon born—Amnon's incestuous outrage—Absalom, in revenge, murders Amnon, is kept in banishment—Joab's stratagem effects his return—Three years' famine for the slaughter of the Gibeonites by Saul—The atonement—Rizpah

CONTENTS. vii

CHAPTER X.

ABSALOM'S REVOLT 158
Absalom's ambitious design—He steals the affections of the people—Causes of disaffection—Absalom at Hebron—Ahithophel—The insurrection breaks out—David leaves Jerusalem, sends back the Ark with the priests—Hushai—Ziba—Shimei's insult—Ahithophel's evil counsel adopted—His further plan defeated by Hushai—David informed of the movement in Jerusalem, arrives at Mahanaim, is supported there by friends—End of Ahithophel—Battle of Mahanaim—Defeat of rebels—Absalom slain by Joab—News brought to David—His grief for Absalom—Joab rouses David to action—The ten tribes submit to David—Judah also invites his return—Shimei, Ziba, and Mephibosheth—Barzillai—Dissension between Israel and Judah—Revolt of Sheba—Amasa made commander, murdered by Joab—Sheba slain—Joab reinstated

CHAPTER XI.

THE CENSUS 185
Administration of the kingdom—The census ordered, its guilt; its progress and completion—Gad's message to David—Three days' pestilence, stayed at Jerusalem—Purchase of Araunah's threshing-floor on Moriah—An altar raised there.

CHAPTER XII

CLOSING YEARS 193
Quiet times—Preparations for building the Temple—David's declining health, last song—Adonijah's conspiracy, supported by Joab and Abiathar—Conspirators at Enrogel, proclaim Adonijah king—News brought to David—He has Solomon proclaimed king, anointed, and enthroned—The conspirators disperse—Adonijah spared—David's last injunction to Solomon respecting religion—Advice concerning Joab and Shimei—Care of Barzillai—Plans and details of the Temple—David's last public address—Solomon's second anointing—David's death, funeral, tomb

CHAPTER XIII.

CHARACTER 205
David, as man, his mental characteristics—David, as king, results of his reign—David, as psalmist, his influence on psalmody—David, as prophet—As type of Christ—Conclusion.

CHAPTER I.

EARLY LIFE.

Bethlehem—Family of Jesse—David's life as shepherd—Samuel's circuit—He arrives at Bethlehem, selects and anoints David—David's early training.

> "Earth has many a noble city;
> Bethlehem, thou dost all excel:
> Out of thee the Lord from heaven
> Came to rule His Israel"

THUS sang our forefathers in old time, celebrating the little town in which Jesus, the Redeemer, was born. The history of Bethlehem begins with the birth of Benjamin, bought by the death of his mother between three and four thousand years ago, and it is connected with the sweet story of Boaz and Ruth, the ancestors of David The appearance of the place to-day is very much the same as it was in those early ages. Standing on a long narrow ridge of grey limestone, its limits have been controlled by the necessities of the site; and travellers who have examined the present little town agree in regarding it as a type of the ordinary Jewish country town, affording a true picture of such a place when it was the scene of the old Bible story. On this spot about B C. 1088, when Troy had fallen, but its war was yet unsung by Homer's verse, was born David, the king, poet, prophet, whose history we are about to narrate

David was the youngest son of a family of ten, the children of one Jesse, a householder and small proprietor, and, as Jewish tradition tells,[1] a weaver of sacred carpets, who lived at Beth-

---
[1] "Targ Jonathan," on 2 Sam xxi 19. "Dictionary of the Bible," i. 202.

lehem and farmed land in the neighbourhood. The genealogy of his family is given in the Book of Ruth, and repeated by St. Matthew and St. Luke, and from it we learn that Jesse was the grandson of Boaz by his Moabitish wife Ruth, and was descended from that Salmon, prince of the house of Judah, who espoused Rahab, "the harlot," in the time of Joshua. Thus, through some of his immediate ancestresses, David was allied to foreign races, and in after-years used this connection for the preservation of his own and his parents' lives. The remembrance of the relationship was not without influence on the character of the future monarch. It enlarged his sympathies, raised him above the selfish isolation of the Hebrew, enabled him to utter from the heart those aspirations for the conversion of the Gentiles which are found interspersed among his poems. It was almost a prophetic instinct that prompted the people's prayer at the marriage of Boaz and Ruth, when they said (Ruth iv. 11, 12): "Do thou worthily in Ephratah, and be famous in Bethlehem: and let thy house be like the house of Perez, whom Tamar bare unto Judah, of the seed which the Lord shall give thee of this young woman." The name David is generally taken to mean "beloved"; and as the youngest of so large a family he may well have been the darling of his parents, though not equally acceptable to his brothers, between most of whom and himself there was a great discrepancy in age. Of his mother we know nothing,[1] and of his brethren little more than the names. The eldest, Eliab, an imperious and ill-tempered man, was afterwards made head of the tribe of Judah.[2] The names of the others were Abinadab, Shammah or Shimmeah, Nethaneel, Raddai, Ozem There was one other son, who probably died young, whose name is not given [3] By a different mother [4] there were also two daughters Zeruiah and Abigail, the eldest of the

[1] The expression, "son of Thine handmaid," in Psa lxxxvi 16, and cxvi. 16, has been taken to imply that David's mother was a woman of piety and devotion, but there is no evidence to prove that either of these Psalms was written by David, and the latter is most probably of post-exilian date.

[2] 1 Chron xxvii 18, where he is called Elihu.

[3] Eight sons are mentioned 1 Sam xvii 12 Comp ibid xvi 10.

[4] The name Nahash in 2 Sam xvii 25 ("Abigail the daughter of Nahash") is either that of Jesse's wife, or has crept into the text instead of Jesse To suppose that Nahash, the king of the Ammonites (1 Sam xi 1), is meant seems to be a most improbable idea. Jesse, a pious Israelite, would not have married the concubine of an idolatrous enemy.

family. The former was the mother of the three celebrated warriors, Joab, Abishai, and Asahel ; the latter of the ill-fated Amasa. These nephews of David, being nearly of his own age, were admitted to the closest companionship, and play an important part in the subsequent history of their illustrious uncle. The possessions of Jesse comprised numerous flocks of sheep which were pastured on the slopes and hills in the neighbourhood. To tend and guard these was the charge of the youngest of his sons. This was no light task, though the position of the shepherd, disesteemed in comparison of military pursuits, was but a humble one, and usually assigned to the least conspicuous member of a family. Not that the occupation of shepherd was anything but honourable among Eastern people, and especially among the Israelites themselves. The sons and daughters of the greatest of their patriarchs had exercised this calling ; the great Prophet Moses himself had kept the flocks of Jethro ; but in a turbulent age and in an unsettled state of society the arts of peace are apt to be disparaged, and the strong right arm is somewhat unduly esteemed. The duties of a shepherd in this unenclosed country were, however, sufficiently onerous, and required the exercise of many soldier-like qualities. In the early morning he led forth the flock from the fold, marching at its head to the spot where they were to be pastured ; here he watched them all day, taking care that none of the sheep strayed, and, if any for a time eluded his watch and wandered away from the rest, seeking diligently till he found and brought it back. In those lands sheep require to be supplied regularly with water, and the shepherd for this purpose has to guide them either to some running stream or to wells dug in the wilderness and furnished with troughs. At night he brought the flock home to the fold, counting them as they passed under the rod at the door to assure himself that none were missing. Nor did his labours always end with sunset. Often he had to guard the fold through the dark hours from the attack of wild beasts or the wily attempts of the prowling thief There was no little peril in the occupation. David himself mentions (1 Sam xvii 34 ff.) how that he had rescued a lamb from a lion on one occasion and from a bear on another, and had slain the wild beasts with his own hand. There were also marauding tribes to resist, who were always ready to swoop down upon unguarded posts, and to plunder homesteads and carry off cattle. Such was the employment in which David passed his early years. That he was no mere shepherd boy, with hopes and aspirations which never reached beyond the petty concerns of his lowly occupation, was plain for all to see. There was something in this bright-eyed youth which made others feel their inferiority and stirred the spleen of commoner natures ; while those who were capable of appreciating excellence acknowledged the graces of his person, the nobility of his sentiments, the charm of his eloquence.[1] This pastoral avocation was a good training for the future ; it cultivated those faculties, virtues, and graces, which were needed for the destiny he had to fulfil. The bodily powers were exercised and braced by a hardy life in the open air ; courage and self-reliance became habitual in the presence of constant danger and responsibility ; dexterity in the use of rustic weapons, the bow and the sling, was acquired. Then the solitariness of the long day, the absence of distracting cares and interests, encouraged reflection and self-communing. As he wandered on the breezy uplands, as he watched the play of light and shadow on the distant mountains, as he gazed into the blue depths of the cloudless sky, his thoughts arranged themselves in rhythmic form, and he sung his hymn in praise of the Creator of this wonderful world to the glories of which his heart was newly opened. To him the heavens declared the glory of God and the firmament showed His handywork ; day unto day uttered speech, night unto night showed knowledge. It was the voice of the Lord that he heard in the thunder, powerful and full of majesty, that brake in pieces the cedars of Lebanon and shook the very wilderness. His own insignificance in the midst of the wonders of creation made him feel more keenly his dependence upon God and augmented his simple faith. Inspired by thoughts like these he sang in after-years :

> " When I consider Thy heavens the work of Thy fingers,
> The moon and the stars which Thou hast ordained ;
> What is man, that Thou art mindful of him ?
> And the son of man that Thou visitest him ? "

And his trust in God shines beautifully forth :

[1] 1 Sam. xvi. 18.

> "The Lord is my shepherd ; I shall not want.
> He maketh me to lie down in green pastures,
> He leadeth me beside waters of rest.
> He restoreth my soul,
> He guideth me in the paths of righteousness for His name's sake."[1]

It was in these lonely hours, as he watched his father's sheep, that he attained that skill in minstrelsy which early attracted the notice of his neighbours and contemporaries. The particular instrument which was the constant companion of his wanderings and the vehicle for the outward expression of his highest thoughts, was the *kinnor*, a small harp of triangular shape like a Greek Delta, having eight or ten strings. To the accompaniment of this instrument he sang his praise to God, poured out his soul in supplication, uttered his fervent aspirations after righteousness, and signified his faith and trust in Jehovah, the covenant Lord. In this simple, innocent life David passed his early years, educating himself for an unknown future, cultivating those manly noble qualities which should fit him for the eminent station to which God should call him. He might have said with the good poet Wordsworth :

> "Wisdom and Spirit of the universe !
> Thou Soul, that art the Eternity of thought,
> And giv'st to forms and images a breath
> And everlasting motion ! not in vain,
> By day or star-light, thus from my first dawn
> Of childhood didst thou intertwine for me
> The passions that build up our human soul ;
> Not with the mean and vulgar works of Man ;
> But with high objects, with enduring things,
> With life and nature , purifying thus
> The elements of feeling and of thought,
> And sanctifying by such discipline
> Both pain and fear,—until we recognize
> A grandeur in the beatings of the heart."

When David was some fourteen or fifteen years old there came a startling interruption to his quiet uneventful life. As he was one day tending his flock in the immediate neighbourhood

[1] Psa. viii. ; xix. ; xxiii. , xxix. We may regard such Psalms as expressing David's sentiments without deciding absolutely concerning their authorship. So in other cases.

of Bethlehem, he was summoned home by an urgent message.
The great judge and prophet Samuel, now with his father, had
desired his immediate presence at a sacrificial feast then about
to commence. Samuel, it seems, was accustomed to visit various
localities at uncertain intervals for the purpose not only of
holding courts of justice and redressing grievances, but also of
celebrating religious services, and offering sacrifices. Religious
matters were at this period in an abnormal state. No sanctuary
had taken the place of the destroyed shrine at Shiloh, the ark
was deposited in one spot, the tabernacle in another; and in the
abeyance of discipline and the enforced inaction of the regular
priesthood, the prophet was permitted or authorized to perform
sacerdotal functions, and by circuiting among the outlying
population to keep alive in the land the knowledge of God.
Ostensibly on one of these irregular visits Samuel had come to
Bethlehem. Really he had been sent by the Lord to anoint one
of Jesse's sons as the future successor to Saul whose disobedience and self-will had led to his rejection from the kingship of
Israel. Not that this successor was to depose the reigning sovereign, and at once assume the royal power; many years were to
elapse before the vacancy of the throne was to open the way
to his peaceful accession. Meantime in God's wise Providence
the future monarch was thus early to be designated, the nomi-
nation being kept from the cognisance of the jealous Saul by
occurring during this religious visitation of Samuel. The
sudden appearance of the venerable prophet, carrying in his
hand the long horn or phial filled with sacred oil, and driving
before him a heifer adapted for sacrifice, filled the rustic
villagers with dismay. Why had he penetrated to their
secluded home? Had any among them been guilty of a crime
which the Judge had come to investigate and punish? Or,
now that the breach between the king and the prophet had
become notorious, would they incur the monarch's displeasure
by welcoming the seer? Disquieted by such reflections, the
elders of the place went forth to meet him trembling, but he
calmed their apprehensions, assuring them that he had come
to sacrifice unto the Lord, and bidding them prepare themselves
for the ceremony by the usual purifications so as to be ready
to join with him in the offering and the consequent feast.
Specially he invited Jesse and his sons to be present with due
preparation, he himself going to their house and superintending

their purification. Either during this lustration, or in the interval between the act of sacr. and the feast, Samuel felt himself impelled to discover which of the young men was destined for the throne. He took the horn of oil in his hand, and probably without distinctly announcing his purpose demanded of Jesse that his sons should present themselves singly before him. When he saw Eliab, the eldest, approach; and marked his noble mien, his handsome countenance, his goodly stature, untaught by woful experience how little reliance could be placed on outward appearances, he said to himself, "Surely the Lord's anointed is before me." He was wrong. The Lord seeth not as man seeth. Bodily advantages weigh not with Him; He looks to the heart, the moral excellence. Eliab was not the chosen one; nor was Abinadab, nor Shammah, nor any other one of the seven brethren. Perplexed by this seeming failure, Samuel asked whether these were all the sons that Jesse had, and was informed that there was yet another, the youngest, a boy of no account who was employed in keeping his father's sheep. "Send and fetch him," said the prophet, "for we will not sit down to table till he come hither." David accordingly was hurriedly summoned, and entered the august presence, knowing nothing of what was in store for him. See him standing before the aged prophet, with his fair, pure complexion, his auburn hair, his light but athletic frame, his open guileless countenance, his bright eyes, his whole appearance goodly to look upon. This was the chosen one; the inward voice whispered, "Arise, and anoint him, for this is he." And Samuel obeyed the impulse, took the horn of sacred oil, and anointed David in the midst of his brethren. Only the members of his own family were present on this occasion, and if they understood anything of the important bearing of this ceremony, the danger of its disclosure and the feeling of clanship would alike prevent them from divulging it. It was expedient indeed that some witnesses should be present, who might, when necessary, testify to the unction; but these witnesses were such as were most likely to keep the matter secret, and to publish it only when it would most redound to the credit and glory of their family and their town. It is however almost certain that the brethren knew nothing of the motive of the ceremony. Plainly Eliab would never have spoken to David in the arrogant and contemptuous tone which he used on the occasion of the fight with Goliath, if he had had any true conception of his young brother's high destiny. Probably his friends saw in the ceremony only David's designation to the prophetical office ; they inferred that he was thus admitted as a member of the School of the Prophets which Samuel had founded. In this supposition they were partly correct ; but there was much more in the circumstance than this. The sacred narrator says . " The spirit of the Lord came mightily (overpoweringly) upon David from that day forward ;" and referring to this event long afterwards, when the monarchy had fallen on evil days, a Psalmist sings: " I have found David My servant ; with My holy oil have I anointed him " (Psa. lxxxix. 20). Doubtless, if Samuel left the brethren in ignorance of the exact nature of the anointing which they witnessed, he imparted its significance in whole or in part to David ; otherwise its utility towards his training for future dignity would have been impaired. Man must correspond to God's gifts, or their efficacy is impeded. The consciousness of being considered worthy of a noble destiny is a powerful stimulus to a noble life. Though inspiration came upon David with sudden and peculiar power, it did not force his will or deprive him of the mastery of his own actions ; it enhanced his natural faculties, but did not overbear them with might irresistible. The Holy Spirit which then came upon him raised in him high hopes and aspirations, and gave him strength to live up to them ; new powers awoke , intellectually and morally he became a new man ; all that was good developed quickly and firmly ; all that was of baser character passed away or became entirely controlled. Kingly virtues readily bloomed in that kindly soil. Government of self was the fitting prelude to the rule of others; he learned gentleness, charity, accessibility, sincerity ; he rose superior to selfish interests, and saw that the objects of one in authority ought to be the honour of God and the good of the community All these high wishes and purposes were fostered and directed by Samuel in the school at Ramah. Here, whenever he could be spared from his home duties, he became a diligent student, and the good old prophet, so grievously disappointed in his first venture, lavished all his care to mould this promising youth into a " man after God's own heart," a worthy ruler under the Theocracy. He taught him not only reading and writing, but also instructed him in music and poetry scientifically, so that the vague utterances and uncertain strains of the shepherd boy took form and substance, and became the regular and enduring psalms and melodies of the finished poet and harpist. And, more than all, he taught the neophyte the law of the Lord, made him conversant with the past history of the nation, drew thence lessons of life, warnings, encouragements, made him wise with the wisdom from above. And the venerable seer loved this pious manly youth who met his advances with answering affection, and looked to him as guide and teacher on all occasions in his earlier life.

Thus David grew on, daily advancing in holiness and righteousness ; as his bodily vigour developed, and his intellectual training progressed, so continually new strength and grace were communicated to his soul, enabling him to realize the unseen and conform his desires and conduct to the highest standard. And surrendering himself to the Divine impulse, and guided in action by the counsels of Samuel, David made no effort to assert himself or to publish his claims to the royal dignity ; he continued, when he was not in the school at Ramah, to tend his father's sheep and to act as the least esteemed in the family circle, being quite content to leave the development of his future career to the pleasure of the Lord, and well assured that He would show the way to the accomplishment of His purpose in His own good time

CHAPTER II.

INTRODUCED TO SAUL.

Philistines invade the land—Elah—Goliath—David sent to the camp, is introduced to Saul, fights with and kills the giant—Defeat of the Philistines—David's interview with Saul—Friendship with Jonathan—David returns home, is summoned to Court to relieve Saul's melancholy madness.

OF David's first introduction to King Saul tradition gave differing accounts,[1] but it seems most probable that it took

[1] The difficulties connected with David's first introduction to Saul and his early connection with the Court are very great, and have never been satisfactorily elucidated. These difficulties have been occasioned by the last editor of 1 Samuel having adopted various documents, some concerned with the life of Saul, others with that of David, and inserted them in his work without endeavouring to make out of them one consistent story, or arranging the facts in strict chronological order. The principal discrepancies in the present Hebrew text are these: in chap. xvi. 19 ff., David is made known to Saul as a skilful musician, is sent for to Court, beloved by the king, made his armour-bearer, and his father Jesse is requested to allow him to be continually with the king. In chap. xvii. David is at home in time of war, is sent casually to the camp on an errand to his brothers, where he is regarded as a mere shepherd-boy unaccustomed to the use of military weapons, and is quite unknown to Saul and Abner. Observing these discrepancies, and endeavouring to reconcile them, modern editors have exhausted their ingenuity in theories and accommodations which still leave some difficulties unsolved. Without recounting these, I may state at once that the most plausible arrangement is one revived and adopted by Hummelauer in his lately published commentary on the Books of Kings. This writer suggests that the fight with Goliath was the occasion of David's introduction to Saul, his position as Court musician and armour-bearer being obtained subsequently. The seeming dislocation in chronology is

place on the occasion of a great national event. When he was some eighteen or twenty years old, the restless Philistines gathered their forces and invaded the territory of Judah, with the view of regaining the supremacy which they had lost by the defeat at Michmash and under subsequent operations of the warlike king of Israel. Marching up the broad valley of Elah (so named from the terebinths growing there, as it is now named Wady-es-Sunt from its acacias), which runs north-west from the Judæan hills near Hebron to the sea, they pitched their camp near Shochoh, the present Shuweikeh, on the west side of the valley, at a place called, from the frequent encounters there occurring, Ephes-dammim, "Boundary of blood," and now represented by the ruin Beit Fased, "House of bleeding."[1] To meet this inroad Saul led forth his troops, taking up a position on the eastern side of the valley facing the enemy In this valley there exists a curious ravine worn by winter torrents some twenty feet across, and having steep banks ten or twelve feet high. This ghor effectually separated the hostile armies, so that for forty days they had rested opposite one another, not risking a general engagement. Not that the Philistines were idle. They did their utmost to provoke a combat in which the advantage would be wholly on their side

accounted for by the supposition that the portion of chap. xvi. which contains the mention of David's summons to Court to soothe the diseased mind of the king is the termination of the History of Saul, the author of which intends only to show how Saul lost God's favour, how David was anointed as his successor and came to be noticed and to take part in public affairs. Chapter xvii. commences the History of David from the beginning, recounting what happened before his attendance on the king, repeating some facts already mentioned The earliest MS. of the Septuagint, the Vatican, omits the following passages which are now found in the Hebrew, viz., chap. xvii. 12-31, 41, 48 (partly), 50, 55-58 ; xviii. 1-5 and other portions of this chapter. The text thus arranged probably represents the original Hebrew, the additions being made, possibly from authentic sources, at a later period. The Vatican text makes a complete and consistent narrative, as a cursory examination will show , and if it were expedient to tamper with the Hebrew text and correct it by the Greek, a straightforward story might at once be set forth If, however, we desire to maintain the integrity of the present Hebrew text, the explanation of Hummelauer seems to be the one that most fairly answers objections This I have accordingly adopted here.

[1] "Quarterly Statement," 1875, p. 191 f. , ibid. 1880, p 211 f. , Conder, "Tent Work," ii. 160.

Among their troops was a man of gigantic stature, Goliath by name,[1] a descendant, possibly, of the Anakim who on their dispersion by Joshua took refuge in the cities of Philistia (Josh. xi. 21). This warrior whom the Philistines put forth as their champion was indeed a formidable antagonist. The Targum makes him boast of being the hero who slew Hophni and Phinehas in the former war and carried off the ark, and who had often led the Philistines to victory on subsequent occasions. But even without the addition of this terrible reputation there was enough in his very appearance to inspire fear. His height is said to have been " six cubits and a span," which, taking the cubit at eighteen inches and the span at half a cubit, would make him nearly ten feet high. Instances of like extraordinary stature are quoted by commentators from Pliny[2] and other ancient authors; and our own country has produced one John Middleton, born at Hale in Lancashire, A.D. 1578, who was nine feet three inches tall and possessed of extraordinary strength, and whose portrait is preserved in the buttery of Brasenose College, Oxford. The armour of Goliath, which the Israelites retained as spoils and examined with natural curiosity, is minutely described by the historian. On his head was a helmet of bronze or copper, probably, as the Philistine accoutrements were imported from the west, of the shape with which Grecian monuments have made us familiar, covering the head and nape, but leaving the face wholly exposed. His body was defended by a coat of mail composed of small

[1] There is great doubt whether this giant's name was Goliath, the record usually calls him simply "the Philistine," and in 2 Sam. xxi. 19, Goliath of Gath is said to have been slain during David's reign by Elhanan. Probably, as Ewald suggests, the champion's real name was lost, and in the course of time that of the giant slain by Elhanan was transferred to David's antagonist. See a different solution in 1 Chron. xx. 5, adopted by the Authorized Version, 2 Sam xxi 19.

[2] "Hist Nat." vii. 16. Here we read that in the reign of Claudius Cæsar an Arab came to Rome who was nine feet nine inches high, and in that of Augustus there were in the city a man and woman even taller. Many of us must remember the Chinese Chang who was seven feet eight, and Keil mentions the appearance of a giant in Berlin in 1857 who quite equalled Goliath in stature. We read of others of Goliath's family notorious for their enormous size and strength, and the Israelites in their early wars had often to encounter these prodigies, though they could never meet them without dismay (Deut. ii. 10 ff., iii. 11 ff., 2 Sam. xxi. 15 ff., 1 Chron. xx. 4).

plates of metal fastened on a surface of cloth or leather, and overlapping one another, such as we may see in the representations of Assyrian warriors. This was of enormous weight, "five thousand shekels of brass," equivalent to two hundredweights of our measure, a ponderous equipment which must have rendered him unwieldy and slow in movement. The corselet, covering front, back, and sides, descended to the knees, and was there met by greaves of copper fastened by clasps or thongs round the calf and ankle, and thus defending the leg. His huge shield, large enough to protect the whole body, and formed of hide stretched on a wooden or osier frame bordered by metal, was borne by an attendant. For offensive purposes he carried first a spear with a shaft or handle of such extraordinary size that it is hyperbolically described as "like a weaver's beam," *i.e.*, the ponderous piece of wood to which the warp was attached in the loom. The spear's head, formed of iron or of the same metal as the other arms, weighed six hundred shekels, or eighteen pounds avoirdupois. Besides this weapon he had a sword girt at his side, and a javelin[1] slung across his shoulders. Such was the champion, who, relying on his brute strength and his impenetrable armour, had these many days been defying the ranks of Israel. "Why," he cried to them, as he stood forth in his threatening panoply in front of the gathered host, " Why are ye come out to set your battle in array ? Am not I the Philistine champion, and ye servants to Saul ? Let us decide the war by single combat. Choose you a man for you, and let him come down to me. If he be able to fight with me and kill me, then will we be your servants , but if I prevail against him and kill him, then shall ye be our servants and serve us." Such challenges were not unusual in olden days, though the proposed combatants were usually more equal in size, strength, and skill. Thus Paris, in Homer, offers to fight with Menelaus ; Turnus, in Virgil, with Æneas ; thus in Roman story the Horatii and Curiatii rest the fate of their respective countries on the issue of the battle between them.[2] But Saul had no hero in his army willing to cope with

---

[1] The Authorized Version renders *kidon*, "target" , but evidently some offensive weapon is meant, and Goliath would not have had two shields, or have gone into battle without some missile. The word occurs in the sense of "javelin," Josh viii 18 , Job xxxix 23, xli. 29, and elsewhere

[2] Homer, "Il." iii 67 ff , Virgil, "Æn " xii 13 ff., Livy, i. 24 f.

this Philistine champion, and for a long time Goliath was able to exhibit his monstrous proportions and to vaunt his prowess unchecked. The opponent who eventually arose came from a most unexpected quarter.

Among the warriors who had answered Saul's summons on the invasion of the country were the three eldest sons of Jesse. Their father's old age was sufficient reason for his declining active service in person, and his other sons were employed at home on the farm or in distant pasturages. In these wars, the troops, which were drawn from a very narrow circle, were not supported at the king's expense, but provided their own rations as they best were able. In the case of Jesse's sons, it was the old man's custom to send them provisions by the hand of David,[1] as Bethlehem was only a few miles distant from the encampment It was on one of these occasions that the event happened which decided David's future career.

Some time having elapsed since Jesse had communicated with his three sons, he determined to send David to carry them some necessary supplies and to see how they fared. With the simplicity of primitive times the narrator specifies the provender thus forwarded. There was an ephah (something less than a bushel) of parched corn, that is, grains of wheat roasted in an iron pan before they had become hard and dry, and forming a very palatable article of food still much used in this country; then there were ten loaves of bread, the large, round, flat cakes which the Jewish peasants make to this day; besides these, there was a present to the captain of their division, consisting of ten slices of dried curd,—the whole store being just such as would be furnished by a country farm. After telling David that he would find the troops in the valley of Elah,[2] and bidding him bring some token from his brothers which, in default of a letter, might assure him of their welfare, and that they had duly received the provisions, he despatched him on his errand Nothing loath to change the monotony of his pastoral life for the

---

[1] The words "David went and returned [went to and fro, R V] from Saul to feed his father's sheep at Bethlehem" (1 Sam. xvii 15), have seemed to many commentators to refer to the statement in ch. xvi. 19 concerning David's attendance at Court in the capacity of musician; but they are better explained as referring to his visits to the army in order to carry provisions to his brethren.

[2] Verse 19 is really part of Jesse's speech.

excitement of a visit to the scene of war, David, leaving his
flock in the hands of a servant, set out at the dawn of day with
an attendant to drive the ass that carried the victuals which were
to be conveyed to the army. When he arrived in the neighbourhood of the camp, which was surrounded by a rude fortification
composed of waggons arranged in a circle, he heard the Israelite
war cry as some troops were led forth on a skirmish with the
enemy. Fired with patriotic ardour, he hastily leaves his
servant with the luggage in the camp, and hurries to the front
where he knows that he will find his brothers. While he was
greeting them in the midst of their comrades, the Philistine
champion came forth as at other times in the valley in front of
the ranks, and repeated his boastful challenge. David's
attention was at once called to this spectacle, and the people
around began to tell how Saul had made lavish offers to any
one who would meet the Philistine, promising great riches, and
the hand of his daughter, and exemption from taxes and
personal service. Fancying that this might be mere rumour,
David asked the truth from others of the soldiers, and heard
that it was even so. And now the spirit that was in him began
to arouse the heroic impulse. Should the heathen thus insult
the Lord's inheritance? Should there be no champion found
to take away this reproach from Israel? Should this uncircumcised Philistine, a foul idolater, presume unchecked to defy the
armies of the only living and true God? Thus indignant, and
glowing with faith in Jehovah, he murmured, as he passed from
group to group amid the despondent, gloomy soldiery. So
early and strongly awoke in his breast feelings and aspirations
which are usually the outcome of maturer age, jealousy for the
honour of God, zeal for his country's welfare, eager desire to do
her service, a noble ambition to attempt an enterprise which
tried warriors declined, and absolute trust in the favour
and direction of heaven. His words exhibited a quiet
confidence that the Philistine would be vanquished, because
he was impiously fighting against God, and implied that a
champion would be found to uphold the righteous cause.
Hearing David thus talking with the bystanders, his eldest
brother, Eliab, was greatly incensed. He was a man of a
jealous disposition, narrow-minded and worldly, and had no
sympathy with David's high motives and aspirations. He
remembered the unction at Bethlehem without fully understand-

ing its import; he had often been forced to acknowledge the virtue and prowess of his young brother, and he had nourished thoughts of suspicion and envy which now culminated in angry words. Was this presumptuous stripling come to perform some deed of daring, which he, who was twice his age, had shrunk from attempting? "Why art thou come down hither?" he angrily asks "And who is taking care of that little flock of sheep which our father entrusted to thee, not one of which he can afford to lose? I know thy impudence and the malice of thy heart. The errand on which thou hast nominally come is all pretence, it is to see the battle, to witness bloodshed that thou art present here." Eliab should have looked at home, and marked the beam in his own eye; the presumption and malice, of which he accused his innocent brother, were very apparent in his own words. But David gently replies, by soft answer endeavouring to turn away wrath. "What have I now done? Is there no cause?" that is, "You know how fond I am of adventurous risks, and that it would be no vain boast were I to assert that if I were a soldier in this army, I would not tamely submit to this insult."[1] And he turned from his cold, unsympathizing brother to make further inquiries about the challenge, receiving the same answer as before. It was not long ere the words and bearing of this bold youth were reported to Saul, who accordingly sent for him to see if he was inclined and able to carry out the action which his language seemed to promise. Thus, in his simple white shepherd's dress, with his open, ruddy countenance and fair hair, with no weapons but his sling and staff, David stands before King Saul. With modest but firm confidence, he speaks: "Let not my lord's heart fail within him on account of the Philistine; I, thy servant, will go and fight with him." Something of the faith which animated David inspired Saul to place the honour of Israel in the hands of this youthful champion; he was disposed to allow the combat; but looking on the almost boyish hero, and contrasting him in his mind with the gigantic foe, before

---

[1] The above is Klostermann's explanation of the clause, obscure from brevity, "Is there not a cause?" Other interpretations are these · "It was only a word," I was only speaking about the challenge and doing no wrong. "Is not this a public matter, about which every one is speaking?" "Is not my father's command a sufficient cause?"

giving his consent to the duel, he puts forward its difficulties and dangers. "Thou art not able," he says, "to go and fight with this Philistine; thou art but a shepherd-boy, and he has been a warrior from his youth." David makes no boast of warlike skill or prowess, but he recounts his combats with wild beasts while keeping watch over his flock; how that, unaided, he had slain a lion and the much more formidable bear, and he affirms that the Lord will aid him to be equally successful in the fight against this heathen in spite of his brutal strength, because he had dared to defy the armies of the living God. Won by the youth's quiet confidence, and recognizing in him a power and a spirit beyond nature, Saul consents to his proposal "Go!" he cries, "and the Lord shall be with thee." But at the same time he will omit nothing that might help him in this momentous contest The young champion shall not be armed less securely than his opponent. So he gives David his own dress, the coat, like the buff-coat of mediæval times, worn under the armour, and to which the sword was attached, and the mail corselet and helmet, and wishes him thus completely equipped to go forth. David, who was lightly made and unused to have his movements fettered by the weight of armour, took a few steps thus encumbered, but found that he could not hope to fight successfully dressed in this panoply. If he were to prosper, it must be by superior activity, not by strength of arm or impenetrability of armour. So he doffed the assumed weapons, and taking with him only those with which he was familiar and in the use of which he was eminently dexterous, his sling and his club, he set forth on his expedition. It was not foolhardiness, or mere love of adventure, or thirst for fame, that prompted the enterprise. A strong religious principle was the moving power. In his eyes it was utterly unworthy of a nation that believed in Jehovah thus to cower before mere brute force, forgetting in whose hands lay the issue, and that God defends the right, it was abhorrent to all his notions that a foul idolater, an uncircumcised Philistine, should flout the armies of the true worshippers of the Lord, and he blushed for his countrymen's little faith in trembling at this boastful pretender. This national disgrace he resolved to wipe out in reliance on the protection and aid of heaven. The position was not of his own seeking He had come to the camp ignorant of what was going on. He had seen the crisis

No one but himself had looked upon it in the right light, as a conflict between light and darkness, truth and error, religion and idolatry The Providence of God had led him so to view it ; and he rose to the occasion, resting his cause on the succour of Him in knowledge of whom the being and continuance of Israel were bound up Purity of motive supported his faith , past experience in private life inspired him with confidence in an enterprise undertaken for the honour of God and the love of His people. And humanly speaking, the conflict was far from hopeless Provided his arm was strong and his aim was steady, the sling was the best possible weapon to employ against an adversary whose might was irresistible, and with whom in close combat he could not expect to cope

Setting out he soon arrived at the ravine which, as we have said, crossed the valley and formed a barrier between the opposing hosts. Descending into this at one of the few places where a descent is practicable, he chose five smooth stones from the water-worn pebbles with which the sides and channel are covered, and placing them in the wallet that hung at his waist, climbed the opposite bank, and presented himself suddenly on the Philistine side of the valley Here was the giant seated in front of the army after uttering his insulting challenge As his eye lighted on David and he perceived that he was advancing in hostile fashion, he rose from his seat indeed, but he openly exhibited his disdain of such an antagonist Was this the champion whom the Israelites had pitted against him, a mere youth, pretty indeed and fair to look upon, but one whose cheek was not bronzed with military toil, who could have had no experience in war, and who came to the fight armed with a club ? " Am I a dog," he exclaimed indignantly, " that thou comest to me with staves ? Come to me, and I will give thy flesh unto the fowls of the air, and to the beasts of the field." And the giant cursed David by the God whom he adored, blaspheming the holy name of Jehovah. The youth was not alarmed at this bluster, or at the closer sight of the monster. Like a hero in ancient story he answered taunt with taunt. "Thou comest against me with sword, and spear, and javelin ; but I come against thee in the name of the Lord of hosts, the God of the armies of Israel which thou hast defied " And he goes on to pronounce an assurance of victory over him and his people, "that all the earth may know that there is a God in Israel ; and that all this assembly may know that the Lord saveth not with sword and spear ; for the battle is the Lord's, and He will give you into our hand" This was the young warrior's confidence. Often in after-life did he think on this occurrence, and in many a psalm express the feeling with which he entered on the conflict.

> "There is no king saved by the multitude of an host,
> A mighty man is not delivered by much strength.
> Our soul hath waited for the Lord ,
> He is our help and our shield
> For our heart shall rejoice in Him,
> Because we have trusted in His holy name" (Psa xxxiii 16, 20, 21)

Slowly the encumbered giant advanced to meet his agile foe, thinking with one thrust of his ponderous lance to end the fight But David never contemplated coming to close quarters. He saw the only vulnerable spot in Goliath's frame, the face which was not protected by the visor of mediæval helmets. Surely with one of these five stones he could strike him from a distance Many Israelites were skilled in the use of the sling. In the time of the Judges (xx 16) we read of seven hundred chosen men of the tribe of Benjamin, who, left-handed, could sling stones at an hair-breadth and not miss. David's dexterity stood him now in good stead. Despising his boyish antagonist Goliath did not condescend to have the protection of the shield-bearer to cover his face, but came on with a careless confidence to meet his fate, perhaps not perceiving the sling in David's hand. While the two were at some distance apart, the youthful hero loaded his weapon Thrice round his head he whirled the thong, and then with all his strength and with an inward prayer for success he hurled the stone. The missile flew true to the mark , full on the forehead it struck the giant and with such force as to sink into the bone. Stunned and insensible Goliath fell prone upon the earth Seeing the effect of the blow, David ran up, and stood over the prostrate Philistine, and having no sword of his own, took that of his adversary and with it cut off his head, which he raised aloft in sight of the two observant armies What an exulting shout arose from the Israelites as they saw this token of victory ! What terror and dismay filled the hearts of the Philistines at this unexpected spectacle ! They had agreed to the terms of the combat because the result was to them a foregone conclusion ; they had no fears as to the issue ; and this utter frustration of all their hopes struck them with sudden panic. Surely, it was a great victory. It restored Israel's faith in the unseen Jehovah who had shown Himself so evidently on His people's side ; it taught them in what spirit to resist their enemies; it pointed to an ideal theocratic king. The Greek translators of the Old Testament have appended to the end of the Psalter a psalm, which they assert that David composed on this occasion. There is no Hebrew original of this poem extant, and it is probably not genuine, but it accords well with the history, and is of very ancient date. "This psalm was written by David's own hand, and beyond the number [*i e.*, the 150 genuine Psalms], when he fought the single combat with Goliath." Such is the title. The following is the ode : " I was little among my brethren, and the youngest in the house of my father. I used to keep my father's sheep , my hands made an instrument of music, and my fingers fitted a psaltery. And who shall report it unto my Lord ? He is the Lord, He heareth. He sent His messenger (angel), and took me from my father's sheep, and anointed me with the oil of His anointing. My brethren were fair and tall, but the Lord was not well pleased with them. I went out to meet the Philistine, and he cursed me by his idols ; but I drew his own sword, and cut off his head, and took away the reproach from the children of Israel."

The immediate effect of David's victory was the utter defeat of the Philistines. Panic-stricken, the armies of the aliens were turned to flight ;[1] they rushed down the valley, some taking refuge in Gath which stood at its mouth on a towering chalk-hill, others making their way to Ekron, far away to the north, pursued and slaughtered up to the very gates, so that David's threat was made good : " I will give the carcases of the host of the Philistines this day unto the fowls of the air, and to the wild beasts of the earth ; that all the earth may know that there is a God in Israel."

Meantime Saul was naturally anxious to know more about this youthful champion. When he had sent him forth to the combat, he had inquired of Abner, his general, whose son he was , but Abner could not inform him But after the battle Abner sought out the hero, and found him stripping the giant

[1] Heb. xi. 34.

of his armour ; and he brought him to Saul with the head of
Goliath in his hand, grim trophy of his victory. To the king's
inquiries David replied that he was a son of Jesse the Bethle-
hemite. A long conversation ensued, of which no record
remains, but it was of such a character and displayed so
favourably David's modesty, patriotism, and piety, that
Jonathan, Saul's son, who was present at the interview and
already inclined to regard with kindness a youth so distinguished
for courage and beauty, conceived for him the most powerful
affection, so that, in the words of the sacred writer, "the soul
of Jonathan was knit with the soul of David, and Jonathan
loved him as his own soul." Here commenced that life-long
friendship between these two young men which is one of the
most beautiful episodes in history. Heart answered heart;
perfect confidence reigned between them, no jealousy ever
darkened the prospect of their friendship; alike in religious
aspirations and in patriotic desires they moved on side by side,
doing their duty to God and the community. The prince saw
in David a kindred spirit, one who had the same intense trust
in Jehovah, the same confidence in the future of Israel, the
same passionate love of his country "Each, too," as Dean
Stanley says, "found in each the affection that he found not in
his own family" To mark this friendship, either now or at
some later period, Jonathan bestowed on David his own
princely dress, the long outer robe which was the usual garb of
the wealthier classes, and the military accoutrements, including
girdle, sword, and bow. This was the greatest honour that he
could confer upon his friend, and showed how he would have
every one know in what light he regarded him and the value
which he set upon his friendship.[1]

From some unexplained cause, either from wilful forgetfulness
of his lavish promises, or deeming David too young and too
insignificant to fill the position of son-in-law, Saul let the youth
return to his home at Bethlehem, taking with him, as the sole
reward of his services, the spoils of the giant whom he had
slain.[2] Of these, the sword was afterwards dedicated in the
Tabernacle at Nob, where we shall again meet with it, and

[1] Comp Esth vi 8 , Homer, " Il." vi. 230 ff.

[2] The words, "he put his armour in his tent" (1 Sam xvii 54), imply
that he took it home It is improbable that David, or indeed any of the
Israelites, had tents in this campaign See Dean Payne Smith *in loc.*

Goliath's head was taken to and preserved at Jerusalem when that city fell into David's hands. For a short time the boy-warrior resumed his pastoral occupations, but ere long he was summoned to Court in order that he might by his minstrelsy allay the king's fits of melancholy madness. Since his rejection Saul had fallen into a state of gloom and depression which at times assumed the form of mania, and to his attendants appeared like demoniacal possession. For such a disease, to which medicine offered no cure, the only palliative known was music; and the courtiers, alarmed at symptoms which daily became more serious, advised the wretched monarch to have recourse to this expedient. On his consenting to the proposal, one of them, who may have been Jonathan himself or a fellow-student in the School of the Prophets at Ramah, suggested that David would be just the person required for such an occasion,[1] for he knew him to be cunning in playing, and, what would make him doubly acceptable to the warlike king, a mighty, valiant man, referring, doubtless, to his recent fight with Goliath Besides this, he was comely in appearance and eloquent in speech, and, as all his actions proved, the Lord was with him Hearing all this, and remembering what he had himself seen of the young hero, Saul despatched messengers to Jesse desiring him to send his son David to him at once The old man could not but comply with the monarch's request, and in accordance with the simple manners of the age he forwarded with his son a little offering from the produce of his farm, some bread, and a skin of wine, and a kid These articles may represent either the present without which no great man in the East can be approached, or the cost of David's maintenance for the short time that he was to remain with the king. Thus was the youthful shepherd transferred to a new sphere which should have supreme influence in his future career and educate him for his

---

[1] The occasion that led to David's first introduction to Saul would very naturally be explained in different ways by different writers The military annalist would ascribe it to his prowess in the fight with Goliath, the civil writer, prophet or priest, would find it in the exercise of his musical talents The final compiler presents both accounts without any attempt at reconciliation In my "Samuel and Saul" I have given the usually received view of the sequence of events, but further consideration has satisfied me that the theory in the text is the most probable solution of the difficulties which encumber the existing accounts. See "Samuel and Saul," pp 161 ff, and note p. 163

high destiny ; thus he learned the course of public events and the secret springs of political action , his intellect was sharpened by contact with other minds , he was taught how to deal with men ; in a very severe school he was trained for trial, and conflict, and suffering ; by many a stroke was fitted for his place in the Church of God.

The mission of David was for a time successful. Under the spell of his minstrelsy and songs and eloquent utterances, the restless, irritable temper of Saul was calmed, the nervous system was soothed, the morbid melancholy was cheered, and for a time the mental disease which was already wasting his energies was checked. As David, with rapt, poetic fervour, poured forth to the accompaniment of his tuneful harp strains of faith and love, a new spirit entered the heart of the miserable king , he seemed to be set back again in happier times, to be living a purer life; harmony was restored to his disturbed nature, and he felt himself capable of rising to higher things. So satisfied was Saul with the good effect produced upon his mental state by the young musician, and so great an affection did he conceive for the gallant youth, that he requested Jesse to allow him to enter the royal service, and to be permanently attached to the Court Henceforward David seldom visited his native place, as a more stirring life opened before him, and affairs of moment occupied all his time and required all his energies. This change in his fortunes formed the subject of many a national ode. Thus in the longest historical Psalm (lxxviii.) we read :—

> " He chose David also His servant,
> And took him from the sheepfolds ;
> From following the ewes that give suck He brought him,
> To feed Jacob His people, and Israel His inheritance."

This was the second stage in his discipline From the repose and monotony of the life at Bethlehem, from his lonely communings with nature and with God, he is transported to new scenes, placed amidst new associations, which enriched his ideas, amplified his experience, and gradually fitted him for the position to which he was called.

CHAPTER III.

LIFE AT COURT.

David's rapid advancement—Saul jealous of David, plans his death, offers him Merab as wife, substitutes Michal on certain conditions—David fulfils the conditions and marries Michal—Renewed schemes of Saul—Jonathan's expostulation leads to a temporary reconciliation—Saul again threatens David's life—David saved by Michal, flees to Rama—Futile attempts to arrest him there—David's interview with Jonathan—Saul's enmity proved irreconcilable—The friends' parting.

THE war with the Philistines lasted many months, or more probably one or more years, and during all this time David was in close attendance upon Saul, took part in military expeditions, and won much distinction by his bravery and prudence in all matters with which he was concerned. The king was much attached to him, and made him one of his armour-bearers, an honourable office like that of squire in the Middle Ages, and usually conferred on warriors of tried valour. There were, doubtless, many who arrived at this distinction. Joab, we read (2 Sam xviii. 15) had "ten young men that bare his armour," and the king had a still larger number, so that the title became an honorary one, and connoted few duties or emoluments From this he was soon promoted to a higher command, and the management of many minor operations was entrusted to him Success accompanied all his undertakings, and envy and detraction at present were non-existent or silent in the face of such notorious merits. Even the courtiers, who were mostly Benjamites, and would be naturally jealous of the advancement of a member of another tribe, were won over by his gallant conduct and modest bearing. Far beyond the precincts of the Court his great abilities were acknowledged, thus early he showed his power over the hearts of men, no one disputing his claim to advancement, all agreeing that his rapid promotion was entirely well deserved, so that he was "accepted in the sight of all the people," and "all Israel and Judah" (for the distinction between the two already existed) "loved him." But in the case of Saul this friendly feeling was soon clouded by jealousy; and the cue once given was followed by the sycophants and time-servers who hang upon men of rank. On the final return of the troops, when the Philistines were expelled from the country and the war was concluded, the conquerors were received with triumph, and a general rejoicing took place [1] From all the cities the women came forth to escort the victors home with music, song, and dance. As they beat their tambourines and struck their triangles and moved with solemn, religious dance, they sang a song of victory, answering each other antiphonally with the refrain:

> "Saul hath slain his thousands,
> And David his ten thousands"

Thus was shown the feeling with which the young hero was regarded, which involved the comparative disparagement of the king. Saul was quick to perceive this, and was greatly incensed. Should this stripling, whom he had himself advanced to his present eminence, be reckoned at ten times his worth? "What can he have more but the kingdom?" he indignantly asked He saw that the affection of the people that had once been his,

[1] This ovation was not held, as our version (1 Sam. xviii 6) seems to intimate, on the return of David from the slaughter of Goliath, but on the conclusion of the war which may have occupied some years Thus there was ample time for the development of David's military talents, and the growth of his popularity before the jealousy of Saul was aroused by the women's acclamations The words "It came to pass as they came, when David returned from the slaughter of the Philistine," are not opposed to this view If we regard the second clause as genuine (and there is good reason for considering it a mere gloss), "the Philistine" is equivalent to "the Philistines," and refers to the nation, not to any individual, and the special mention of David denotes that the conduct of the war had chiefly devolved upon him, and that he was regarded as the master-mind of the campaign.

the admiration which had hitherto followed him, were transferred to David, and from this day forward, in his secret heart, he cherished a feeling of malignant jealousy against him. Brooding on this matter, and giving himself up to his evil passions, Saul on the next day was seized with one of his attacks of insanity; and on David, as usual, presenting himself with his harp to soothe the monarch's mind, he could not control the murderous impulse that arose within, and brandishing the spear which he bore as the symbol of sovereignty, he threatened to pin him to the wall. Twice did David escape this danger, withdrawing himself from the king's sight, but continuing his duties about the Court, as he considered the menaced assassination to be a symptom of temporary insanity, and not a proof of deliberate enmity and hatred. God had placed him in his present position, and he would never leave it till it became absolutely untenable, or he felt himself summoned by the same authority to another post. To Saul's dislike of David was now added a feeling of fear. He felt that the youth was under Divine protection, that the grace which he himself had forfeited was poured in abundant measure upon his rival, while he seemed powerless to injure him. A superstitious dread of this gallant, successful, beloved leader took possession of his soul, and his thoughts were continually engaged on planning his ruin and death. He could not ignore his great services; he was himself too much influenced by popular reputation to openly oppose the claims of one so highly valued, but he removed him from his presence for a time by giving him a high command, and making him captain of a thousand, that is, of one of the great tribal divisions. But such a position only gave David further opportunity of distinguishing himself and winning the affection of the army. Hitherto Saul had avoided the fulfilment of his promise to give his daughter in marriage to the conqueror of Goliath; now inspired by the hope that under the prospect of such an alliance David might undertake some rash enterprise and therein lose his life, he offers him his elder daughter, Merab, on condition that he would fight valiantly against the enemies of the Lord; saying to himself, "Let not mine hand upon him, but let the hand of the Philistines be upon him." In calling the Philistines "the enemies of the Lord," he wished to enlist David's patriotism and religious feeling on his side, calculating that his piety might lead him to destruction.

Whether David saw through the crafty design or not, he answered humbly, yet confidently, as one who felt the highness of the honour proposed, and trusted to the Lord to carry him safely through all contingencies. "Who am I?" he said, "and what is the condition of my father's family in Israel, that I should be son-in-law to the king?" He could not refuse the offer, for it was one of value and dignity, and opened to him a path of increased usefulness, but it was in many respects embarrassing. Merab does not seem to have entered heartily into the proposed arrangement. There was no love between the young people, and David objected that neither he nor his family were of sufficient importance to aspire to such a connection; and suddenly, either from the caprice which marked Saul's character, or owing to a new fit of jealousy, on the appearance of another suitor who was able to offer a substantial dowry, the negotiation came to an end, and Merab became the wife of Adriel, a native of Abel-Meholah, a town in the Jordan valley ten miles south of Bethshean, and the birthplace of the great prophet Elisha.[1] Of the melancholy fate that befell the offspring of this marriage we shall read hereafter But the base device of luring David to ruin by means of marriage was still continued. Saul discovered with satisfaction that his younger daughter Michal, attracted by the graces of his person and the gallantry of his conduct, had fallen in love with David, and he made it clear to the latter that he would be willing to accept him as son-in-law. David, who had now had experience of Saul's fickleness and ill faith, returned no, or an evasive, answer to this proposal. Not deterred by this rebuff, the king desired his courtiers, as if of their own motion, to persuade David to accept the offered honour. The youth answered discreetly that he was fully aware of the greatness of the privilege thus presented, but he was poor, and unable to offer the dowry which the king would expect from a suitor for the hand of his daughter. He might indeed have claimed his bride without purchase money in accordance with the royal proclamation before the combat with Goliath, but he was too generous and took too low an estimate of his own merits to press this point, and contented himself with expressing his inability to comply with the usual custom of making an ample offering to the parents of the bride. This was just

[1] The paragraph about Merab (1 Sam xviii 17-19 and 21 partly) is wanting in the oldest MS. of the Septuagint

the answer that the treacherous Saul desired. "Tell him," he said to his servants, "that I require no dowry from him, but one hundred foreskins of the Philistines, to be avenged of the king's enemies." And he appointed a certain time during which the agreement was to hold good, thinking that David would thus be driven to undertake some rash and foolhardy expedition in which he might lose his life The proposition exactly suited the adventurous spirit of the young hero. If he saw the treacherous design of the king in thus exposing him to imminent danger, he had firm trust in the protection of Jehovah, and hailed the opportunity of punishing the oppressors of Israel. He also felt confident that when he returned successful, the promised reward could no longer be withheld, and that the close relationship thus established between himself and Saul would lead to a return of that friendship and confidence which personally he had done nothing to impair In the existing condition of affairs between the Israelites and the Philistines no formal declaration of war was needed : raids on both sides were of frequent occurrence without the motive of any new or urgent provocation. So David gathered his men together, made an incursion into the enemy's country, slew double the number required, and ere the stipulated period was expired, presented the ghastly proofs of his exploit before the king. It was a barbarous state of society which allowed a prince to exact such a dower, and found a suitor prepared to execute so cruel a demand. If we meet with instances of extraordinary virtues and marvellous endowments in some of the "Men of the Bible," we must remember that they were not altogether superior to the feelings and opinions of their contemporaries, that they were imbued with the spirit of their age and country, only modifying national prejudices by an intense realization of an overruling providence, and faith in the guiding and protection of the covenant God In the case of David it was characteristic to sympathize with every human feeling, to realize every phase of human nature. The part of patriot was a noble one to play; to slay the enemies of Israel by any means and under any circumstances was to fight the Lord's battles ; the idea of cruelty in inflicting this vengeance never crossed his mind ; there was a duty to be done ; the details of its performance were of no concern

Saul could not delay his consent to the marriage, now that

his savage condition was fulfilled ; and Michal was wedded to
David, the affection with which she regarded her husband being
a fruitful source of annoyance to her jealous father. But in the
face of public opinion and in consideration of his eminent
services he could not withhold further advancement from his
son-in-law. Accordingly he conferred upon him the office of
captain of the king's body-guard, a post which was only
inferior to that of Abner, the general-in-chief, and gave
him a seat with Jonathan at the royal table. In revenge for the
late raid, and perhaps thinking that David would take advantage of the relaxation from military service allowed to a newly
wedded man, the Philistines made a fierce attack on the
Israelites. But the young commander did not allow domestic
ties to interfere with public duties ; now, as always, he was
ready to meet the enemy, and to risk his life in the contest.
Success attended all his efforts , his popularity increased with
every fresh campaign , reluctantly Saul was compelled to own
that the Lord was with him , and feeling that he was a dangerous rival, and possibly a competitor for the throne, he was
more than ever determined to effect his destruction. No longer
attempting to disguise his design, he speaks openly to Jonathan
and his courtiers of the necessity of putting this traitor to death.
The loving heart of Jonathan is filled with apprehension for
the safety of his friend , he communicates to him his father's
intention, and not knowing to what sudden measure the king's
hatred might have recourse, he advises David to conceal himself somewhere near at hand till he had expostulated with his
father, and endeavoured to win him from his evil purpose. David
being thus temporarily secured, Jonathan sought an interview
with his father, and modestly but earnestly pointed out the
wickedness and impolicy of his conduct. He whose death he
meditated had been a faithful servant to the king, and had
done him no wrong , nay, he had often risked his life in his
country's service, and had wrought great deliverance in Israel ;
let not the king shed innocent blood and deprive himself of
the great stay and glory of his kingdom. This intercession of
the one, who, if Saul's suspicion was well founded, would be
most injured by David's pretensions and popularity, had an
immediate influence on the king's better feelings ; he repented
of his murderous design, and swore solemnly that he would
spare his life "As the Lord liveth, he shall not be put to

death." With great gladness Jonathan carried the good news to his friend; a temporary reconciliation was effected, and David renewed his attendance on the king's person, and resumed his important command in the army.

This happier condition of affairs did not long continue. Another important success of David in a battle with the Philistines awoke in Saul a furious jealousy. Giving way to this evil feeling he was seized with a paroxysm of insanity, and when David, as usual, attempted to soothe him with music, the wretched monarch, losing all control, hurled his spear at the minstrel with murderous intent. David eluded the blow, and the missile fixed itself harmlessly in the wall. But he saw danger in the king's presence, and withdrew himself to his own house, in the lower part of Gibeah, the royal palace being in the upper city. Saul was not to be thus baffled of his purpose, he had now thrown off all disguise, and determined to have the life of his enemy. He dared not openly break into the house and murder him, lest the people should rise to the rescue of their favourite, but he surrounded the habitation with his emissaries, ordering them to keep strict watch and slay him in the morning as soon as he appeared outside the door. He may have had some superstitious scruples about effecting a forcible entrance into a house at night, like that which prevented the Philistines from seizing Samson at Gaza (Judges xvi. 2), but he took what he considered certain means of securing his prey. To encourage him in his evil purpose, and to foment the feeling of enmity, if ever it slumbered for a time, there was a band of cowardly courtiers, themselves envious of the youthful aspirant, and ready to promote any machination that tended to his overthrow. The state of matters is well described in Psalm lix., which the Title (probably erroneous) ascribes to this period. Thus the Psalmist says:

> " Deliver me from mine enemies, O my God;
> Set me on high from them that rise up against me.
> Deliver me from the workers of iniquity,
> And save me from the bloodthirsty man.
> For, lo, they lie in wait for my soul,
> The mighty gather themselves together against me;
> Not for my transgression, nor for my sin, O Lord.
> They run and prepare themselves without my fault;

> Awake thou to help me, and behold ;
> Even thou, O Lord God of hosts, the God of Israel.
> They return at evening, they make a noise like a dog,
> And go round about the city.
> Behold, they belch out with their mouth ;
> Swords are in their lips,
> For who, say they, doth hear?"

David's trust in the Lord's protection was not ill-founded Deliverance arose from a member of his own household. Michal had somehow become aware, probably through her brother Jonathan, of the conspiracy against her husband, and she took means to save him Josephus[1] asserts that he was to be brought formally to trial for treason, and his condemnation secured by some underhand means. Whether this was so or not, Michal saw that there was no safety but in immediate flight ; to this expedient she persuaded him to have recourse. As the front of the house was guarded, and the door carefully watched by the royal servants, she let her husband down from a window in the rear (the house probably standing on the city walls), as the spies were saved at Jericho, and St. Paul at Damascus, and he got safely away unperceived. To afford time for the escape another stratagem was employed by this true woman, whom love made skilful in device and secret in action. Finding that David did not come forth as they expected, the guard inquired where he was. Michal answered that he was sick and in his bed. She had prepared a life-size image, one of the household Teraphim, with the usual goat's-hair cap[2] worn by sleepers and by invalids, laid it in a bed and covered it with a mantle ; and when the soldiers showed some incredulity about David's sudden indisposition, she led them to the chamber door and pointed to the figure in confirmation of the story. The dim light and the distance contributed to make the delusion perfect, and the guards reported to Saul that his son-in-law was confined to his house by illness This did not content the vindictive tyrant, and he ordered the satellites to bring David,

---

[1] "Ant." vi 12 4.

[2] The LXX with a little change in the reading give, "She placed a goat's liver at his head." This reading is adopted and enlarged upon by Josephus ("Ant " vi. 11 4), the idea being that the liver palpitated for some time after the death of the animal, and thus the spectators were deceived into believing that the image in the bed was breathing

bed and all, up the hill into his presence. The Oriental bed is little more than a pallet or strip of carpet, so the command was easy to execute; but when, forcing their way into the sick chamber, the soldiers attempted to arrest the culprit, the deception was discovered. Saul was highly incensed at the fraud, and sending for Michal reproached her bitterly for letting his enemy escape. A worthy daughter of her father, she is ready with another falsehood to screen her complicity, and asserts that she had acted thus under compulsion, her own life being threatened if she did not aid her husband's flight. " He said unto me," she affirms, " Let me go ; why should I kill thee ? " It seems strange to hear of Teraphim, the images of ancestors preserved usually for superstitious purposes, in the house of the pious, God-fearing David. Two solutions of the apparent anomaly are conceivable. Either David was so accustomed to the presence of these statues in the mansions of all heads of families, that he had never regarded them as unlawful or considered to what impious purposes they were applied by many of his countrymen, and so allowed them to adorn his chambers, though he made no other use of them; or they had been brought surreptitiously by Michal from her father's house, and without David's knowledge set up in the women's apartments. Bishop Wordsworth suggests that hereby a *nemesis* overtook the treacherous king. " Perhaps," he says, " Saul, forsaken by God and possessed by the evil spirit, had resorted to *Teraphim* (as he afterwards resorted to witchcraft); and God overruled evil for good, and made his very *Teraphim* (by the hand of his own daughter) to be an instrument for David's escape."

Fleeing from Gibeah, David betook himself to his old friend and counsellor Samuel, at Ramah, and told him without reserve all that had befallen. It was a great crisis of his life. Should he surrender his public career, rid himself of the dangers to which he was exposed, and devote all his energies to music and poetry, and the prophetical office? Not such was the advice of Samuel. The Lord had other work for him, work for which his training was gradually fitting him, and which would be set forth in due course. Meantime, as a temporary asylum and a place seemingly secured by its sanctity from any open assault, Samuel took him to the prophetical college which he had established in the immediate vicinity of Ramah, and which from its consisting of a cluster of separate dwellings was called Naioth

LIFE AT COURT.

or Nevaioth ("dwelling"). Here in the exercise of religious duties, in communion with kindred spirits, in intercourse with such friends as Gad and Nathan, who were probably residing there at that time, and in imbibing wisdom and instruction from Samuel, David passed a few weeks in peace and satisfaction.

This rest was not long undisturbed As soon as the place of his refuge was known, Saul sent messengers to arrest him, the desire of vengeance overcoming his scruples at invading the peace of the sanctuary and violating the great prophet's abode. There ensued a very different result from what he had anticipated. The emissaries arrived at Naioth, entered the great hall, where the inmates assembled, with the full intention of seizing David, whom they expected to find among them ; but when they looked on the company of prophets gathered there, not youths only, but men of mature age, arranged in choral bands, with the venerable Samuel at their head, and when they heard their psalms and hymns and fervid utterances, they were seized with religious enthusiasm, and, forgetting their errand, joined in the prophetical exercises, and moved and sang and spake as ecstatically as the regular members of the school. Informed of this unsuccessful attempt, and refusing to see therein a warning against further pursuit of his enterprise, Saul sent messengers a second time on the same errand, with the same result. Baffled in like manner a third time, Saul was highly incensed at the frustration of his purpose, and having no longer recourse to messengers, set out himself for Naioth But the Holy Spirit whom he had grieved, and against whose influence he had striven, overpowered his stubborn will. Before he arrived at Naioth he too was seized with religious excitement , and when he came into the presence of the assembled choir, the enthusiasm that affected him was so powerful, that "he stripped off his clothes, and prophesied before Samuel, and lay down naked all that day and all that night." Thus the Spirit of God pleaded with him ; and though nothing now could permanently influence him for good, he renounced his present intention, or perhaps had altogether forgotten it, and returned to Gibeah, leaving David unmolested. The feelings which inspired David at this critical period found utterance in a psalm which has been the comfort of many a storm-tossed soul :

> "In the Lord put I my trust;
> How say ye then to my soul,
> Flee as a bird to your mountain.
> For, lo, the wicked bend the bow,
> They make ready their arrow upon the string,
> That they may shoot in darkness at the upright in heart . . .
> The Lord is in His holy temple,
> The Lord, His throne is in heaven ·
> His eyes behold, His eyelids try, the children of men.
> The Lord trieth the righteous .
> But the wicked and him that loveth violence His soul hateth . . .
> For the Lord is righteous , He loveth righteousness ,
> The upright shall behold His face " (Psa xi.)

What counsel Samuel gave to his young friend and whilom pupil we know not for certain; we can only judge of its tenour from succeeding circumstances. An armed resistance he certainly did not advise. Such an action, undertaken by this popular hero, might indeed have succeeded, but only at the cost of a bloody civil war and much suffering to the people. Not violent measures, but peaceful endurance, and renewed efforts at reconciliation, were the purport of his recommendation. In quietness and confidence was to be David's strength. He was, as he was well assured, to succeed to the throne, but he was to do nothing to precipitate events; he was to wait the Lord's time, and in due course the way would be made clear.

Saul left Ramah without making any personal promise to David, and the latter, in the uncertainty of the future, and anxious to know what treatment to expect, went secretly to Gibeah to take counsel with his dear friend Jonathan. The details of all that happened at this time, and the account of the interviews between these two noble youths are very full, and were evidently furnished to the narrator by one of the persons concerned. Conscious of his own integrity, David begins by asking what wrong he was accused of committing that the king thus persistently sought his life. Jonathan, in spite of all that had befallen, cannot believe that his father in his saner moments would contemplate such a crime, or still persist in his murderous intention. "God forbid," he cries, in horror of such a supposition , "thou shalt not die." He goes on to say that his father does nothing whatever without telling him, and that if he had any design against David he would be sure to make it known to him privately. Guileless himself, Jonathan could not think evil of Saul. But David, taught by sad experience, had looked deeper into the king's heart, and had seen too plainly the bitter hatred and treachery that lurked therein. Knowing the deep love that the two youths had for one another, Saul would not be likely to impart to his son his fell purpose against the friend of his heart; and David reiterates his conviction of the certainty of Saul's deadly animosity, adding solemnly: "As the Lord liveth, and as thy soul liveth, there is but a step between me and death." Deeply impressed with the consciousness of his friend's peril, Jonathan asks what he wishes him to do; and between them they concoct a plan for testing the king's real disposition towards his son-in-law. The next day was the festival of the New Moon, which was celebrated at Gibeah, not only with the accustomed ceremonies, the blast of trumpets and the offering of sacrifices,[1] but also with a solemn banquet attended formally by the royal family and the highest officers of state, this latter part of the celebration extending over two days. Notwithstanding all that had passed, Saul fully expected David to take his part in this celebration. Whether a temporary and superficial reconciliation had been effected by Samuel, or whether the king remembered little of the violence which he had shown during his maniacal attacks, he evidently saw no reason why his son-in-law should be absent on this occasion. It was proposed by David to use this expectation in order to ascertain Saul's sentiments, whether he was, in truth, softened by recent events, or still retained his murderous intentions in his saner moments. David was to absent himself from the festival, remaining concealed in the neighbourhood during its continuance, and if Saul inquired the reason of his absence, Jonathan was to say that he had given him leave to pay a hurried visit to Bethlehem in order to attend the annual family sacrifice; if Saul was satisfied with the excuse, it would show that he harboured no malicious design; if, on the other hand, he should be greatly enraged, it would be a sign that his feeling of hatred was unchanged. The annual celebration at Bethlehem was doubtless a fact; in the absence of any central sanctuary and the general abeyance of discipline, the sacrifices, which, according to the Mosaic prescriptions, ought to have been offered at the Tabernacle, were now celebrated at the

[1] Numb. x. 10; xxviii. 11-15.

tribal centres, and the family of Jesse made use of the altar at Bethlehem. To this annual festival David had been invited; and though it might have been out of his power to attend it, he scrupled not to use the invitation as an excuse, the prevarication being a fault of which the lax morality of the age would take no notice. But it is not at all improbable that he really did spend at least one day at his father's house, the interval allowed being quite long enough to permit the double journey To secure Jonathan's compliance with his request, David reminds him of the friendship between them, confirmed, as it was, by the solemn invocation of Jehovah's name, and he adds that if Jonathan believes him to be a traitor and plotter against the royal house, he had better slay him with his own hand, and not deliver him to his father. "God forbid," cries the generous prince, "that I should think evil of thee. If I knew that evil were determined by my father to come upon thee, and did not tell thee—" and he leaves his sentence unfinished in his overpowering emotion [1] Then feeling that many difficulties lay in the path, not the lightest of which was the means of communicating necessary intelligence, he leads his friend into the open country where, without fear of listeners, they might freely discuss the situation. After duly weighing various plans, Jonathan promises with an oath to make a full investigation into his father's plans, and to find means to convey information of the result. And then satisfied that David will one day occupy the throne of Israel, and fearing that he might carry out the usual Oriental custom of destroying the family of the previous dynasty, he conjures him to show kindness not to himself only, but to his descendants when he should be no more. The method of communication was ingenious and calculated to disarm suspicion, if, as was possible, the king ordered his proceedings to be watched. On the third day from the present meeting about the same time, David was to go and hide himself in a certain place behind a well-known heap of stones; thither Jonathan would come, attended by a boy, with his bow and arrows. He would shoot thrice as if at a mark, and tell the lad to run and fetch the arrows; if he said, "The arrows are on this side of thee," David might show himself in safety, but if he cried, "The arrows are beyond thee," David must fly at once, as his death was determined. Thus unsuspected he might

[1] "Speaker's Comm.," 1 Sam. xx. 9.

LIFE AT COURT. 37

communicate with his friend even if spies were in the neighbourhood; should no witnesses be present, he would not miss the opportunity of once more conversing with him mouth to mouth.

At the appointed time the New Moon was celebrated, and the royal feast was spread. The chief table was arranged for four, the king's place being near the wall furthest from the door, his son's on the right, the great general Abner's on the left, and David's opposite. On Abner's entrance Jonathan arose, as if to do honour to this respected chieftain, and took David's seat facing the king.[1] The move was made in order that Saul might be induced the readier to notice and comment upon the absence of one of the guests, and thus relieve his son's anxiety for the fate of his friend In this hope he was disappointed. Saul made no remark the first day. This was a sacrificial feast of which no one might partake who had contracted legal or ceremonial defilement;[2] and thinking that this was the reason why David was not present, he asked no question. But whereas such pollution lasted only till night-fall, and on the second day of the festival the place of David was again vacant, Saul could no longer restrain his vexation, and turning to his son demanded impatiently why this "son of Jesse," as he called him, had not appeared either yesterday or to-day. Jonathan gave the excuse which had been prepared, adding that he had been summoned to this family gathering by his eldest brother, acting for his father Jesse. Saul had intended at this festival, when surrounded by his own fierce and devoted adherents, to effect the destruction of his hated rival. At the unexpected frustration of his design, he no longer attempted to conceal his real feelings, and addressing Jonathan with the coarsest abuse ordered him immediately to produce David and deliver him up to death , for he saw that David had suspected his design, and that Jonathan sympathized with him and connived at his evasion; and the full bitterness of his apprehension and jealousy comes to the surface in the vehement words · "Do not I know that thou hast chosen the son of Jesse to thine own

[1] This seems to be the most satisfactory way of explaining the difficult expressions in 1 Sam xx 25 Jonathan must have sat opposite to Saul, or the latter could not have cast his spear at him (ver 33), and one can thus see why it is said especially, "Jonathan arose, and Abner sat by Saul's side."   [2] Lev. vii. 20, 21.

shame and unto the shame of the mother that bare thee? For as long as the son of Jesse liveth upon the ground thou shalt not be established nor thy kingdom;" *i.e.*, he will either now usurp the government, or wrest it from thee after my death. Thus he thought to set Jonathan's private interests in opposition to his friendship, to make him see that the two were incompatible. But the young prince had recognized the leading of Providence in the rapid rise of David, and he was not one to fight against God. He was a true patriot, and that which was most for his country's good was right in his eyes, whatever might be the effect on his own fortunes. Undeterred by his father's furious language, wholly uninfluenced by selfish considerations, and desirous to probe to the depth his hatred for David, Jonathan replies by the question: "Wherefore shall he be slain? What hath he done?" To this gentle pleading Saul returned no answer in words; a paroxysm of fury seized his soul, and brandishing his ever-ready spear he threatened to slay his gallant son even as he sat at the table. There could no longer be any doubt of the king's relentless animosity against his son-in-law, when he was prepared to murder his own son for taking the part of the absent culprit. Jonathan arose from the table in fierce anger, left his food untasted, and retired to his own chamber. He was deeply grieved not only at the public insult offered to himself before the assembled guests, but also and chiefly at the groundless aspersion cast upon his friend David, who, though ingenuous, upright, innocent, had been openly denounced as a secret traitor and plotter, deserving of immediate death.

Rising early next morning, Jonathan with a sad heart proceeded to carry out the programme arranged before with his friend. He strolled with his boy to the appointed rendezvous, where David was hidden, shot the arrows, and gave the desired intimation; and then finding that there were no prying eyes to observe his movements, he sent the lad home, that unnoticed he might hold a last interview with his beloved friend. As soon as David perceived that Jonathan was alone, he came forth from his hiding-place, and falling on his face he did obeisance to the prince, calling him the saviour of his life.[1] Jonathan raised him from the ground, and the two youths embraced with the fondest affection, mingling their tears to-

[1] Josephus, "Ant." vi. 11. 10.

gether, till David was completely overcome with emotion[1] "Go in peace," said Jonathan at last, being forced to bring the mournful interview to an end ; " and what we have sworn both of us in the name of the Lord, saying, The Lord be between me and thee, and between my seed and thy seed for ever—" He could not finish the sentence ; sobs choked his utterance. He was parting with one whom he loved as his own soul, whom he might never see again ; he was leaving him in distress and danger, henceforward a fugitive and an outlaw, liable at any moment to capture and a violent death , he was returning to a Court now become odious, to a father for whom his filial affection had received a severe shock, from whom he might expect distrust and ill-will, and who, he saw, was determined to continue that wilful course which would end in total alienation from God, in ruin to his kingdom and himself. Well might he go back to the city, lonely, depressed, sorrow-stricken.

As for David, when he left the spot, he had no time to indulge his grief ; he had to provide measures for his safety. He was to commence the untried life of a public enemy, where all men's hands might be against him, and every energy of mind and body was needed to save his life from destruction. His service with Saul had taught him some things which were of eminent use in the training of the future king. He had learned how to handle soldiers in the field, how to order the battle and to employ his forces to the best advantage ; he had learned how to command, to make his influence felt, to bend to his will the various minds with which he came in contact ; he had learned prudence ; he knew how to temper the suggestions of impetuous youth with the sagacity of deliberate counsel. Flattery and fame and high distinction had not marred the simplicity of his character ; he had had experience of envy and detraction, and could hold his own amid the annoyances and temptations of the Court But not yet was his education complete. Hardship and suffering were to brace his energies and try his patience ; many a keen stroke, many a heavy blow, was needed to fit this goodly stone for the Master's use ; and the record of many months now following is a tale of bitter trial.

[1] "Until David exceeded" (1 Sam xx 41) This may also mean that David wept even more bitterly than Jonathan. Klostermann, thinking that a note of time is wanted, reads, "until it was high day." The Sept. Version may perhaps mean, "until great exhaustion."

CHAPTER IV.

OUTLAW LIFE IN JUDÆA.

David at Nob—Received by Ahimelech, Flees to Gath; Takes refuge in Adullam—Destruction of Nob—David relieves Keilah—At Ziph—Last interview with Jonathan—David at Hachilah and Maon—In imminent peril—Spares Saul's life at Engedi, and expostulates with him—Carmel—Nabal and Abigail—David marries Abigail—Spares Saul's life a second time—Saul regrets his persecution, and promises to cease from further pursuit.

TURNING sorrowfully from his friend, leaving wife and home and the high position so laboriously won, David commenced the life of an outlaw, which he was constrained to continue for many years. Whither now was he to direct his footsteps? He dared not visit Bethlehem, as Saul would naturally seek him there first of all, considering him to be still with his family, as Jonathan had led him to suppose. Ramah was no longer a safe asylum. He could not again subject the venerable Samuel and the sacred college to the violence of a mad and capricious tyrant, whose frenzy at any moment might assume a homicidal form. His native soil seemed to afford no safe resting-place. Was he to abide in some foreign territory till happier times? His pious mind revolted at making such a decision without Divine direction. He would seek counsel from the Lord; he would ask an oracle at the priest's mouth. The ark, indeed, was perhaps still resting at Kirjath-jearim, but the Tabernacle and the sacerdotal staff were at Nob, a height near Jerusalem, only a few miles from Gibeah, and the regular worship of Jehovah was here celebrated with some of its ancient splendour

The high priest at that time was named Ahimelech, who is either a brother of, or possibly the same person as, that Ahiah who was with Saul in the camp at Michmash (1 Sam. xiv. 3). He was a man of a timid nature, not inclined to risk offending the imperious monarch under whose protection he lived. Knowing this man's character, and fearing that if he appeared as a fugitive from the vengeance of Saul, the priest would decline to receive him or to supply his pressing wants— food and arms—David had recourse to a subterfuge, which, while it answered his immediate purpose, was the cause of a terrible calamity to the innocent community at Nob, and of the bitterest sorrow to himself.

Seeing the king's son-in-law arrive suddenly in hot haste, unattended and evidently distressed, Ahimelech was alarmed, and hurriedly inquired the meaning of this unexpected visit. David reassured him by professing to have been sent by the king on a secret expedition, of which no one but himself was to know the object; he added that his attendants were concealed in a neighbouring spot, and that he had been obliged to start so suddenly as to have had no time to provide himself with food or arms. He entreated Ahimelech to furnish these necessaries That David was guilty of falsehood in a portion of this statement is, of course, evident. Doubtless it was true that he had appointed some of his friends and trusty followers to meet him in a certain spot, the rest was pure invention. Tried by the lax morality that obtains in questions of war and politics, the lie would be called prudent and necessary; and at the time David may have so regarded it. We have a higher standard by which to judge such infringements of the law of truth, and we must unhesitatingly condemn the artifice, while we acknowledge the strength of the temptation that occasioned it. The sacred narrator records the failings of his hero, showing that, excellent as he was, he was not superior to human infirmities, and we who read the history now learn to look for a perfect example, not in any hero of the Old Testament, or saint of the New Covenant, but in one only character—the man Christ Jesus.

Ahimelech, who knew something of the king's enmity against his young commander, might have had some suspicion of the true state of the case, but David's statement satisfied him; and to the fugitive's demand for five loaves, or food of some kind, for the use of himself and his hungry followers, he answered, that he would willingly have supplied them had he been able, but that he had no bread at all save the hallowed shewbread, which was the weekly perquisite of the priests on the presentation of the twelve new loaves every sabbath day. Even if this day on which David arrived was the sabbath (which seems very improbable), when the labour of making ordinary bread could not be undertaken, other food might naturally have been expected to be available. But there seems to have been no common victuals whatever in Ahimelech's house It speaks plainly of the poor estate of the sacerdotal order in those days, and the little estimation in which its members were held, that such poverty should have been allowed. Had tithes been duly paid, had the people flocked to the sanctuary with their offerings and sacrifices, destitution such as this could not have occurred. Even this bread was not legally available for David's use. It was to be eaten in accordance with the Levitical enactments (Lev. xxiv 9) by the priests only and in the holy place; but the rigour of the Law was often relaxed; the stale bread was taken to the priests' houses, and perhaps on some occasions given even to lay persons. Ahimelech professed himself willing to strain a point in David's favour (charity being greater than rubric[1]), if he and his companions were free from ceremonial impurity. Having in view the occurrence of the late festival and their hurried journeying since then, David could assure him that this was the case, and the priest, overcoming his scruples, gave what was required. As for arms, he had none to offer but the sword of Goliath, which the young champion at the close of the first campaign had himself dedicated in the Tabernacle as a thank-offering to the Lord to whom he owed his victory. "There is none like that," said David; "give it me" It had once before been a pledge of victory; it might be so again in his hands. And as it was of no extraordinary size, and was doubtless of fine temper and serviceable form, the young warrior grasped it with joy as a trusty friend in this emergency. One more boon he craved; he desired the high priest to inquire of the Lord for him by Urim and Thummim, putting his question in such a way as not to compromise the inquirer or convey any information of which it was expedient that he should remain in ignorance. Ahimelech saw

[1] Matt xii 3 f., Mark ii. 25–27.

nothing unusual in this request ; David was engaged in the king's business ; he had often before this consulted the oracle for him ;[1] and he willingly did so now. What the answer was we are not told. But David could not linger at Nob. He had seen there one of Saul's most devoted and unscrupulous attendants, Doeg, an Edomite, who held a position of some importance in the royal household. This man, having been detained at the Tabernacle either by the performance of a vow, or, as some suppose, in order to be examined by the priests for a suspicion of leprosy, had not known anything of the latest proceedings at Gibeah ; but David was well aware that he would carry an unfavourable report to his master of all that had transpired at Nob ; he therefore hastened to leave the sanctuary and seek an asylum elsewhere. Certain that as soon as Doeg's information reached Saul, active measures would be taken against him, David, in his great perplexity and overwhelmed by the imminent danger to which he was exposed, took a precipitate determination of fleeing for refuge to the nearest Philistine city. This chanced to be Gath, which, as we have seen above, stood towering over the entrance of the valley of Elah. The lord of this place was named Achish, his official title, as the heading of the Thirty-fourth Psalm teaches, being Abimelech As some years had passed since the defeat and death of Goliath, and David in his modest estimation of himself never considered that his person was well known among his national enemies, he determined to offer himself to the Philistine's service[2] Probably Saul's cruel tyranny had already driven many Israelites to a similar measure, and deserters were by no means unknown. Concealing his name and relying on his identity remaining undiscovered, he openly entered the town, though he had formed no plans for the future and had not considered what his next step would be. There seemed at the moment less danger in the midst of enemies than amid his own countrymen, and he may have thought to make himself acceptable as a minstrel or in some other peaceful capacity at this Court. But his calculations were quickly overthrown. The

[1] 1 Sam xxii 15 "Have I to-day begun to inquire of God for him?" is Ahimelech's answer to Saul's accusation.

[2] It is certain that this account in 1 Sam xxi refers to quite a different occasion from that recorded in chap xxvii The circumstances are so distinct in many particulars that the former cannot be regarded by any unprejudiced reader as a distorted version of the latter.

Gittites at once recognized him as the famous Israelite general who had been celebrated in festive songs throughout the land. They called him the real king of the country, and exultingly seized and brought him before Achish as one who could do him good service against his hereditary foemen. Too late David perceived the dilemma in which he was involved. He was welcomed as one who had broken irretrievably with Saul; he was received as a traitor and a deserter. If he did not maintain this character and take active part against his own country, his life would be sacrificed. But the idea of such treachery was inconceivable; it never entered his mind as a debatable question. Whatever might be his wrongs, however cruel and unjust and unmerited the treatment which he experienced, he had no thought of righting himself by siding against his fatherland; he was always content to commit his cause to the Lord whom he served. His feelings at this crisis are expressed in the Fifty-sixth Psalm:

"Be merciful unto me, O God, for man would swallow me up;
All the day long he fighting oppresseth me
Mine enemies would swallow me up all the day long;
For they be many that fight proudly against me.
What time I am afraid,
I will put my trust in Thee
In God I will praise His word,
In God have I put my trust, I will not be afraid;
What can flesh do unto me?"

To avoid the consequences of his rash act in putting himself in the power of his enemies, David had recourse to an expedient, which, however mean and unworthy, has been often practised, and among an Eastern people was calculated to insure his safety. He feigned himself mad, drummed on the doors as if playing an instrument of music, let his spittle fall down upon his beard, and assumed epileptical attacks when seized by strange hands. Similar stories, in the case of Ulysses, Solon, Brutus, are well known to every reader of classical history. David had had frequent opportunities of seeing paroxysms of real madness while attending upon the miserable Saul, and could doubtless imitate with painful accuracy the symptoms of such a malady. He completely deceived the Philistines. Then, as now, insane persons were regarded as peculiarly possessed and protected by heavenly influences. Such an one would not be harmed whatever his nationality might be, at the same time his services were useless, and Achish dismissed him with contempt. "Wherefore," he demands of his servants, "have ye brought this mad man to me? Do I lack mad men, that ye have brought this fellow to play the mad man in my presence?" The king's question receives painful significance if it was true, as the Jewish legend tells,[1] that his own wife and daughter were insane.

Convinced at last that his person was too well known for him to appear openly, either in his own land or that of the enemy, David had no recourse but to seek a refuge in some district thinly inhabited, and where the nature of the country would make it difficult to follow or surprise him. Standing where he did, at the gates of Gath, his decision was quickly made About two miles up the valley of Elah, at the foot of a limestone hill, stood the ancient Canaanitish city of Adullam (now Aid-el-ma), surrounded by a labyrinth of *wadys* and defiles, the sides of which are honeycombed with caves, partly natural, partly excavated by the primeval Troglodyte inhabitants. In this district, most conveniently situated for one in his position, hovering on the confines of Israel and Philistia, David found refuge, taking up his abode in what was known as "the cave, or fort, of Adullam" The animosity of Saul had extended to all that were connected with the fugitive by ties of blood or companionship, and their safety lay in cleaving to him and following his fortunes. That many, even a whole family, should suffer for the fault of one, was no unusual occurrence, so, fearing the vengeance of the king, David's brethren and kinsfolk fled from Bethlehem and joined him at Adullam Among the refugees were many who afterwards became celebrated for daring or military skill, and notably his own three nephews, the sons of his sister Zeruiah, Joab, Abishai, and Asahel Besides these, there was a motley crowd, composed of persons who, for various reasons, were dissatisfied with the present state of things, and voluntarily placed themselves under this young leader. The government of Saul was not favourable to the arts of peace He was a soldier and nothing more. Domestic prosperity, the administration of justice, the upholding of the Law, were matters about which he little concerned himself. Many had suffered from his

[1] Quoted by Bishop Ellicott, *in loc.*

arbitrariness and tyranny; many had experienced the weight of his resentment, owing to their attachment to David. The terrible weight of debt, unrelieved by the enforcement of the Law against unrighteous usury, pressed heavily upon many; others saw with dismay whither Saul's perverseness was driving the nation, and hoped to force a reform by joining in a revolt. Gradually all such disaffected persons flocked to David, and in no long time a band of four hundred men looked to him as leader. It must have been a herculean task to mould these discordant and unsatisfactory elements into a harmonious whole; yet, ably seconded by friends of unusual abilities, he accomplished this feat. It was not, as many among his followers supposed, with any intention of undertaking operations against the tyrant from whom he and they had suffered much wrong, that he organized this force; his purpose was equally prudent and patriotic. He knew the weakness of Saul's kingdom; he saw how greatly it was exposed to attack, not only from the restless Philistines, but also from the prowling, nomadic tribes that roamed the southern desert ; and he resolved to use the men who unsolicited had united themselves to him, in order to form a little army which might guard the frontiers of his beloved native land. To effect this required much skill and patience; nor was it till after many months' labour that he could congratulate himself on having under his command a body of resolute soldiers whom he could trust to execute his orders in perfect discipline and to accomplish any enterprise which lay in man's power.

Meantime a refuge had to be provided for his father and mother, whom well-grounded fear had driven from their home at Bethlehem, and who, at their advanced age, could not share their son's perilous and vagabond life. From the hills that arose above the place where he was lurking could be seen, on the eastern horizon, the blue mountains of Moab. With the people of this country he had certain affinity through his ancestress Ruth, and to the king of this land he determined to commit his parents till he knew what God would do for him. Convinced of the justice of his cause and that he was destined for high position, he firmly believed that the Lord would ere long put an end to his wanderings and enable him to relieve his parents from all anxiety. The temporary eclipse of faith from which he had suffered in the first moments of terror and perplexity had passed away ; and he was again the bright hopeful youth who had full confidence in the Divine leading and reliance on the Divine love The asylum which he found is called Mizpeh, " watch-place," a name applied to any height. This was probably some citadel or town south of the Arnon towards the lower part of the Dead Sea. Saul had made war on the Moabites (1 Sam xiv. 47), and driven them from their northern possessions, but the animosity with which he persecuted David would make the latter acceptable to the Moabite king. He willingly afforded the required shelter, and there for a time the fugitive leader himself found a home.

From this peaceful respite, which would indeed soon have been broken by solicitation to act against his countrymen, David was aroused by a message brought by the Prophet Gad. This personage, here first mentioned and afterwards well known as " David's seer " (1 Chron. xxi 9), had probably become acquainted with the hero at the College of Naioth, and was now sent, perhaps by Samuel, to bid him leave his present residence among aliens and to betake himself to the land of Judah Henceforward the fugitive had at intervals the support and prestige of the presence of this man of God, and the outlaw band could look for direction from one who was inspired by the spirit of prophecy, and whose absorbing interest in the fate of this young leader induced him to note all the events of his life and to record them for the instruction of posterity.[1] There was work for David's little army in their native country, harassed by foreign marauders, distracted by internal dissensions ; there was protection to be afforded, there was reputation to be won— further and important education for the future king So from Moab he moved to the forest, or thickets, of Hereth, a locality on the edge of the mountain chain of Hebron, possibly identified with the modern Kharas, in which the name survives, and only a few miles from his former quarters at Adullam. Sad news reached him here. Suddenly into his camp came flying in terror and sorrow, Abiathar, one of the sons of the high priest Ahimelech, who had befriended David at Nob. The treacherous Doeg had carried to Saul his malignant report of what he had seen, and the miserable king, suspecting a plot and frantically jealous of all who afforded any countenance to his fugitive son-in-law, had wreaked his vengeance on the innocent

[1] 1 Chron. xxix 29

priest and his family. Nay, he had commissioned the unscrupulous Doeg to take an armed force to Nob, and to destroy all whom he found there. So well did the Edomite execute the atrocious command, that of the sacerdotal family none escaped the sword save Abiathar, who brought the harrowing intelligence to the camp at Hereth. Thus the doom on the house of Eli was being fulfilled. It was with extreme sorrow that David heard the account of this sacrilegious massacre. He felt that he was in some degree the cause of the catastrophe, and he received the survivor with all the sympathy and regard which his situation naturally evoked, enhanced as they were by the thought that friendliness to him had been punished so terribly. "Abide thou with me," he said to the young priest, "fear not; for he that seeketh my life seeketh thy life; for with me thou shalt be in safeguard." From that day forward, until almost the end of life, Abiathar continued David's trusty friend and companion; and having brought with him the ephod with the Urim and Thummim, he acted as priest during David's chequered career, and, when need arose, consulted the Lord for him in the appointed manner. Tradition has referred Psalm lii. to this period, to which in some respects it is appropriate. Doeg's villany and Saul's tyranny seem to be adumbrated, while the faith and courage which breathe forth are the sweet Psalmist's own sentiments.

" Why boastest thou thyself in mischief, O mighty man?
  The mercy of God endureth continually.
  Thy tongue deviseth very wickedness,
  Like a sharp razor working deceitfully. . . .
  Thou lovest all devouring words,
  O thou deceitful tongue.
  God shall likewise destroy thee for ever,
  He shall take thee up, and pluck thee out of thy tent,
  And root thee out of the land of the living . . .
  But as for me, I am like a green olive tree in the house of God;
  I trust in the mercy of God for ever and ever
  I will give Thee thanks for ever, because Thou hast done it,
  And I will wait on Thy name, for it is good, in the presence of Thy saints."

The atrocity perpetrated by Saul at Nob alienated from him the minds of all the pious among the Israelites, and many more, despairing of the present government, joined the outlaw and put full confidence in his leadership. An opportunity of testing his skill arose almost immediately. Three miles south of Adullam, built on a steep hill above the valley of Elah, stood Keilah (Kila), a fortified city, mentioned in Joshua (xv. 44) as one of those that appertained to Judah in the Shephelah, or Lowland. It was now harvest time, and the inhabitants were gathering their produce, when the Philistines from the neighbouring plain made a sudden raid, and seized the corn already stored in the threshing floors, and drove off the cattle. In such emergencies, it was no longer to Saul that the people turned ; David was their refuge and hope. That such was his mission he himself felt, encouraged and directed in this conviction by the prophet whom he now had in his company. On being informed of the inroad, he at once was ready to repel or to punish it. But he would not undertake the business without Divine guidance. Theocratic government was the foundation of his public life and actions, he must know God's will before he took in hand any new enterprise. By means of the high priest[1] he inquired of the Lord whether he should go and smite these Philistines, and was encouraged to go. But his followers held back, not indeed through fear of a defeat ; they had too much confidence in their leader to have any doubt concerning the immediate result of the expedition, but they hesitated as to the expediency of moving from the mountainous district where they could provide for their safety if pursued, and exposing themselves in the champaign which offered no facilities of concealment. That the course enjoined would occasion the enmity of the Philistines did not influence David at all ; but as the objection of his troops, now increased to six hundred, was reasonable, he, in their presence, made a second inquiry of the Lord, and was told emphatically that he might safely go, and that the Philistines would be delivered into his hand Upon this assurance he undertook the exploit, defeated the Philistines with great slaughter, relieved Keilah, and recovered the cattle that had

[1] Our present Hebrew text (1 Sam xxiii 6) makes David joined by Abiathar with the ephod at Keilah, whereas in chap xxii 20 it is implied that the priest arrived before the expedition to Keilah If the former is correct David's inquiry must have been made not by Urim and Thummim, but by means of the Prophet Gad But in xxiii 6 the words, "to Keilah," are probably an interpolation The LXX read "It came to pass when Abiathar, son of Ahimelech, fled to David, then he went down with David to Keilah, having the ephod in his hand."

been driven off. Here for a time he remained as a protection to the neighbouring farmers and peasants. But ere long he received information through some friend at Court (probably Jonathan) that Saul was gathering a large force to besiege him while in Keilah, thinking that he could not escape. This report being confirmed by the Divine oracle, David asked whether the inhabitants would deliver him up to Saul, and was assured that they would do so if he remained among them. The Keilites, doubtless, had taken to heart the warning given by the destruction of Nob, and fear of a similar fate overpowered the natural feeling of gratitude to their benefactor, and disposed them to sacrifice sentiment to material advantage. Selfishness begets cowardice and deters men from undertaking obvious duties. Nothing, therefore, remained for David but to quit this ungrateful city and to return to the hill country of Judæa, where he might more readily baffle pursuit. It was an anxious life that he now led, requiring unusual courage, watchfulness, and self-denial. He had no fixed abode, "went whithersoever he could," eluding Saul's incessant efforts for his capture, and at the same time carrying on a guerilla warfare against the Philistines and the border tribes. Of this toilsome and perilous existence the sacred writer gives some notable episodes.

Driven by circumstances from Keilah, David moved his little force southwards into the wild country that is called the wilderness of Judah, and extends from the mountains of Judah to the Dead Sea. Passing Hebron, he pitched his camp in the desert of Ziph, about four miles south of that town, where an isolated rounded hill still bears the name of Tell Zif. This spot was selected from its position, which obviated all fear of a sudden surprise. Overgrown itself in parts with thickets and forest, it commanded an extensive prospect, and no enemy could approach unseen. At Choresh (Khoreisa) in this neighbourhood occurred the last interview with Jonathan, the tried friend who remained true and loving unto the end. His father's pursuit of David gave the prince the opportunity of being in his neighbourhood without suspicion, and he eagerly availed himself of it to "strengthen" his friend's "hand in God," and to renew the solemn covenant already made between them. Jonathan and many others with him were convinced that David was designated for the kingdom, and that, however lowly his present state, final success was inevitable. The mad self-will of Saul, the alienation of Samuel and of the best among the people, the manifest tokens of weakness and decay in the kingdom, these and such like facts compelled all thinking men to see that a change of rulers was necessary and imminent, and they turned their eyes and hopes on David as one who was worthy to be the king of Israel, and who was under Divine direction in all the actions of his remarkable career. Such was the view which Jonathan took of present circumstances; this conviction he desired to impart to the beloved fugitive, who indeed required some consolation and support to enable him to endure the evils of his precarious position. The constant persecution to which he was subject, the ingratitude of his own countrymen, the indefiniteness of the period of his future advancement, though they could not shake his faith, often made him despondent. Inexpressibly grateful at this moment was the assurance of Jonathan's unabated love, and the confidence entertained by him and others, that God had chosen him, the outlaw, to be king of Israel. The young prince may not have known of the anointing at Bethlehem, but he had long been so convinced that David was specially selected for a high destiny, that he looked forward with contentment to seeing him in his father's seat; and then, with rare disinterestedness, he spoke calmly of resigning his own claims to the throne in favour of his friend: "Thou shalt be king over Israel, and I shall be next unto thee; and that also my father knoweth." He spoke out of the fulness of his heart, quite prepared to accept the inferior position which he proposed for himself. To all such plans the fatal battle of Gilboa put a termination. His self-abnegation was never brought to the test, nor was David tried by feeling that his advancement was achieved only by dispossessing his trusty friend of his legitimate inheritance. The future was mercifully hidden from the eyes of these two loving unselfish youths; and ere they parted they repeated the vow of life-long friendship, looking forward to a time not far distant when they could meet without fear in happy intercourse, uninterrupted by jealousy and suspicion and disunion.

After the interview with Jonathan, which had cheered and strengthened his depressed spirits, David betook himself to the hill Hachilah (El Kolah), a long ridge that runs out of the Ziph plateau towards the Dead Sea. Here is a country indescribably wild and dreary, a waste of chalky ridges, scored by innumerable watercourses, and separated by broad valleys, without a tree or a spring to break the monotony of the cheerless wilderness. This desert is terminated on the east by a range of cliffs rising abruptly from the shore of the Dead Sea to a height of 2,000 feet.[1] Through this desolate region David was now roaming, not unmarked by watchful eyes. Some of the Ziphites, who were thorough partisans of Saul, and who knew nothing of the outlaw's delegation to the kingdom, and regarded him as a rebel against lawful authority, observing his movements in the distance, sent word to the king that they had found his enemy, and offered to guide him to his capture. There is no reason for loading these people with abuse as malignant evil-doers and traitors. From their point of view they were merely doing their duty as loyal subjects. And they may have had special cause of gratitude towards Saul for freeing them from the dangerous inroads of the Amalekites, which their town, at that time unfortified, was wholly unable to resist. Of this deliverance they had a constant reminder in the monument which the king had set up in their neighbourhood on his return from the slaughter of the Amalekites.[2] They probably also felt that the presence of David's troops was a constant burden and drain on their resources, and were glad to free themselves from the necessity of contributing to their support. Saul gladly availed himself of their services; and so successfully did they perform their offered task, that David was surprised, and only saved from destruction by the news of a sudden raid of the Philistines, which opportunely called off the pursuers in another direction. He had moved a few miles south to the vicinity of the town of Maon (Main), which stands on a curious conical hill, from the summit of which opens a very extensive prospect. From this spot Saul's advance was perceived, and David, knowing the country well and anxious to avoid a collision with the royal forces, hastened to get on the opposite side of the great gorge, called then Sela ham-Mahlekoth, "Cliff of Division," and now Malaky, which lies between Hachilah and Maon, and which Saul could not pass except by a detour of many miles But having a large body of troops at his disposal, the king, dividing his forces, prepared to beset both ends of the pass, and the escape of the fugitives would have been hopeless but for the

[1] Conder, "Handbook," p 213

[2] 1 Sam. xv. 12 Ziph was fortified by Rehoboam, 2 Chron. xi. 8. Weiss, "David u. seine Zeit," 95, 96

OUTLAW LIFE IN JUDÆA.

providential interruption already mentioned. This remarkable escape deepened David's trust in Divine protection, and encouraged him in hope of final success The memory of this event long continued, and the name by which thenceforward the ravine was known, reminded future generations of the fact that he who made Israel a great kingdom was once a miserable fugitive whose life was daily in utmost peril. David himself embodied his feelings at this crisis in a psalm (liv), the title of which refers to the event, and which the Church interprets of Christ by appointing it to be said on Good Friday.

> "Save me, O God, by Thy name,
> And judge me in Thy might
> Hear my prayer, O God ,
> Give ear to the words of my mouth.
> For strangers are risen up against me,
> And violent men have sought after my soul ;
> They have not set God before them.
> Behold, God is my helper ,
> The Lord is of them that uphold my soul.
> He shall requite the evil unto mine enemies :
> Destroy Thou them in Thy truth
> With a freewill offering will I sacrifice unto Thee,
> I will give thanks unto Thy name, O Lord, for it is good.
> For He hath delivered me out of all trouble,
> And mine eye hath seen my desire upon mine enemies "

Distrusting the neighbourhood of the Ziphites, David removed eastward to the shore of the Dead Sea, where amid the heights of Engedi (Ain-Jidy), "Fountain of the Kid," he found, as he hoped, a securer refuge. The district over which he had to pass offered great difficulties even to his active and light-armed followers, being composed of steep limestone ridges seamed by torrent beds and divided from each other by deep valleys The hot spring of Engedi, which issues from the side of a mountain about 600 feet above the Salt Sea, and half a mile from the middle of its western margin, fertilizes the neighbouring land to a very remarkable extent, and forms an oasis in this desolate country which has made it widely celebrated The sides of the ravines which lead to Engedi are full of caverns, both natural and artificial, which are at this day used as retreats by robbers and shepherds. One such cave is graphically described by Tristram : "A fairy grotto of vast size, under a trickling water fall, with a great flat ledge of rock overhanging it, dripping with stalactites, and draped with maiden-hair fern. Its luxuriance was wonderful. We gathered many tresses of its fronds a yard long; and yet the species is identical with our own. The sides of the cliff, as well as the edges of the grotto, were clothed with great fig-trees, hanging about and springing forth in every direction, covered with luxuriant foliage, and just now budding into fruit. Mingled with these were occasional bushes of *retem* [broom], with its lovely branches of pendent pink blossoms waving their sweet perfume all around. To reach the grotto we had to force our way through an almost impenetrable cane brake, with bamboos from twenty to thirty feet long, and close together. No pen can give an adequate description of the beauties of this hidden grotto, which surpasses anything Claude Lorraine ever dreamt."[1]

It seemed almost impossible for Saul with his heavy-armed troops to follow the fugitives to this inaccessible retreat. Yet hate accomplished a task from which military experience would have shrunk, and the king led three thousand picked warriors into these mountain fastnesses, and arrived safely in the neighbourhood of Engedi. And here, had he had to deal with a less generous foe, he might have paid for his rashness with his life. David with a portion of his force had taken up his abode in one of the numerous caverns; to this same cavern by chance Saul one day, leaving his troops, betook himself for privacy's sake. Coming into the dark grotto from the bright sunshine without, he did not perceive the outlaws who were clustered in the interior. They, however, saw him plainly, and perceived that he was wholly in their power. Here was an opportunity for exacting a bloody vengeance for all that they had suffered at the tyrant's hands. With an eager whisper they point this out to David, and urge him to take advantage of the situation so providentially ordered, and by one blow rid himself for ever of the oppressor. If, for an instant, the suggestion found favour with the persecuted leader, and he thought of making his way to the throne to which he was destined by the murder of its present occupant, he checked the unhallowed idea with stern decision. The king, however cruelly he had treated his innocent son-in-law, was the Lord's anointed; religion and loyalty alike forbade him to lay hand upon him. The person

[1] "Land of Israel," p 286, see also 377 ff.

of the anointed monarch was sacred. He accordingly repressed, though with much difficulty, the eager desire of his warriors to slay the unconscious king; but, in order to prove to Saul that he had been in his power, and that he had no intention of injuring him, as calumniators represented, he stole forward silently in the gloom of the cave, and while Saul was occupied, he cut off a piece from the skirt of the royal mantle which the king had thrown aside. But when the latter had left the cave, David's heart smote him because he had indulged even a passing thought of harming the monarch, and because he had offered an indignity to the royal person by cutting the robe. So he followed Saul from the cave; and, seeing that none of the hostile troops were at hand, he took the opportunity of asserting his innocence of all offence and endeavouring to allay the rancorous hatred under which he was suffering. "My lord, the king!" he cried aloud, as Saul was slowly walking away. The monarch turned at the once well-known voice, and beheld David doing obeisance and showing every mark of respect as in the presence of a superior. Too surprised to speak, Saul stood and listened while David poured forth eloquent words that witnessed his unshaken loyalty and love. With much feeling he asserts his innocence of the crimes of which he was accused; "Wherefore," he asks indignantly, "hearkenest thou to the calumnies of men who say, Behold, David seeketh thy hurt? To-day thy life was in mine hand, and some bade me kill thee; but I would not put forth my hand against my lord, for he is the Lord's anointed." And to prove his words he holds out the piece which he had cut from Saul's mantle in the cave. Then he goes on to assert his own powerlessness and insignificance, which it is unworthy of the king of Israel to pursue with this animosity; and he ends his appeal by the solemn words: "The Lord be judge, and give sentence between me and thee, and see, and plead my cause, and deliver me out of thine hand." Impressionable as Saul was, he heard these words of his wronged yet magnanimous son-in-law with profound emotion; his heart was touched; the evil spirit was for the moment overpowered, and unwonted tears fell from his eyes. "My son David," he acknowledges with shame and self-reproach, "thou art more righteous than I; for thou hast rendered unto me good, whereas I have rendered unto thee evil. . . . Wherefore, the Lord reward thee good for that thou hast done unto me this day." The impression which he had long entertained, that David was to be his successor in the kingdom, was now changed into sure conviction, and conquering all jealous feelings he gives utterance to this belief, and prays David to swear that when he comes to the throne he will not exterminate his name and cut off all the seed of the family of Kis. Willingly David gave the required pledge, and Saul returned to his home at Gibeah, but without inviting the fugitive to come to the royal city and resume his position there; and David, having had bitter experience of Saul's fickleness and treachery, remained in the mountainous district, removing from place to place as the exigencies of his adventurous life demanded Well might the poet embody his remembrance of the late adventure in words pathetic and trustful:—

"O Lord my God, in Thee do I take refuge,
Save me from all them that pursue me, and deliver me;
Lest he tear my soul like a lion,
Rending it in pieces while there is none to deliver.
O Lord my God, if I have done this,
If there be iniquity in my hands,
If I have rewarded evil unto him that was at peace with me;
(Yea, rather I have delivered him that without cause was mine adversary,)
Let the enemy pursue my soul and overtake it,
Yea, let him tread my life down to the earth,
And lay my glory in the dust.
Arise, O Lord, in thine anger!
Lift up Thyself against the rage of mine adversaries,
And awake for me, in as much as Thou hast commanded judgment."

(Psa vii)

It is evident that Saul at this time could afford little protection to any but the inhabitants of the neighbourhood of his own abode, the rest of the country, and especially the southern districts, were exposed to the incursion of Philistines, Amalekites, Edomites, and other nomad tribes. Against these raids David and his companions contended without intermission, acting as a defence for the shepherds and villagers of the mountainous region of Judæa, and at times extending their operations to the wilderness of Paran,[1] a name applied loosely to the northern

[1] For "Paran" the Vat MS of the Sept reads "Maon," which many commentators have adopted from not understanding that the northern part of the great desert of El Tih extending up to the mountains of Judæa was

portions of the desert of Arabia, where it touches the hill-country of Judæa. From the persons thus protected the outlaws received contributions of provisions, which enabled them to support life in the absence of other means of subsistence.

Among the farmers who had benefited greatly by the defensive measures of the fugitive band was one Nabal, who dwelt in the city of Maon and had extensive possessions at Carmel (Kurmul), about a mile and a half to the north. "One is struck at once," says a recent explorer of this district, "with the fitness which the plateau presents for the adventures of the fugitive bandit chief who was destined to become the king of Israel. The inhabitants, like Nabal of Carmel, are rich in sheep and oxen. The villagers of Yuttah [in this neighbourhood] owned 1,700 sheep, of which 250 belonged to the sheikh. All along the borders of the Jeshimon and Beersheba deserts there is fine pasturage, to which the peasants descend in spring-time, having made some sort of agreement with the neighbouring Bedawin to protect them from other tribes."[1] This Nabal (whose name means "Fool," and whose after conduct proved the appropriateness of the appellation bestowed upon him) was possessed of very large flocks, for he had three thousand sheep and a thousand goats. And while these were pasturing on the wilderness of Carmel, David and his men had not only themselves scrupulously abstained from committing any depredations upon them, but had zealously guarded them from others, so that, as the shepherds acknowledged, "they were a wall unto us both by night and day, all the while we were with them keeping the sheep." Now, once a year it was the custom to hold a great festival when the flocks were brought home for shearing; a banquet was provided for all concerned, and there was no stint of materials for eating, drinking, and making merry. David thinking that he had earned some recompense for his care of Nabal's property, sent ten of his followers with a courteous and modest request that the great sheep-master would give him a small share of the good things that were abundant at this moment There was nothing unusual in such a demand. The support of a body of six hundred followers

loosely thus called There was a valley so named south of Bethlehem, the retreat of Simon the Gerasene in the time of Vespasian Josephus, "Bell Jud." iv. 9. 4.   [1] Conder, "Tent Work," ii. 88.

must have proved a source of much anxiety to their leader, and he must often have had to make similar applications to those whom he befriended, and whose contributions were his chief means of subsistence. Such a requisition would be made at the present day by any Arab sheikh who found a festivity going on in his neighbourhood. Nabal was a churlish, selfish boor, without one generous impulse, uninfluenced even by common gratitude. He rejected David's request with studied insult. Who was this son of Jesse, he asked, that he should think to be fed at his expense? What was he but a runaway servant who had deserted his own lord, and now had the impudence to expect other people to support him? When the young men brought back this insolent answer, David was highly incensed. It was not the mere refusal that galled him, though this was irritating enough; the terms used by Nabal implied that he was a warm partisan of the king, and regarded David as a disloyal rebel, whom he would gladly see hunted down and punished. In hot anger the outlaw, urged on by his fierce and rude followers, swore a solemn oath to take bloody vengeance on the sheep master, who was not only an ungrateful churl, but a vindictive political opponent. Selecting four hundred men to accompany him, he marched at once for Carmel, intending to put to the sword every male in the place. It was a hasty and cruel determination, unbecoming a servant of the Lord, and which, had he executed it, would have occasioned many evil consequences and brought on him a life-long regret. From this sin he was spared by the prudence of Abigail, Nabal's lovely and clever wife. Informed of her husband's folly and of the approach of the exasperated freebooters, she sent forward a copious supply of provisions to meet them ere they reached their destination, and she herself followed with the view of personally deprecating the vengeance of the justly incensed leader. Her policy was successful. Prostrating herself before David, she in the humblest terms makes her petition. The piety and faith of this excellent woman are very remarkable. She has full confidence in the guidance of Jehovah and in the effect of her own intercession in so good a cause. It was the Lord who had sent her to prevent the effusion of blood; not on such as Nabal should David's vengeance be outpoured; may all his enemies be as foolish and insignificant as he; as for the present which she brought with her, it was unworthy of David's acceptance; let him give it to his followers; had she been present when the messengers came they should not have returned empty. Then she expresses her full assurance of the great future that awaits the outlaw. though men are found to seek his life, he shall triumph over all opposition; he shall have a sure house, because he fights the Lord's battles. "The soul of my lord," she says, "shall be bound in the bundle of life with the Lord thy God; and the souls of thine enemies, them shall He sling out, as from the hollow of a sling." And then, with almost prophetic intuition, or as if taught by Samuel himself, she adds : " When the Lord shall have done according to all the good that He hath spoken concerning thee, and shall have appointed thee prince over Israel, this shall be no grief unto thee, nor offence of heart, either that thou hast shed blood causeless, or avenged thyself, and when the Lord shall have dealt well with thee, then remember thine handmaid, and own that I rightly foresaw thy destiny and gave thee good counsel." To such an address David could not be insensible. The propriety and wisdom of the speech were enhanced by the beauty and modesty of the speaker, and the generous hero at once acknowledged his error and agreed to forego his cruel intention It is true that he had taken a solemn vow to execute vengeance on Nabal and his family. Irreligious men like Jephthah and Saul would have kept their promise even when its execution involved the commission of a great crime ; but David, now convinced of the wickedness of his purpose, deliberately breaks his vow in the cause of justice and mercy. He rightly considered that in the case of a wicked vow faith was not to be kept, and that an oath which cannot be observed without a crime is itself impious and unlawful.[1] The outlaws withdrew to their fastnesses, and Abigail returned home in peace But other consequences were to follow. Abigail had not informed her churlish husband of her intention when she set out to intercept the freebooters, and when she arrived at the house she found Nabal in a state of intoxication, and was compelled to postpone her communication till next morning. On hearing from her what had happened, how she had saved him from imminent destruction by her timely intercession and offering of provisions, he was seized with a stroke of apoplexy occasioned either by abject fear of the danger into which his intemperate language had

[1] St. Isidore.

brought him, or by a storm of passion at what he regarded as the humiliation of his wife before a hated renegade, and after lingering in a state of insensibility for ten days, he died. In this event, of which he was soon informed, David recognized the hand of God, who had preserved him from a great crime, and yet had not suffered his enemy to go unpunished. There is no unseemly exultation in this thought Deeply imbued with the truth of God's moral government of the world, and believing himself to be specially the care of Divine Providence, David expects such visible judgments upon the wicked and interprets them in this reverent fashion. So he may have sung under similar circumstances (Psa. lviii. 11):

> "Verily there is a reward for the righteous,
> Verily there is a God that judgeth in the earth."

The impression made by Abigail upon David was great and permanent, such a woman would be a true helpmate for him; pious, modest, prudent, she would aid him in all that was good and warn him against evil Worldly considerations also may have had some part in promoting the connection. She, doubtless, inherited her husband's property as he seems to have left no children, and would bring to her new lord both wealth and influence. David accordingly sent messengers to Abigail conveying proposals of marriage, moved thereto not only by affection for her, but also by the fact that Saul had unlawfully annulled his marriage with Michal and given her to one Phalti or Phaltiel, a chief of the town of Gallim, which lay between Gibeah and Jerusalem. Abigail at once consented to the offer, in terms which expressed with Oriental effusion her reverence and obsequiousness "Behold, thine handmaid is a servant to wash the feet of the servants of my lord." Her respect for the young outlaw and her belief in his high destiny outweighed the consideration of the wandering life which she might have to lead in following his fortunes, and she readily became his wife. Some time before this David had married one Ahinoam of Jezreel, a small village in the mountains of Judah near Maon, his position now being secure enough to enable him to provide for the safety and comfort of the women who accompanied his forces. We shall see hereafter to what crime and misery this unhappy practice of polygamy led in the case of David's family.

The connection with Nabal's property induced David to take up his quarters again in the neighbourhood of Maon and Carmel. This position brought him within the ken of his old enemies the Ziphites, who, knowing nothing of the late reconciliation with Saul, hastened to inform the king of his presence among them, being urged to take action by their fear of the fugitive's vengeance for their former treachery[1] Saul's momentary remorse had been soon checked by a fresh access of insane jealousy. His son-in-law's marriage with a rich heiress which gave him great influence in Benjamin had excited his evil passions, and now the Ziphites' information afforded him an opportunity of cutting off this enemy before he became too powerful. He could not resist profiting by the chance thus offered. Taking with him the 3,000 men, the standing army which he always kept in readiness, he set out from Gibeah for the wilderness of Ziph, where he was told that he should find the band of freebooters. Here he pitched his camp at the foot of Mount Hachilah by the side of a well-known road that led from the mountains of Judæa to the south. David, when first he heard of Saul's expedition, could scarce believe that after all the king's protestations he would again resort to his old persecution ; but being certified by his scouts that this was the case, he moved to a position whence he could look down upon the royal camp, which was, as usual, of a circular form surrounded by a rampart of waggons. Having from this distance carefully observed the situation of the encampment and the arrangement of its details, how that Saul and his chief captain Abner lay in the midst with the troops around them, having also seen that the watches were ill kept and no precaution taken against a sudden surprise, he conceived the idea of making a personal reconnoissance and affording to Saul a fresh proof of his innocence of all offence and his respect for the person of the Lord's anointed. Accordingly he proposed to his brave nephew Abishai and to another

[1] Eichhorn, Thenius, Ewald, Bishop Harvey, and others consider this account to be merely another version of the occurrences narrated in chap xxiii 19–xxiv 22 The stories have certain points of similarity, it is true , but in a pursuit which lasted some years in a very narrow district it is not merely conceivable, but highly probable, that similar scenes should have been repeated There are also such marked differences in details that the two accounts must be taken to refer to separate events The arguments for this view may be seen in Keil, Dean Payne Smith, Kirkpatrick, Chandler, Weiss, &c

of his officers, Ahimelech, a Hittite chieftain who had joined him, that they should pay a visit to the royal post. Ahimelech declined the perilous exploit, but Abishai expressed his willingness to share the danger. It was now night, and guided by the rays of the moon or by the light of the watch-fires still burning, David and his nephew arrived unperceived at the waggon rampart. Inside, the host was wrapped in a deep sleep; as the narrator says, "a deep sleep from the Lord was fallen upon them;" and the two heroes penetrated unto the very centre of the camp where Saul lay sleeping with his spear stuck in the ground at his head (as now-a-days the tent of an Arab sheikh is distinguished by a spear fixed in the ground at the entrance), and a water-bottle by his side. Seeing Saul in this defenceless state the fierce Abishai urged David to let him smite him with the spear; one blow should suffice, he should have no need to strike twice. But, as in the cave of Adullam, David would not consent to such a deed; the person of the Lord's anointed was inviolable; if Saul was to die, his fate must be left in God's hands, no subject might presume to take his life. Having bidden Abishai to carry away the king's spear and water-bottle, David retreated safely from the camp, and "none saw, none knew, none awaked." Mounting a neighbouring hill, at a safe distance from the enemy, he lifted up his voice in the clear evening air which conveyed the words distinctly to the ears of the soldiers on the opposite slope, and in ironical terms reproached Abner for his carelessness concerning his lord's safety. "Answerest thou not, Abner?" he cried; and on the commander asking who was disturbing the king's rest with this clamour, he proceeded: "Art not thou a man worthy of the name? and who is like to thee in Israel? Wherefore, then, hast thou not kept watch over thy lord the king? for there came one of the people in to destroy the king thy lord. This thing is not good that thou hast done. As the Lord liveth, ye are worthy to die, because ye have not kept watch over your lord, the Lord's anointed. And now, see where the king's spear is, and the water-bottle that was at his head." Awakened by the shouting, Saul recognized the voice of the speaker, though the darkness of the night prevented him from seeing his person. "Is this thy voice, my son David?" he cried; and David, aware now that the king was listening, in earnest words pleaded his cause, and showed the folly of this constant persecution of one of his most loyal subjects. What was the cause of this animosity? There could be only two reasons for it (for he himself was innocent of all offence); either the Lord stirred up the king against him, or malevolent men. If the former supposition was true, Saul was giving way to that evil spirit which God permitted to assail him in punishment of his stubborn self-will, and his duty was to pray against the temptation, to appease the Lord by an offering. If, on the other hand, the slanders of evil men had poisoned the monarch's mind, David desires that God will punish them as they deserve (" cursed be they before the Lord "); for by their calumnies they will drive him from his native land, exile him from the sanctuary where the Lord has promised to abide, where alone He is duly worshipped, and force him to take refuge with an alien people among whom he would be in danger of being ensnared in idolatrous practices, or dying a violent death far from all the comfort of true religion. To such an appeal Saul's better self could not but respond , the long-resisted grace of God strove once more with this hardened sinner. Briefly, in broken sentences, he expresses some remorse for his cruel conduct; but he is no longer moved to tears as he was in the former case when his life was so magnanimously spared; he is harder, more unbending now , and though his words sound fair, they are known to be false and treacherous, and such as no one can trust. " I have sinned," he cries; "return, my son David ; I will do thee harm no more, because my life was precious in thine eyes this day; behold, I have played the fool, and have erred exceedingly." Here is no real repentance, but only vexation at mistaken tactics and at a carelessness which had put him again in his rival's power. In token of his unshaken loyalty and good faith David sends back the spear and the bottle which he had taken from the royal camp, and concludes this notable interview by declaring his unalterable belief that God will eventually reward him for his upright conduct and fidelity, delivering him out of all affliction. By all that has happened an unwilling acknowledgment is wrung from Saul that David is blessed by Providence, and that great success awaits him : " Blessed be thou, my son David ; thou shalt both do mightily, and shalt surely prevail " And thus these two, the rejected monarch and the great king of the future, parted, never more to meet in this world , Saul returned to his home at Gibeah, and David resumed his fugitive life henceforward under different circumstances.

We are unable accurately to follow his wanderings at this period; nor is it of much moment to do so, as they are comprised in a very small region, and during their continuance no circumstances of importance occurred. The names of some of the friendly towns or districts which afforded him shelter are given in the catalogue of the places to which he sent presents of cattle from the booty taken from the Amalekites just before the death of Saul[1] Some of these are well known; others are not identified. But all lay in the south of the country, mostly within the territories of Judah and Simeon.

[1] 1 Sam. xxx. 26 ff.

CHAPTER V.

EXILE IN FOREIGN LAND.

David takes refuge among the Philistines, dwells at Gath, removes to Ziklag—His expeditions—The Philistines invade the land of Israel—David marches with them, is sent back to Ziklag, which he finds plundered and burnt, pursues and defeats the Amalekites—Battle of Gilboa—Death of Saul and his sons reported to David—David's elegy.

THE extreme measure to which his last words with Saul had pointed, David proceeded now to put into execution. The life he had lately led was hateful and harassing; no confidence could be placed in Saul's future abstention from persecution, and it was becoming more difficult every day to support his troops and at the same time to restrain them from making reprisals on the king's partisans. His enemies were active and powerful. At their head was Abner, the honoured commander of the royal forces; Doeg, the Edomite, was another and a most malevolent adversary. Psalm vii. tells us of one Cush, a Benjamite, whose words were very bitter against David, and he may be taken as a specimen of his tribe which feared the accession of Saul's rival, and, like the Ziphites, were ready to inflame the king's mind against the outlaw, and to lay plots for his destruction. He was too loyal to promote an insurrection against the existing dynasty, or, as he would have been able to do, to repel force by force; yet how to secure his own safety without bloodshed was a difficult question to solve, while he still remained exposed to secret treachery and open attack. Samuel was dead; the old friend and counsellor who had hitherto supported and guided him had passed away in a good old age; the restraining influence which he had exercised on Saul by his very presence in the land had ceased to be felt, his continual intercessions went up no more, and the tyrant unchecked would now run his wilful course to its miserable termination. Affected by these considerations, David determined to leave his native land and to take refuge amongst the enemies of his people. What such a determination cost him we can ill understand unless we put ourselves in his position, and see what this banishment involved. To a devout Hebrew the land of Canaan was the Lord's sanctuary; here only could He be duly served and acceptable worship offered. Where the Ark and Tabernacle rested there was the presence of Jehovah, and thence were His covenanted graces outpoured. Outside the limits of the promised land, "the inheritance of Jehovah," there was no possibility of joining in the public services so inexpressibly dear to the religious heart of the true Israelite. We learn how precious was this privilege considered from the Psalmist's words on another occasion (Psa. xlii.):

> "As the hart panteth after the water brooks,
> So panteth my soul after Thee, O God.
> My soul thirsteth for God, for the living God;
> When shall I come and appear before God?
> My tears have been my meat day and night,
> While they continually say unto me, Where is thy God?"

In a heathen land, unsupported by the external aids of religion, surrounded by idolatrous environments, customs, and practices, there was great danger of declension from true piety and a subsidence into the habits and feelings of paganism. Such apprehensions and the positive loss of the hallowed joys of Divine worship embittered the exile of the persecuted David, and gave to the wrench from his native land an anguish inexpressible. Whether in deciding on this voluntary banishment he was following Divine direction may be reasonably doubted. The sacred writer gives no hint of any consultation held or advice asked. David "said in his heart," thought within himself, that he should one day perish by Saul's hand, and that there was no better expedient open for him than to escape into a district whither he could not be followed. A temporary distrust of God led him to despair of safety at this crisis. Had he duly weighed the fact that the kingdom was promised to him, that he was destined to succeed to the throne now occupied by his relentless enemy, he would not have feared death at Saul's hands, but would have tarried the Lord's leisure, and awaited the development of events within the confines of his native land. With some infirmity of faith he selected his own way of escape. It was an act of human prudence, overruled indeed by Divine Providence, but fraught with grave dangers and temptations. The country to which he determined to flee was that of the Philistines, both as lying nearest to Judæa, and being inhabited by a warlike people who were able to protect him, and whom Saul, under present circumstances, would be unwilling to attack. The king of Gath, their chief city, was still that Achish with whom David had sought refuge some years before, and from whom he had escaped by feigning madness. But on the present occasion the young Israelite appeared under very different circumstances. No longer a helpless fugitive, unaccompanied and in dire distress, he arrives now at the head of a band of valiant followers, by this time increased far beyond the original six hundred, and "every man with his household," which they brought with them, both with the view of henceforth making their home in this foreign land, and likewise to secure their families from the vengeance of Saul. Convinced from all that he heard that David had finally broken with the Hebrew king, and hoping to enlist his powerful services on his own side, Achish received him gladly, showed him great respect, and assigned to him and his numerous followers quarters in Gath. As soon as Saul heard of this arrangement, he saw that the fugitive was beyond his power, and he ceased to pursue him. Thus David gained the immunity which he sought, but at how dear a cost! By this proceeding he afforded ground for the slanderous reports at which he had been so justly incensed; he was consorting with hereditary foes; what must his conduct be? Who would credit his loyalty under such sinister circumstances? The position was one of appalling difficulty. He was welcomed as the enemy of the Israelites, he could retain the friendship and protection of his new allies only by acting, or pretending to act, against his own countrymen. To such treason he was utterly opposed; the very thought was abhorrent. While the two nations remained at peace, his course was comparatively easy, and he spent his time in exercising his troops, in cultivating the acquaintance of the Philistine chiefs,

and in learning the music of the Gittites. His friendship with
Ittai, who followed him with a faithful troop of his countrymen
in the retreat at Absalom's rebellion, dated from this time. The
Psalms,[1] that in the titles are said to be "set to the Gittith,"
were either composed to a measure or style learned in Gath, or
a companied by an instrument in the manufacture of which the
Gittites excelled and which bore a name so derived. But however employed, the period of the sojourn in the Philistine
capital was irksome and trying. It lowered his spiritual nature,
leading him at every step into fresh falsehood and dissimulation.
To this dark period no psalms are attributed. If in the presence of heathen observances and ceremonial he became
acquainted with certain new musical measures and instruments,
his heart never awoke the poetry of his lips, and the rapture
and devotion of earlier and later days were wholly wanting.
Achish, at much inconvenience, had located him and his
followers in this already populous town, that he might observe
the strangers' conduct and judge how far they were to be trusted;
and David felt himself under constraint, and quite unable to
carry out any plans which he had formed for the relief of his
countrymen from the raids of the desert tribes; at the same
time any refusal to assist in a proposed attack on the Israelites
would at once deprive him of the protection of his present
entertainers. He feared also for the religion of his little troop.
The seductive forms of idolatry to which they were exposed
were hardly likely to be resisted for any lengthened period.
The freebooter's life was not one that conduced to piety or strict
observance of national religion, and the rough soldiers of whom
the troop was composed would only too readily conform to the
customs of those whose good will it had become necessary to
conciliate. Under these circumstances, grounding the request
upon his desire of not burdening the king with the continual
support of so large a body of immigrants, David entreated
Achish to assign him a residence in some country town, where
he could support himself and his followers without drawing on
his host's resources. There chanced to be at this time a town
in the Negeb, or South country, very sparsely inhabited, which
seemed suitable as a residence for the fugitives. This was
Ziklag, a place as yet not identified, but supposed to have been
on the edge of the Southern Wilderness. It had been originally

[1] Psa. viii., xxxi., lxxxiv.

allotted to Judah, but had been transferred to Simeon, and some short time before the present period had been captured by the Philistines, but not occupied by them.[1] This town, probably at David's expressed desire, was assigned to him permanently; and the sacred historian, writing after the division of the kingdoms of Israel and Judah, mentions that it remained up to his time an appendage to the crown of the latter. Hither David removed, happy in being free from the observation of jealous courtiers, and relieved from the embarrassments consequent on his equivocal position; and here he remained for more than a year, being the closing period of Saul's reign.

In this situation, though the vassal of Achish, David acted virtually as a petty king, cultivated the arts of peace and war, learned more skill in ruling men and in organizing such miscellaneous materials as those of which his followers were composed. Under his auspices Ziklag became not only a centre of military operations undertaken in defence of threatened territory, but a refuge for the oppressed, a rallying point for all who saw in the government of Saul the imminent danger of a national collapse, and placed their hopes in the conduct of this new leader. So it came to pass that the news of his settlement here brought many adherents to his standard.[2] From Saul's own tribe came a valuable contingent of archers and slingers who could use either hand in the management of their weapons. Some of them, as being kinsmen of Saul, David at first received with suspicion, but they at once quieted his scruples with an assurance of loyalty: "Thine are we, David, and on thy side, thou son of Jesse: peace, peace be unto thee, and peace be to thine helpers; for thy God helpeth thee." Others joined him from the central district of Manasseh, and others again from the region beyond Jordan, even swimming the swollen river in their eagerness, many of them being of high authority in their own tribes, and bringing with them numerous followers, so that in a short time his little troop swelled "until it was a great host,

[1] Josh. xv. 31, xix. 5, 1 Chron. iv. 30 Ritter, "Allg Erkunde," xvi 132, identifies Ziklag with Tell el Hasy, a remarkable hill some few miles north-east of Gaza, of which a description is given by Robinson, "Researches" ii. 390. Weiss is inclined to agree with this identification, taking the Brook Besor (1 Sam. xxx 9) to be the Wady Sheriah, which debouches on the sea-coast near Gaza Dr. Thomson places it far away to the south; others fix it west or north-west of Beersheba.

[2] 1 Chron. xii. 1-22.

like the host of God." Having appointed captains over his army and reduced it to certain discipline, he proceeded to employ it in checking the inroads of the predatory tribes of the south. Among these are specified the Geshurites, Gezrites, and Amalekites. These last had in some degree recovered from Saul's devastating attack, and in company with the other peoples, had made raids on the neighbouring territory of Judah. The Geshurites are named in Joshua (xiii. 2, 3) as dwelling between Ekron and Egypt. They were an extensive nation, and some of them were found in Gilead and in other parts of Syria. The Gezrites, or Gerzites, were the remains of a once powerful horde that gave its name to Mount Gerizim. They were all nomad Arab tribes, roaming over the northern part of the Desert of Paran, and living partly by plunder, like their descendants, the present Bedouins. To check these marauders David led out his forces and inflicted upon them crushing defeats, took their sheep, oxen, asses, and camels, in which their wealth consisted, plundered their other effects; and that no report of his proceedings might reach the Philistines' ears, he put to the sword every man and woman in the devastated district. Such a measure may have been necessary as a matter of worldly precaution, but it was a cruel deed, unworthy of a high-minded chieftain. Thus one wrong step involves other transgressions; as one lie too often has to be supported by other falsehoods. He had commenced a course of duplicity, and could maintain his consistency only by this barbarous bloodshedding. Even good and high-minded men seem to have cherished very lax ideas of morality in their treatment of aliens and idolaters. It is possible indeed that he may have satisfied his conscience by the consideration that he was simply executing the vengeance which had been pronounced upon the Amalekites; but the impartial critic can hardly acknowledge the force of this plea in the face of the distinct statement. "David saved neither man nor woman alive to bring them to Gath, saying, Lest they should tell of us." The connection of David with the Philistines implied corresponding duties. His feudal lord exacted from him not only military service, but a report of the expeditions which he made, and a certain portion of any plunder that he took. A true account of his late enterprises he could not give; he considered himself compelled to prevaricate. So on various occasions to Achish's inquiry in what direction his raid was made, he answered that it was levelled "against the south of Judah, or against the south of the Jerahmeelites, or against the south of the Kenites," thus leading the king to suppose that he had attacked the southern territory of Judah and its dependencies. There was a Jerahmeel who was the eldest son of Hezron, Judah's grandson, and the Jerahmeelites were his descendants, an offshoot of the tribe of Judah, and settled in the Negeb. The Kenites were of the stock of Jethro, and had faithfully followed the fortunes of the Israelites, living under their protection, and probably paying a certain tribute for the privilege To assault these was to embroil himself with his tribesmen and friends, and Achish, fully crediting David's insinuations, believed that the fugitive was now become odious to his countrymen, and would be his faithful vassal for ever. The deception was the easier by reason of there being no captives taken who might have made awkward revelations. Naturally these would have formed a most important part of the booty, being of much value as slaves; but David's barbarous policy saved none such alive; and the Philistines accepted the loss with grim satisfaction, deeming that such conduct only rendered wider and more impassable the breach between him and his former friends.

The reign of Saul was now approaching its disastrous conclusion. The long-suffering of God had waited vainly for his repentance, and the end was at hand. The Philistines had recognized his weakness and instability, the failure of his military energy and the general decadence of his power; and they determined to make a grand effort to crush him at one blow and to regain their old supremacy. Their successes of late years had been marked; they were now able to change the theatre of war, and in place of occupying their time in petty raids on isolated districts of Judah, they marched northwards along the coast, collecting their forces on the road, and then turned inland to the plain of Esdraelon, thus invading Israel from the north. Here would have been a grand opportunity for David, had he still been in the country at the head of his band of chosen warriors In such an emergency the voice of the nation would have called upon him to act in defence of his native land so seriously menaced; Saul could not have opposed his championship, and under such a leader the battle of Gilboa would have had a different issue, and the recognition of his claims by all Israel would not have been so long postponed, nor obtained at the cost of civil war. But the course of duplicity in which he was involved led to further complications, and, but for Divine interposition, would have forced him to take part in inflicting that disastrous defeat which culminated in the death of Saul and his sons. Achish made much of him, and hoped for great things from his experience. So the valiant outlaw, whose help and presence were so highly valued, was directed by his liege lord to accompany the expedition with the troops under his command. There was no way of evading this command The dilemma in which his duplicity had placed him must be met. He could not ask counsel of the Lord. As a temporary expedient he answered Achish in ambiguous words: "Thou shalt know what thy servant will do." Achish sees in this reply a promise of prowess in his service, and at once engaged, if the young chieftain exerted himself on this occasion, to give him the captaincy of his bodyguard, one of the most distinguished posts in the army. Generous and open-hearted, and influenced by sincere admiration of the exile, the Philistine king fears no treachery on his part, and is pleased to afford him an opportunity of showing his military skill and valour against his ungrateful countrymen. This very confidence and absence of all suspicion on the part of Achish added a new pang to the regret with which David, not for the first time, viewed his present proceeding. Displeased with himself, seeing no way out of the difficulty of being false either to his old or his new friends, yet half trusting that some means of release would occur, David followed the king's troops on their march to Jezreel. They had passed the Philistine frontier, and were well on their way towards the battlefield of Esdraelon, where indecision would be no longer possible, when David's perplexity was providentially removed by the interposition of the Philistine lords, who had joined the array from various quarters. Beholding these strangers in the Gittite contingent they were seriously displeased. They by no means shared the feeling of Achish with regard to the refugees; they viewed them with the utmost suspicion. "What do these Hebrews here?" they cry, as these defiled past in their strange arms and accoutrements. It was in vain that the king professed his faith in David's loyalty, and reminded the dissentients that he had lived among them for more than a year without blame;

they would not consent to his remaining in the army; he would turn against them in the battle, and make friends with his late lord by acting the traitor's part. How could Achish expect such an one as David to befriend them—David whose very name was a by-word—of whom it was sung, "Saul has slain his thousands, but David his ten thousands"?

The king did not dare oppose the general wish of his princes. He summoned David, assured him, with an oath, "as Jehovah liveth," that he had full trust in his fealty and honour, but as the lords were suspicious of him, he bade him leave the army and return to his own place, taking no part in the present expedition. David, in order to maintain the character of a partisan of the Philistines, and having a fear that they might refuse to afford him further refuge on their return from the war, answered the king in the tone of an upright man whose honour had been called in question: "What have I done? and what hast thou found in thy servant so long as I have been before thee unto this day, that I may not go and fight against the enemies of my lord the king?" Thus, concealing his own satisfaction at the turn of events, craftily spoke David. The reply of Achish is more than ever flattering. Employing an idea which he had learned from the Israelites, he says: "I know that thou art good in my sight as an angel of God;" but nevertheless he desires him to retire at daybreak, before any fresh levies arrive, and to take with him all his troops, and especially those Manassites who had lately joined him, and were well known as soldiers of Saul's army.[1] David, nothing loath, complied with the request, and set out on his return. God had dealt with him more mercifully than he deserved, rescuing him from great perplexity, and opening a means of escape from a situation when it seemed inevitable that he must either dishonourably break his word or act as a traitor to his country. Very thankfully, his trust in God strongly confirmed, he turned his face southwards. It was none too soon. During his absence a terrible misfortune had befallen his home at Ziklag. This place

---

[1] The expression (1 Sam xxix 10), "with the servants of thy lord that are come with thee," is hardly one that Achish would employ to denote David's usual followers. A man so kindly disposed to the fugitive would not utter such a veiled taunt. Rather, the words refer to the Manassites who, as it is mentioned in 1 Chron xii 19, "fell to him when he came with the Philistines against Saul to battle"

lay probably some fifty miles from Aphek, where the Philistines had mustered their forces; and seeing no cause for special haste, David spent three days in performing the distance. Taking advantage of the undefended state of the country, denuded of its fighting population by the demands of this new expedition of the Philistines, and desirous of avenging the recent raids from which they had suffered, the Amalekites had invaded the southern region both of Judæa and Philistia, and attacking Ziklag, they had plundered and burned the town, and carried off alive all the women and children, the only inhabitants left therein, to sell them as slaves. When the little army of refugees found nothing but a smoking ruin instead of a prosperous city, and the silence of utter desolation where they had expected to meet the embraces and greetings of wives and children, they were seized with dismay; they "lifted up their voices and wept till they had no more power to weep." Then, with that quick revulsion of feeling common in an excited crowd, they seek to lay the blame of the disaster upon some one person, that they may vent their angry feeling in doing him a mischief. The sojourn in an enemy's land had displeased some of David's followers; the serving in the ranks of the uncircumcised Philistines had excited much discontent; and now this unblest campaign had led to the terrible disaster which had befallen them. For all this David was answerable. True, he had suffered no less than they; he had lost his two wives, as they had lost theirs; but the common calamity did not make their grief less savage in its demand for a victim. They gathered round him with cries of vengeance, and threatened to stone him to death. The occurrence was very similar to what had befallen Moses at Rephidim, when the people were ready to kill their leader because they were in want of water to drink (Exod xvii. 4). As Moses acted then, so did David now. Undismayed by threats, knowing whither to fly for aid, he laid the matter before the Lord. At his request, Abiathar, the high priest, invested himself in the sacred ephod, and by means of the Urim and Thummim inquired if the marauders should be pursued and overtaken. The answer was very favourable, promising that the expedition should be successful, and all that was lost should be recovered. Taking six hundred of his veterans with him, without delay David set forth on the track of the enemy. They had found no provisions in their plundered home, and this forced march tried the energies even of this hardy band, so that, on arriving at the ravine Besor, a *wady* (*es Sheriah*) which runs down to the sea-coast a little south of Gaza, and was probably filled with a swollen torrent, two hundred were too fatigued to advance further. Leaving most of the baggage with them, David, with the rest of the troops, continued the pursuit. By and by they found an Egyptian slave lying half dead in the way, who had become faint and unable to travel, and so had been barbarously left to perish by his Amalekite master. After recruiting the famished man with food and water, they learned from him that the raiders had three days' start of them, but he knew the route which they had taken, and promised, on David's engaging neither to put him to death nor to deliver him up to his master, whose cruelty he had good reason to fear, to bring the Israelites to the Amalekite camp. This accordingly he did, and the pursuers arrived unseen in the immediate vicinity of the marauders, whom they found engaged in a scene of the wildest license, feasting and dancing, with no watch kept, and completely exposed to attack David restrained his little band of heroes, who were burning to rush to the rescue of their wives and children, but when the orgies were ended, and the revellers, overcome with wine and gorged with food, were buried in profound sleep, in the early dawn he launched his troops upon them, and a fearful contest ensued. The hardy desert-roamers were not easily subdued. Though taken at a disadvantage, they fought bravely ; and being numerically far superior to the Israelites, they prolonged the resistance till evening put an end to the strife By this time few were left alive Four hundred of their slaves took advantage of the confusion to seize on camels and escape, and these were nearly all that survived the massacre The whole of the captives were rescued ; and besides recovering all that had been carried off, the Israelites gained immense booty, consisting of what the marauders had collected in this extensive raid. The arms, clothing, jewels, were divided among the soldiers, both those who had actually engaged in the fight and those who had been left fatigued to guard the baggage at the torrent Besor About these last a little difficulty occurred. The selfish and the envious, that are to be found in every large body of men, grudged these loiterers their share of the spoil ; it was, in their view, as much as they could expect if they received their wives and children safe and sound. But David would not listen to such mean and narrow proposals. The Lord had dealt graciously with them; they ought to deal generously with their brethren. He makes an appeal to their religious feelings, while he kindly but firmly resists their demand: "Ye shall not do so, my brethren," he says, "with that which the Lord hath given unto us, who hath preserved us, and delivered the troop that came against us into our hand. And who will hearken unto you in this matter? for as his share is that goeth down to the battle, so shall his share be that tarrieth by the stuff: they shall share alike." David was not one to be led astray by popular opinion from the path of justice, and his influence was strong enough to impose his will even on the froward and unruly. And from that time forward it became the rule in Israel that those who took part in the battle and those who guarded the baggage should share alike in the distribution of booty. It was an equitable arrangement, and one that had already been acted upon, as, for instance, in the case of the Midianitish war, where the prey was divided into two parts, one for those who engaged in the fight, and one for the rest of the congregation.[1] The Amalekites had collected in this inroad an immense quantity of cattle, and these, with the recovered herds of the Israelites, made a surprising show. The latter having been separated from the former, a kind of triumphal procession was formed; and as the herdsmen drove forward the Amalekite cattle, they celebrated the victory with an extemporized ode, of which the refrain was: "This is David's spoil."[2] On his return to Ziklag, David disposed of this booty in a wise and politic manner. From it he made large presents to all the cities and districts which had befriended him in his outlaw condition, thus evincing his gratitude, and binding them by closer ties, proving that though he lived among Philistines, his heart was with his own countrymen, and preparing them to support his claim whenever the throne of Israel should be vacant.

[1] Numb. xxxi. 27.

[2] The passage to which reference is made runs in the Hebrew thus: "And David took all the flocks and the herds, which they drave before those other cattle, and said, This is David's spoil." The Sept. gives, "it was said," the Vulg., "they said;" and this is probably the genuine reading.

This, indeed, was the case now, though he knew it not. The fatal battle in Gilboa, which proved so disastrous to the Israelites and the house of Saul, had just been fought. David knew that a decisive conflict was imminent, and was waiting with anxious impatience for intelligence of the result He had not been three days in Ziklag ere news arrived, which turned he song of victory over the Amalekites into a wail of mourning. Suddenly there appeared in the town a stranger with all the outward signs of sorrow, with rent garments and earth upon his head. Brought before David, he prostrated himself and did obeisance, as in the presence of a monarch to whom all reverence was due; and when commanded to give an account of himself, he professed to have come straight from the camp of Israel, having witnessed the issue of the battle. We know from other sources (1 Sam. xxxi.) the true state of the case, how that Israel was disastrously defeated, that Saul's three sons were slain, and that Saul, having in vain endeavoured to make his armour-bearer kill him, took his own life by falling upon his sword. The messenger, who was an Amalekite, and doubtless well acquainted with the general position of Israel, wishing to curry favour with the rising prince, gave a different version of the sad event. The truth is that he was hovering about the battle-field with the intention of plundering the dead, and coming on the scene of Saul's suicide after the battle was over, possessed himself of the king's insignia, and hurried off immediately to Ziklag, thinking, with Oriental cunning, that the surest passport to a new monarch's favour was to prove himself to have been instrumental in removing the last occupant of the throne. The account which he gave was this: The Israelites had been wholly defeated, and had fallen in great numbers; and among the slain were Saul and Jonathan; the body of the latter he saw, as he happened to come on Mount Gilboa He then beheld Saul leaning on his spear and incapacitated for further combat. Saul turned and asked him who he was, and hearing that he was an Amalekite, spake and said to him. "Stand over me and slay me, for anguish hath taken hold of me, because my life is yet whole in me And so," continued the stranger, "I stood over him and slew him, because I was sure that he could not live long after this sore defeat."[1] To

---

[1] There is no question here of a parallel tradition of the same event already narrated. both of which narratives are of equal authority; nor are

confirm the truth of his statement, he presented David with the crown which he had taken from the head and the bracelet from the arm of the murdered king That kings carried their royal insignia into battle we learn from the proceedings of Ahab and Jehoshaphat at Ramoth-Gilead (1 Kings xxii. 30); and we know from the monuments that the Assyrian monarchs wore costly coronets when engaged in active war. The Amalekite brought these trophies to one whom he regarded as the assured successor of Saul, expecting to reap a handsome reward. He was miserably deceived. Not exultation over a fallen enemy was the feeling that David showed, but heartfelt sorrow and righteous indignation. True, his persecutor was dead; but he thought not of this at the moment, nor of the prospect which was thus opened before him. The king whom he admired and had loved was gone , the friend who was as dear to him as his own soul had fallen ; the Lord's people had miserably perished ; comrades and tribesmen were slain by the hands of the Philistines. The deepest grief seized him and his gallant companions ; they rent their clothes, they mourned, and wept, and fasted, not in mere obedience to customary observance, but with a sentiment which came straight from the heart. But there was a stern duty to be performed before the mourning had full scope. Once more David summons the Amalekite to his presence, and hears from his own mouth the account of his deed. It was a grievous crime in David's eyes to take the life of the Lord's anointed. Whether he fully believed the tale or not, he judged the narrator from his own lips. The power of life and death was now in his hands, and he gave sentence against the murderer. "Thy blood be upon thy head," he says ; "for thy mouth hath testified against thee, saying, I have slain the Lord's anointed." And the wretched man was immediately despatched by one of the attendants.

Then David gave vent to the sorrow of his soul for the calamity that had happened, and uttered a mournful elegy, which for tenderness and pathos is unsurpassed. In view of Saul's melancholy life and disastrous death, he forgets all that he had suffered at his hands , he sees only the prince and father

we constrained to attempt, with Josephus ("Antiq " vi 14 7 ; vii. 1. 1), to reconcile the two accounts. Plainly, the Amalekite's tale is a fabrication , the mention of "chariots and horsemen following hard after" Saul is sufficient to stamp the story with falsehood.

whom he had loved and honoured, the Lord's anointed whom he had reverenced as God's vicegerent, the great warrior whose strength and courage and skill were so widely celebrated. But at the thought of Jonathan his heart overflows Bitter tears fall as he recalls what he has lost in him—the truest friend, the most unselfish of men, who made his private interests of no account if he could serve another, his comrade in many a hard-fought field, his trusty counsellor in every difficulty. The lamentation which he uttered at this time was preserved (we may well be thankful for it) in the Book of Jashar, a collection of national songs or ballads, and has been transferred thence by the historian of David's reign It was called "The Bow," both because that weapon is mentioned in the dirge, and also because it was a martial song, and the bow was one of the principal weapons then employed in war, and one in the use of which the Benjamites were especially skilful. And as Moses composed a song and taught it to the children of Israel (Deut xxxi. 19 ff), so David ordered the children of Judah to learn this elegy by heart, that the memory of those whom it celebrated might never perish [1] The ode is divided into two parts, the first lamenting the fall of Saul and Jonathan, the second commemorating the friendship of Jonathan and David. It ends with the sorrowful refrain which had marked the strophes.

> "Thy glory,[2] O Israel, is slain upon thy high places !
> How are the mighty fallen !
> Tell it not in Gath,

---

[1] The Ang Version, "also he bade them teach the children of Judah *the use of* the bow," is plainly wrong Such instruction would have been unnecessary, and the intimation of the fact would here be wholly irrelevant The principal word in a passage often gives a title to the paragraph A familiar instance is "The Bush," in Mark xii 26 Commentators note that in the Koran sections are named from some prominent object mentioned therein, *e g*, The Cow, Rest, Iron, Morning Another and very probable explanation of this verse 18 is given in "The Speaker's Comm ," in an additional note The custom of learning such odes by heart is referred to in 2 Chron. xxxv 25 , Jer ix 20

[2] "Glory," *tsebi*, Vulg , "inclyti," referring to Saul and Jonathan Some have translated the word "roebuck, gazelle," in allusion to Jonathan's speed of foot , but the parallelism shows that both heroes are spoken of here.

Publish it not in the streets of Ashkelon,[1]
Lest the daughters of the Philistines rejoice,
Lest the daughters of the uncircumcised triumph.
Ye mountains of Gilboa,[2]
Let there be no dew nor rain upon you, neither fields of offerings:[3]
For there the shield of the mighty was defiled,[4]
The shield of Saul not anointed with oil [5]
From the blood of the slain, from the feet of the mighty,
The bow of Jonathan turned not back,
And the sword of Saul returned not empty.
Saul and Jonathan were lovely and pleasant in their lives,
And in their death they were not divided;
They were swifter than eagles,
They were stronger than lions.
Ye daughters of Israel, weep over Saul,
Who clothed you in scarlet delicately,
Who put ornaments of gold upon your apparel.

How are the mighty fallen in the midst of the battle !
Jonathan—he is slain upon thy high places.
I am distressed for thee, my brother Jonathan;
Very pleasant hast thou been unto me;
Thy love to me was wonderful,
Passing the love of women.

How are the mighty fallen,
And the weapons of war perished !"

---

[1] Gath and Ashkelon represent the whole Philistine confederacy.

[2] Inanimate nature is bidden join in the universal sorrow.

[3] *I e*, producing fruits whence offerings could be made. Others render: "ye deceitful fields," comparing Hos vii 16; Psa. lviii. 57, and construing the next clause, "for there hath the shield of heroes experienced deceit."

[4] R V., "was vilely cast away." This would be rather a metaphorical expression for the utter collapse of Saul's power than a statement of what literally happened in the battle But the word is best understood as meaning "was polluted" with the blood, that is, of those whom it ought to have defended.

[5] *I e*, anointed with blood, or else cast aside uncared for and not polished or soaked with oil, as shields usually were. The Ang. rendering follows the Vulgate, "as though he had not been anointed with oil " It gives a very good sense, and one quite in agreement with David's view, but it is very doubtful whether the Hebrew will allow this construction.

CHAPTER VI.

KING AT HEBRON.

David removes to Hebron, is anointed king of Judah—Ishbosheth, the rival king, at Mahanaim—Battle at the Pool of Gibeon—Defeat of Abner and death of Asahel—Abner makes overtures to David—Michal restored—Abner assassinated by Joab—David's feelings at this event—Ishbosheth murdered—David anointed king of Israel—Philistines make war—The Well of Bethlehem—Double defeat of the Philistines

WHEN the mourning for the late calamity was ended, it became a question with David whither to betake himself. His home at Ziklag was burnt to the ground; was it worth while to rebuild it? Now that Saul was dead, was it politic, was it right to remain in the land of the Philistines? The victory at Gilboa had given these last possession of a large tract of country; the north submitted to them without a blow, and many of the Israelite cities between the Plain of Esdraelon and the river were deserted by their inhabitants and occupied by the enemy. What the adherents of Saul might do was still unknown. Any hasty or indiscreet movement might provoke a civil war, and weaken the nation when it most needed prudence and undivided counsels. Yet the hero yearned to repair the fallen fortunes of his people, and to be the agent in shedding on the land the light of prosperity; and there seemed at the moment to be no one to take the lead but himself. In this emergency, David, true to the theocratic principle which now again guided his actions, had recourse to the Divine Oracle, and was directed to remove to the town of Hebron. This city, so celebrated in the life of Abraham, was situated among the hills of Judæa, about twenty miles south-south-west from Jerusalem, and about the same distance north-east of Beersheba. Captain Conder describes its present appearance: "In returning to camp we passed through the luxuriant vineyards of the supposed Vale of Eshcol, carefully inclosed between dry-stone walls. The grapes, mellowed by the autumn mists, were in full beauty; the rich, amber-green foliage covered the whole of the open valley; beyond was a stone town, and a fortress gleaming with a recent coating of whitewash, having a tall minaret above. A barren hill and a few grey olives rose behind. Such was our first view of Hebron, the ancient city, which, as the Bible tells us, 'was built seven years before Zoar (or Memphis), in Egypt' (Numb. xiii. 22).... Hebron is a long stone town on the western slope of a bare terraced hill; it extends along the valley, and the main part reaches about 700 yards north and south.... The Sultan's Pool, a large well-built reservoir, occupies part of the valley. West of the city is an open green, surrounded by hills which are covered with olives."[1] This was a place of great importance, both from old association and from its strategical strength, and was well suited to be the capital of the new kingdom about to be inaugurated. David's claim to the throne was well established. The hereditary principle had never been formally laid down; Jonathan, the only likely competitor, was dead; David was endeared to his countrymen by important services rendered for many years, he was a skilful commander, a true patriot; his ambiguous behaviour in the Philistine army was forgiven by his own tribe, or had escaped general observation, and the people felt that they could confide in his leadership. Besides, it was evident that the Lord was with him. His being directed to abide in Hebron was a token that the Lord God of Abraham was his God. The great prophet Samuel had been his constant friend and guide; now the seer Gad was his counsellor; the high priest Abiathar hallowed all his undertakings with his ministrations and consulted the oracle in his behalf. Then the pious in the nation had learned to love his psalms and hymns; found in them eloquent exponents of the hopes and aspirations which filled their own breasts. Thus for the late exile there had arisen a general affection and respect, which could have but one result under the present circumstances. For this high regard was not confined to his own family connections or tribe; the members of his own little army

[1] "Tent Work," ii. 78 f.

spread his fame among their friends far and near ; and many influential persons from the other tribes, notably from Ephraim now rising into importance, followed his fortunes.

With a compact band of comrades, by this time increased to a considerable size, David, according to the Divine warning, moved to Hebron, residing himself with his wives and family in the city, and quartering his followers and their households in the neighbouring towns, which belonged to the district thus called [1] This colonization of the country, authorized by heavenly permission, was followed by formal recognition of his claims at the hand of its chief men. The heads of the tribe of Judah gathered around him, and with one consent elected him king, the election being solemnly inaugurated by the priestly unction. The first anointing by the act of Samuel had been secret, designed to note his Divine commission; the present consecration was a public recognition of him as king of Judah, just as afterwards a third anointing followed when he was acknowledged king of Israel. David was now thirty years old, in the vigour of healthful manhood, strong in faith, purified by adversity, prepared by many varied experiences to fill the position to which he was exalted. From the sheepfold to the throne he has passed by a series of stages which were his education, each of which contributed some trait, left some impression, to stamp upon him the character which has won, not the admiration only, but the warm love of all who hear his history.

The men of Judah were induced to take such immediate steps for the formal election of David by the hostile action of Abner, who had set up a rival pretender to the throne vacated by Saul. On the fatal issue of the battle of Gilboa the soldiers of Israel had dispersed, panic-stricken and despairing ; but the ambitious general Abner was not disposed to succumb to the Philistines, or to see in the fall of Saul and his three eldest sons the extinction of his dynasty. Collecting some remains of the defeated host, he retreated from the country now possessed by the enemy, crossed the Jordan, and took up his position at Mahanaim, carrying with him Ishbosheth, or Ethbaal,[2] as his

[1] "The cities of Hebron" (2 Sam. ii 3). Comp 1 Chron. ii 42 f. So "cities of Samaria" (1 Kings xiii 32).

[2] Eshbaal, "Man of Baal," was altered into Ishbosheth, "Man of Shame," as Meribbaal into Mephibosheth, Jerubbaal into Jerubbesheth, Baal "Lord," having obtained a sinister meaning as the name of an idol

name was originally, Saul's fourth son, and using him as a tool to gather the friends and adherents of the late king. Mahanaim, "two hosts," was a spot celebrated in the history of Jacob (Gen. xxxii. 2, 10), and well fitted by the associations connected with it and its strong position and fortifications to be the rallying point of the dispirited Israelites. It appears to have been one of the most considerable cities of Gilead, appertaining to the tribe of Gad, north of the Jabbok and not far from the Jordan, but its site has not been yet satisfactorily identified. We shall hear of it again in connection with a later episode of David's history. Placing the weak puppet, Ishbosheth, in this secure situation, Abner set himself resolutely to recover the districts seized by the Philistines and to raise the fallen state of Israel The country on the east of Jordan, called generally Gilead, was well disposed to receive any connection of Saul, and being free from hostile invaders at once acknowledged Abner's authority. Then crossing the river he secured the allegiance of the northern tribes, especially that of Asher,[1] delivering them from the yoke of the Philistines, and turning south made various expeditions with good success into the Plain of Esdraelon, and the regions of Ephraim and Benjamin, so that at the end of five years he was able to proclaim his obedient tool king "over all Israel," except Judah, retaining in his own hands all the realities of power. But it was a very partial sovereignty. His troops seem to have been composed chiefly of Benjamites, and to have been of scanty numbers; and he never had sufficient confidence in the Western tribes to remove his kinglet from Mahanaim and place him in any of the central cities of Palestine.

The first act of David on being anointed king of Judah was to make inquiries respecting the fate of his predecessor's remains. Had they received fitting funeral honours, or what had become of them? He was informed that the Philistines,

[1] The Hebrew reads "Ashurites" (2 Sam. ii. 9), which must be a corruption of "Asherites" (Judg. 1. 32) , the LXX read "Thasiri" or "Thasur", the Vulg. has "Gessuri"; so the Syriac. This last term (=Bridgeland) applies (Deut. iii. 14; Josh. xii. 5, xiii 13) to a district east and west of the Jordan, north of the Lake of Gennesaret, not the same as Geshur, with whose king David formed an alliance. It is not at all probable that Abner went out of his way to attack these people, when he had so much already on his hands. The name Asher seems to be used to include al the north-western tribes.

after the battle of Gilboa, had found the bodies of Saul and his three sons, and, after cutting off their heads, had hung them on the wall of Bethshan, which was a city on the edge of the Plain of Jezreel, about four miles west of the Jordan, afterwards called Scythopolis and now Beisan. He was further told that the inhabitants of Jabesh-Gilead, the city rescued by Saul in his first military adventure, mindful of what they owed to the slaughtered monarch, had sent forth a party by night, taken the corpses from the wall where they were exposed, and carried them safely to their own town. Here, lest further insult should be offered, they burned them, though cremation was not a Hebrew custom, and buried the bones under the well-known tamarisk tree which stood in the city. Hearing of this honourable act David sent a solemn embassy to thank the Jabeshites for their pious care of the dead, and to assure them that he would never forget their kindness; at the same time he took occasion to notify his own accession to the throne of Judah, and to urge them to have the courage to acknowledge his claims and to hold Gilead against all opponents. No mean spirit of revenge found place in his breast; as he had grieved sincerely over Saul's miserable fall, so he rejoiced sincerely at the honour paid to his remains By this proceeding he also showed that he had no wish or intention to punish Saul's adherents, but, on the contrary, was favourably disposed towards them. Thus, also, he proved his loyalty to Saul and the futility of the charge of rebellion brought against him. He had never been wanting in respect to the late monarch, and now took only legitimate means to be recognized as his successor after popular election. His politic appeal seems to have led to no result. Gilead became the headquarters of the rival prince and made no demonstration in David's favour. And he was content to wait. In quietness and confidence lay his strength. He knew he was destined to be king of Israel, and that the way to the throne would in time be made open without any attempt of his to force the course of events. We may well note his absolute dependence upon God's direction, which led to this acquiescence in a state of things which to most men in his situation would have appeared intolerable. When he heard of Ishbosheth's pretensions, he took no further steps to assert his own claims, though he might reasonably have held them to be superior to those of any other, and with his great military abilities and his experienced troops might easily have made them good against all competitors. Though, conscious of Abner's hostility, he never relaxed his watchfulness or allowed his followers to forego their soldierly habits and training, he undertook no active operations against the opposite party, and directed his general, Joab, to avoid all acts of hostility, and to spare the effusion of his countrymen's blood. For five years this policy was successful, and collisions between the rival forces were, if not wholly avoided, at least reduced to local skirmishes of slight consequence. But this state of inaction, where two antagonistic parties existed in a region of comparatively limited extent, could not continue for ever, and a chance encounter at length led to serious results.

Meantime, David continued to prosper; his moral influence and his material power daily increased. In order to enlarge his connection and to strengthen his authority he made various marriages, and while he continued at Hebron he became the father of six sons In addition to the two wives whom he brought with him, Ahinoam and Abigail, the former the mother of his first-born Ammon, and the second of Chileab (or Daniel as he is called, 1 Chron. iii. 1), he espoused Maachah, the daughter of Talmai, king of Geshur, a region of Syria, northeast of Bashan, between Hermon and Damascus, by which alliance he secured a supporter in the neighbourhood of his rival's kingdom. It was a marriage formed on political grounds, contrary to the spirit of the Law, and it bore bitter fruit. The offspring of this union was Absalom, the son who usurped his father's throne and wrung his father's tender heart with keenest sorrow. Another son also, Adonijah, born at this time of another wife, Haggith, attained an unenviable notoriety in much the same fashion. Two other wives are mentioned as married in this interval, but nothing more than their names, Abital and Eglah respectively, is known about them. Eglah indeed seems to be called specially "David's wife,"[1] and hence some have thought that she is the same as Michal, Saul's daughter; but there is no reasonable ground for the supposition, and the assertion at the end of the list, probably, merely implies that all the six women named were not concubines, but David's legitimate wives.

Five years and more had passed since the death of Saul, and

[1] 2 Sam iii 5, 1 Chron. iii. 3.

Abner now proclaimed Ishbosheth king of Israel,[1] and thought himself powerful enough to reduce Judah to obedience. With this view he organized a new expedition, and marched from Mahanaim with a strong body of troops towards Gibeon (El Jib), a famous city in the territory of Benjamin, situated on a rounded hill some five miles north-west of Jerusalem, and therefore bordering on the district subject to David's authority. David, though he had carefully abstained from any aggressive measures against the house of Saul, was prepared for any emergency, and pushed his forces northwards under the command of his warlike nephews, Joab and his two brothers Abishai and Asahel, to anticipate and resist an actual invasion of his little kingdom. The rival armies met at the Pool of Gibeon, a large reservoir fed by a spring from the perpendicular rock on the south-east of the town. On the opposite sides of this pond the hostile forces took up their positions in full sight of each other. Neither party showed any eagerness to commence hostilities; and Abner, seized with a momentary compunction at shedding kindred blood, and relying on the skill and valour of his Benjamite troops, proposed that the contest should be decided by single combat. Both parties must have felt that an internecine civil war would be a fatal source of weakness and give a great advantage to their implacable enemies the Philistines. Like Mettius Fuffetius in the parallel story of the Curiatii and Horatii,[2] Joab agreed to the proposal. Twelve young men were selected from either side, and meeting on neutral ground between the armies, they fought with such courage and ferocity that not one survived. The scene of this sanguinary encounter long bore the name of Helkath-Hazzurim, "Field of edges," "Sword-field." As this combat of champions had decided nothing, a general engagement ensued, and Abner suffered a severe defeat, and found himself constrained to fly towards the river, having no secure refuge in Western Palestine. Among the pursuers of the vanquished host was Asahel, the youngest

[1] In 2 Sam. ii. 10 it is said that Ishbosheth reigned two years. If this reading is correct, the reign must be reckoned from the time when his dominion over all Israel was established. The age attributed to him in the same passage, "forty years," must be a misreading; he was probably not more than twenty, or even less, at this time. The verse looks very like a gloss introduced in conformity with the usual practice of giving such information at the commencement of a king's reign. Comp. 1 Sam. xiii 1, 2 Sam v 4, 1 Kings xiv 21, &c [2] Livy, i. 23-25

of David's three nephews, a skilful warrior, like Achilles, "swift of foot" as a wild roe. Fired with the ambition of slaying a celebrated leader, this youth pursued Abner with persistent vigour, and though twice warned by the stern Israelite, who was loath to slay one so closely related to Joab, to turn aside and be content with some inferior prey, he persevered in his purpose, until Abner, losing patience and seeing that one of the two must be sacrificed, turned and struck the stripling a blow with the shaft of his spear, meaning probably to disable rather than to kill his opponent. But the veteran's hand was heavy; the weapon was probably pointed, or shod with metal; and the stroke was fatal. Pierced through the belly, Asahel fell on the roadside weltering in his gore. As the soldiers came successively to the scene of this disaster, they stood rooted to the spot, awestruck at the untimely fate of this promising youth. But Joab and Abishai, who had not passed that way, and so had missed the piteous sight, continued the pursuit, until as evening drew on they arrived at the waste pasture-land that lay on the east of the city of Gibeon. Here Abner with the remnant of his forces, consisting of some valiant Benjamites, had taken a commanding position on an eminence, and on Joab's approach he called for a truce. "Shall the sword devour for ever?" he cried. "Knowest thou not that it will be bitterness in the latter end?" And he urged Joab to stop the pursuit, and not drive them to desperation and aggravate the animosity of the rival tribes. Joab, who had had orders from David to spare as far as possible the effusion of blood, hearkened to this remonstrance, at the same time assuring Abner that, if he had not asked for quarter, they would have continued the pursuit all through the night unto the dawn of another day. But now, sounding the retreat, he drew off his forces, and allowed the enemy to make good their escape through the Arabah and up one of the ravines debouching on the Jordan to Mahanaim. He himself returned to Gibeon, and mustering his soldiers, counted and buried his slain except Asahel, whose corpse was taken to his father's city, Bethlehem, and honourably interred there. Only nineteen of David's veterans had fallen, while the loss on the side of Abner, whose troops were raw and inexperienced, amounted to three hundred and sixty men. Having performed the funeral obsequies of his brother, Joab marched to Hebron to make his report to David.

But he had conceived in his heart a deadly hatred of Abner and a keen desire of revenge which nothing but blood could satisfy. The opportunity which he sought was offered ere long.

Between the rival factions of David and Ishbosheth a state of hostility continued. There was, indeed, little open warfare, but partisanship ran high, and while the incompetence and weakness of the latter became daily more apparent and drove many former adherents to desert his cause, David's popularity largely increased, and a conviction everywhere spread that he was the divinely appointed heir to the throne, and the only man fit to rule the nation and to unite the divided tribes into one solid community. So, as the historian says, " David waxed stronger and stronger, and the house of Saul waxed weaker and weaker." An instance of political stupidity on the part of Ishbosheth precipitated the catastrophe which had long been impending.

A quarrel about a woman led Abner to break with the house of Saul and transfer his allegiance to David. He had long known and had been convinced that it was God's will that the throne of Israel should be occupied by the son of Jesse; but he had resisted this conviction, and either in wilful obstinacy or from self-interested motives, had set up Saul's son as his father's successor, and supported his pretensions with all the ability and means at his command. Now, in a moment of pique, he treacherously conspires to overthrow the puppet whom he had fostered. Among the concubines of Saul was one Rizpah, a foreigner, the daughter of Aiah, a Hivite. This woman, who had accompanied Ishbosheth to Mahanaim, Abner married. In Oriental eyes, to appropriate a member of the late king's harem is equivalent to aspiring to his throne, and is considered virtually treason,[1] and though there is nothing to prove that Abner meditated any such design, the weak fool who bore the name of king, and who did not realize wherein consisted the sole strength of his position, took this view of the matter, and coarsely accused his great general of gross treason. Indignant at the charge, and at the same time not altogether sorry of a valid excuse for deserting the ungrateful princelet, Abner fiercely answers. " Am I a despicable partisan of Judah?[2] I, who this day am showing kindness to thee and thy father's house, and have not delivered thee into the hand of David, and

---

[1] Comp 2 Sam xii 8, xvi 21, 1 Kings ii 22, Herod iii 68 and 83.

[2] Literally " Am I a dog's head belonging to Judah?"

yet thou chargest me with a fault concerning this woman?"
And then he swore a solemn oath to do his utmost to carry out
the will of Providence, to translate the kingdom from the house
of Saul, and to set up the throne of David over the whole
people from Dan even to Beersheba. Cowed by Abner's
violence, and trembling at the result of the storm which he had
awakened, the miserable Ishbosheth answered nothing. Events
precipitated themselves. Determined on his new course, Abner
wasted no time in inaction. He sent messengers at once to
David, asserting that the kingdom was at his disposal, and
offering to put it in David's hands if he would make a league
with him, and give him assurance of full consideration. David,
who was not above profiting by the quarrels of his opponents,
received these overtures with satisfaction, and professed his
willingness to form a league with his correspondent, adding
only one condition, that his former wife Michal, forcibly taken
from him and married to another man, should first be restored
to him. For this stipulation many reasons may be given. It was
a test of Abner's power and of the genuineness of his overtures
of reconciliation; it served also to recall to men's minds the circumstance that David had paid her dowry with the lives of Philistines—a politic reminder rendered expedient by his late dealings
with Achish. There may have been a lingering affection for the
wife of his youth who had saved his life from her father's fury; it
was also unseemly and derogatory to his honour to allow another,
and a private man, to possess the consort of a king. Had
David been in an inferior station, the matter would have had a
different complexion, and Phaltiel, Michal's second husband,
might have not been disturbed in his domestic arrangements.
Under present circumstances the restitution was necessary. It
was also most judicious. Hereby was shown the new king's
close connection with the fallen dynasty, and that he bore no
rancour against the house of Saul; and thus the goodwill of
the northern tribes was conciliated, and the way opened for
a peaceful accession to the throne. Abner assenting to this
condition, David sent a formal message to the nominal king
and head of the family, Ishbosheth, demanding the restoration
of his wife as an act of justice. The weak prince had no
power to refuse this reasonable request. Abner was accordingly
commissioned to fetch her from her home at Gallim, where she
had lived in much affection with Phaltiel, who accompanied

her on her journey with many tears as far as Bahurim, on the eastern slope of Mount Olivet, and would not even then have torn himself from her side but for Abner's stern command. "Go, return." Before this, Abner had held communication with the heads of the northern tribes, many of whom had long been favourable to David, and were only withheld from openly declaring for him by the strong will and vigorous measures of Ishbosheth's general. He had also opened negotiations with the tribe of Benjamin, which, as being most closely connected with the house of Saul, might be inclined to offer opposition to the transference of the kingdom. But though some might fear thereby to lose dignity or worldly advantage, really little choice was left to them; between David supported by Saul's great leader, and Ishbosheth deserted by him who alone had maintained his tottering cause, there was no comparison; and the chieftains intimated pretty generally what their decision would be. Elated by this success, Abner, accompanied by a picked body of twenty men, possibly representatives of some of the tribes, escorted Michal to Hebron and delivered her to David. He was received with great honour, entertained at a sumptuous feast, and dismissed with a special mission to convene a meeting of the tribes by which David might be accepted formally as king. Gladly he departed on this errand, anticipating a happy result to his machinations, and not without hope of establishing for himself an influential position in the new kingdom. Hardly had he quitted Hebron and set out on his journey, when Joab returned from some warlike expedition loaded with booty, and eager to make his report to David. He was disagreeably surprised by the news of Abner's visit, which seemed likely to lead to results inimical to his private interests. Immediately on hearing of it, he rushed into David's presence, and with little show of respect upbraided the king with having been deceived by a traitor who had come as a spy, and ought to have been treated as an enemy and not dismissed in peace. Waiting for no reply to his remonstrance, he, without his lord's knowledge, sent messengers after Abner with an intimation that David wished for a further interview. The Israelite general, who had started by the usual road to the north, was overtaken at the Well of Sirah (*Ain Sareh*), about a mile from Hebron, and fearing no treachery, relying on David's good faith, left his escort there, and at once returned with the messengers. Joab and Abishai were waiting for him at the city gate. In seeming friendliness they greeted him; and taking him aside under pretence of having some private communication to make, Joab slew him in cold blood. Thus he revenged the death of his brother Asahel, though public opinion did not sanction this treacherous murder, as Abner had killed that youth in self-defence, and all knew that Joab committed the crime in order to rid himself of a possible rival who might supplant him in the king's favour. It was with the utmost indignation and horror that David heard of this atrocity perpetrated by his unscrupulous nephew. Joab had made himself too necessary to be dealt with as he deserved; the plea of *vendetta* would palliate the crime in the eyes of the people, who at any rate would not have been willing to exchange their own leader's life for that of Abner. Such considerations ensured the impunity of the offender, but David took immediate steps to disavow all complicity with the deed. In the heat of the moment, while asserting solemnly that he and his kingdom were guiltless, he imprecates a fearful curse on Joab and his family. Looking for temporal punishment of crime, he prayed that blood-guiltiness might attach itself to Joab's house, "Let there not fail from it one that hath an issue, or that is a leper, or a cripple that leaneth on a staff, or that falleth by the sword, or that lacketh bread" Then he commanded a public mourning to be held by Joab and all the people, while they carried the dead man to an honourable sepulchre in Hebron, and his own tears fell fast at the grave, and he refused to join in the funeral feast, fasting and weeping till sunset. Over the fallen hero he raised a more enduring monument than any stone-cut record by uttering an elegy, one strophe of which is enshrined in the eternal pages of Scripture.

"Should Abner die as a fool dieth?
  Thy hands were not bound, nor thy feet put into fetters;
  As a man falleth before the children of iniquity, so didst thou fall."

The king's sorrow affected the bystanders; they wept with him; they were gratified to see that he abhorred the bloody deed of Joab. And not only they, but the distant tribes also recognized his sincerity, and soon acquitted him of all complicity in the crime To his own friends he speaks his mind more freely, showing his own tender heart which he calls weakness, and complaining of Joab's pitilessness, and adding a kind of apology for leaving the guilty persons unpunished "Know ye not," he says, "that there is a prince and a great man fallen this day in Israel? And I am this day weak though anointed king; and these men the sons of Zeruiah are harder than I. The Lord reward the wicked doer according to his wickedness." The last words were the expression of his strong conviction that justice would be done, assuming the form of a prayer that the vengeance which he was unable to take might be executed by God's interposition.

The death of Abner left matters in much confusion. The negotiations with the northern tribes which he was commissioned to complete were necessarily interrupted, and David's supremacy seemed likely to be still longer delayed. Many at first believed that Abner had been slain by David's command, and were disposed to repudiate the author of such treachery. Disabused of this notion, they were yet not determined how to act. An unexpected event solved the difficulty The utter helplessness and inefficiency of Ishbosheth deprived of his only stay, became patent to all his adherents ; and being convinced of David's innocence of Abner's murder, and reflecting on his many claims to their support, the Israelites generally wished for a change if it could be effected without civil war Among the leaders in Ishbosheth's army were two Benjamites, Baanah and Rechab, natives of Beeroth (*El-Bireh*), originally a Gibeonite city nine miles north of Jerusalem, alloted to the tribe of Benjamin, and occupied by members of that tribe when deserted by the old inhabitants These men, who had been living lately at Gittaim, came to the determination to assassinate their weak prince, thus removing the obstacle to a peaceful settlement of the kingdom (the only other direct heir to the throne being a lame child of tender years, Mephibosheth the son of Jonathan), and, as they thought, securing for themselves the favour of the new monarch Connected as they were with Gibeon, and perhaps of Canaanite descent, they may also have had a blood-feud with Saul on account of his massacre of the Gibeonites (2 Sam xxi. 2), which they proceeded thus to avenge They came to Mahanaim at mid-day, when the king was taking his siesta in an inner chamber. It happened that on this day the customary tribute of wheat was being brought into the granary,[1] and there were many persons coming and going in the palace. Among the porters the two Benjamites passed unheeded, as they probably carried sacks with them the better to conceal their purpose; they penetrated easily to the interior of the house, found Ishbosheth asleep, slew him as he lay, and having beheaded him, put the head into their sack, and made all speed to Hebron. Here they presented themselves to David with the ghastly proof of their deed in their hands, expecting a rich reward for delivering him from the rivalry of the son of that pitiless enemy who had sought his life, on whose seed Providence had avenged his persecution. But they were soon undeceived. Their crime awoke David's warmest indignation. With a solemn asseveration, "As the Lord liveth who hath redeemed my soul out of all adversity," he recalls the parallel case of the Amalekite who boasted that he had slain Saul, and how he had treated him. One who was under the protection of Providence needed not man's crime to advance his rights. These murderers had assassinated an innocent, inoffensive person, and expected to be rewarded for their deed; they should indeed have a reward, but the payment should be death; thus should the guilt of this atrocity be expiated. And he ordered them to be executed and their carcases to be hung up in the sight of all at the much frequented Pool of Gibeon, only mutilated of the feet that had carried them to the scene of the murder, and of the hands that had done the deed. To the head of Ishbosheth he gave honourable burial in the tomb of Abner at Hebron.

Now at length there was hope of a peaceful settlement of affairs. All things pointed to David as the only possible head of the nation. The Philistines were restless, and disunion at this moment might be fatal. A leader must be found, and here was one in every respect eligible. He was of common descent, "of their bone and flesh," he was a tried and well approved commander in many a hard fight, he was the chosen

---

[1] The A V. has (2 Sam iv 6), "As though they would have fetched wheat." The LXX, followed partly by the Latin Vulgate, give a paraphrastic explanation "Behold, the woman who kept the door was cleaning wheat, and she slumbered and slept, and the brothers came unobserved into the house." For the interpretation given above see Klostermann *in loc.*

of the Lord, who had said to him by the mouth of the prophet, "Thou shalt be the shepherd of my people Israel, and shalt be a captain over them." Led by these considerations, the elders of Israel, with their followers in very large numbers, assembled at Hebron and offered allegiance to David. The Chronicler (1 Chron. xii. 23 ff.) gives a summary of the warriors who presented themselves from each tribe on this momentous occasion. They numbered, he says, 331,300, including contingents of Levites headed by Jehoiada and Zadok. A great festival was held, at which David entered into a solemn league with the representatives of the community, and was then anointed king of all Israel. For three days the assembled troops were hospitably entertained, supplies of provisions being contributed not only by the neighbouring inhabitants, but being forwarded from the most distant tribes; Issachar, Zebulon, and Naphtali, sending caravans of asses, mules, oxen, and camels, laden with meal, figs, raisins, wine and oil, and herds of sheep and oxen to be killed for food. "And there was joy in all Israel."

Thus after so many years of patient expectancy, so many and so various trials and reverses, without any attempt to hurry matters to a more speedy issue, waiting always the Lord's good time, David arrives at that position to which as a youth he had been designated, and for holding which becomingly events had trained him in marvellous fashion. "In the fulness of time," says Ewald, "and at the right moment, in perfect vigour of mind and body, he grasped the supremacy which was offered him, after having passed through every stage of power and honour, and every inward test of heavy trial and varied strife. But though he was the most worthy of gaining the prize, and by far the greatest man of his time, yet both the real facts of the case and his own consciousness combined to warn him that he had only reached this lofty position by his reverence for the Holiness which had once for all been embodied in the community of Israel, while Saul, on the other hand, had fallen through despising it; and so he was clearly urged by these striking examples, above all things to seek true welfare hereafter even on the 'throne of Israel' in nothing but a faithful clinging to the 'rock of Israel' and his 'shining light' (Psa. xviii 28-30), and then he might expect a more and more glorious development of the new period of his kingly career. . . . Now that, true to that Holiness, he had reached, by wise and persevering effort, the furthest point of the power and glory which lay right before him, the first question which had to be decided was, whether at this height he would still suffer himself, as king, to be led by the same spirit of Jahveh that had raised him so far, or whether, in the power of unprecedented greatness, he would banish that spirit from him in proud self-reliance." His after life shows how he stood this test.

For seven and a half years David had reigned at Hebron, during which time the Philistines had left him in peace Whether he actually paid them tribute, continuing the vassalage to which he submitted at Ziklag, cannot be determined. They at any rate regarded him as neutral, if not friendly, judging his position by the hostile relations between himself and the house of Saul. But when David became king of all Israel, and the northern tribes who had fought for their freedom so fiercely and so long submitted themselves to his rule, the Philistines saw that David was their friend or vassal no longer; they recognized that in him they had henceforth an uncompromising enemy supported by the strength of all the country. They watched with apprehension the scene at Hebron, and only waiting till the unusual gathering had partly dispersed, they made such a sudden and unexpected attack on that city that David was compelled to retire before them.[1] He retreated to a frontier fortress in the neighbourhood of Adullam,[2] while the enemy occupied the valley of Rephaim, on the west and southwest of Jerusalem, between that city and Bethlehem, thus intercepting his communication with the northern tribes, and having the support of the warlike inhabitants of Jebus. While he was waiting here for a favourable opportunity to attack, there occurred an incident which the narrator has preserved as an instance of David's piety and self-denial, and of the love

[1] The events narrated 2 Sam xxi 15 ff, xxiii. 8 ff, 1 Chron. xi. 10 ff., xx 4–8, occurred at this time before the capture of Jerusalem This we gather from the facts, that, had Zion been in David's hands, the Philistines would not have been able to hold the valley of Rephaim or to occupy Bethlehem, and that the accounts of the battles point rather to single combats and isolated deeds of prowess, than to the operations of a regular army such as David afterwards possessed.

[2] 2 Sam v. 17, where "the hold" is Adullam. This paragraph joins on to verse 3. Comp xxiii. 13–17, 1 Chron. xi. 15 ff.

with which he was regarded by his followers, who shrank from no danger or sacrifice in order to gratify his lightest wish. In this time of inaction, on a hot and burning day, his mind turned to the home of his boyhood, and to the sweet well of water (now represented by an extensive cistern north-west of the town) which had so often refreshed him in his youth.[1] Thoughtlessly, perhaps, he gave utterance to the wish of his heart. "Oh that one would give me drink of the water of the well of Bethlehem!" The words were heard by those around, and three of the heroes of his army at once resolved to gratify his desire. They made for the hostile camp which lay between them and Bethlehem, forced their way through the outposts, reached the well, secured some of its precious water, bore it safely back, and presented it to their beloved prince Touched to the heart at this proof of their devotion, he received the cup graciously at their hands, but he would not drink of it It had been won at the imminent risk of life by these brave warriors; it was thereby consecrated, as it were, to God, and might not be used for any meaner purpose. "Shall I drink," he cries, "the blood of the men that went in jeopardy of their lives?" So he poured it out as a libation before the Lord. As St Ambrose says. "Daniel overcame nature by not drinking when he thirsted. and he thus taught his army by his example to endure thirst, and showed them that he would not expose his soldiers to danger in order to gratify any ambitious desires of his own. To him the water would have no sweetness, being tainted with the taste of the death of his friends."[2]

Desirous of Divine direction, David through the high priest inquired of the Lord whether he should himself attack the Philistines, and whether the attack, if made, would be successful. Both questions being answered in the affirmative, he made his preparations accordingly. Collecting all available forces, he flung himself upon the Philistines encamped on a height in the valley of Rephaim. Irresistible as the outbreak of waters through a breach in a dyke, his attack resulted in a complete victory; the heathen fled with the utmost precipitancy, leaving the images of their gods which they had brought with them into the field to aid them in the fight, and which the Israelites took among the spoil and afterwards burned as the Law ordained.[3]

[1] Conder, "Tent Work," i. 287. [2] Quoted by Wordsworth *in loc*.
[3] Deut. vii. 5, 25; 1 Chron. xiv. 12.

The scene of this event was known afterwards by the name Baal-Perazim, "Lord of breaches," an appellation which recalled the resistless onslaught of the Israelite warriors; or, as David put it in his religious manner, "The Lord hath broken forth upon mine enemies before me, as the breach of waters." Here was a reversal of the disaster that had attended the introduction of the sacred Ark into the camp of Israel in Eli's time; thus was wiped out the disgrace of that sad capture. But the struggle was not ended by this battle. The Philistines organized a second campaign, and again occupied the valley of Rephaim. Many acts of individual bravery occurred in these wars, some of which the historian narrates in his accounts of David's mighty men (2 Sam. xxi., xxiii.; 1 Chron. xx), but our space forbids their insertion here. On the present occasion the Philistines were in too great strength to be attacked openly in front; and David was warned by the Divine oracle to make a detour and take them in the rear, choosing the time for the onslaught when he should hear in the neighbouring mulberry-grove a rustling like the marching of an army. This would conceal the sound of their approach, and was to be considered a sign that Jehovah was leading them to victory. In agreement with this counsel, David, marching to Gibeon,[1] attacked the enemy from the south, and inflicted upon them another severe defeat, chasing them with great slaughter all the way to Gezer (*Tell Jezar*), a Canaanite city not far from Ekron, between the Lower Beth-horon and the sea. By these and similar operations the power of the Philistines was much broken; and after one other heavy disaster, to be recorded hereafter, they gave up all hope of subduing the Israelites, and for the future confined themselves to their own possessions in the lowlands.

[1] Not Geba, as is now read 2 Sam. v. 25, which is too far to the east, but Gibeon, as in Sept. here, and in 1 Chron. xiv. 16. Comp. Isaiah xxviii. 21.

CHAPTER VII.

KING AT JERUSALEM.

Capture of Jerusalem—The seat of government established there—Removal of the Ark from Kirjath-Jearim—Perez-Uzzah—Ark brought to Jerusalem—Michal's insulting words—Organization of priests and Levites—Psalmody—Military organization—Civil administration—David proposes to build a temple; is forbidden to undertake it, but is promised a great future—Mephibosheth.

THE most pressing need at this time was a new capital. Hebron was too far south and in other respects unsuitable for the headquarters of a kingdom extending from Dan to Beersheba. On the confines of Benjamin and Judah stood the ancient city Jerusalem, built on a cluster of hills surrounded on most sides by deep valleys, and well-nigh impregnable To capture this fortress would be an enterprise worthy of David's renown, one sure to be popular with all Israel, and especially with those two tribes, one of which had constantly supported him, and the other connected with Saul it was sound policy to conciliate or, if necessary, to overcome. But the undertaking was an arduous one. Already an important town in Abraham's time, Jerusalem had obtained a pre-eminence among the south-Canaanitish states; its king, Adonizedek, had been defeated and slain by Joshua, and Judah had conquered and occupied some portion of the city. Subsequently, however, it had been seized by the old inhabitants, the Jebusites, who still retained possession of it. From its position it formed a natural bulwark against invasion from the north and west, whence attack was most to be feared, and would prove to be a suitable metropolis for the united people of Israel and Judah Making a great levy of all his available forces, David marched on Jerusalem, attacking it from the north, the only side not defended by deep valleys. The Jebusites, confiding in the strength of their position, met his attempt with jeers and derision: "Thou shalt not come in hither," they cry; "but the blind and the lame shall keep thee off," *i.e.*, a garrison of cripples will be sufficient to defend the fortress; and Josephus[1] says that they actually manned the walls with such Their boast, however, was a vain one. David had offered to give the chief command to the brave warrior who should effect an entrance into the citadel (perhaps by a subterranean channel which was known to exist), and should hurl from its walls the defenders, "the lame and the blind," as he calls them, repeating the words of the Jebusites.[2] Joab, conspicuous for all deeds of strength and daring, led the forlorn hope, stormed the citadel, and was rewarded with the generalship of the army (having hitherto commanded only the six hundred), the black deed at Hebron being counterpoised by these subsequent services. Thus was taken the "stronghold of Zion, that is, the hill on the north-west of Moriah, separated from it by the Tyropœon valley (a ravine at that time some hundred feet deep), and known by the various names of Zion, Acra, The Lower City, and the City of David. The Upper City lay to the south, and Moriah on the east was probably not yet built upon.[3] The memory of this notable capture and of the impregnability of the fortress was preserved by the common proverb used in the case of a strong-built, well-defended edifice "Blind and lame come not into the house," *i e.*, it needs good sight and supple limbs to effect an entrance.[4] In the stronghold thus gallantly won the king took up his residence; and, to secure the city on the only exposed side, he extended the fortifications of the work called "The Millo"[5] to the right and left, thus cutting off all

---

[1] "Ant " vii 3. 1.

[2] Such is a probable interpretation of the very obscure passages (combined) 2 Sam. v. 8 and 1 Chron. xi. 6

[3] Vexed questions concerning the topography of Jerusalem cannot be examined here. The conclusions assumed above are those defended by Colonel Warren in "Transact of Soc of Bibl Archæol," vol vii. pp 307 ff

[4] So in effect Klostermann (2 Sam. v 8) The Sept and the Vulg. interpret "the house" of the Temple But no such exclusion was ever practised (Comp Matt xxi 14), and such a proverb, if the fact were true, could not have arisen before the Temple was built.

[5] The word always has the article, the LXX. call it "The Acra." It

approach from the north, and completing the defence of the whole. What was ruinous in the interior Joab repaired at his own expense, and covered much of the unoccupied ground with buildings. The quarter of the city thus fortified and rebuilt was called "The City of David," while the name Zion came to be used in poetry and solemn utterances to signify what we term Jerusalem as a whole. The conquest of this important fortress, and the establishment of the seat of judgment there, conferred such glory on David that the whole country yielded willing obedience to him; he "waxed greater and greater," and the Lord was with him; for he recognized his true position, that he was raised to the throne, not for his own aggrandizement, but for the sake of his people Israel; and the marked success that attended all his undertakings proved that he pleased God and stimulated him to continue in the right way. Foreign nations sent their congratulations. The Phœnicians, who had helped the Philistines in their recent wars, saw reason to reverse their previous policy, and were now anxious to be on friendly terms with a nation that was growing in strength and commercial importance. So we read that Hiram, king of Tyre, the father or grandfather of Solomon's ally, was foremost in offering friendly aid towards the erection of David's various buildings, not only forwarding materials, as cedars, but providing skilled workmen to carry out his designs.

At this great crisis of David's life, feeling his responsibilities, undazzled by the sudden sunshine of prosperity, but only the more resolved to rule justly and piously, to purify his own heart and to encourage holiness among his people, he may well have given utterance to these noble aspirations in the words of the Hundred-and-first Psalm.

> "I will sing of mercy and judgment;
> Unto Thee, O Lord, will I sing praises.
> I will behave myself wisely in a perfect way;
> Oh, when wilt Thou come unto me?
> I will walk within my house with a perfect heart.
> I will set no base thing before mine eyes;
> I hate the work of them that turn aside;
> It shall not cleave unto me.

---

was probably an earth-work surmounted by a tower, and was in existence when David took the city (See 1 Kings ix 15, 24, xi. 27, 2 Chron xxxii. 5)

> A froward heart shall depart from me ;
> I will know no evil thing
> Whoso privily slandereth his neighbour, him will I destroy ;
> Him that hath an high look and a proud heart will I not suffer
> Mine eyes shall be upon the faithful of the land, that they may dwell with me,
> He that walketh in a perfect way, he shall minister unto me.
> He that worketh deceit shall not dwell within my house,
> He that speaketh falsehood shall not be established before mine eyes.
> Morning by morning will I destroy all the wicked of the land ;
> To cut off all the workers of iniquity from the city of the Lord "

The new kingdom had received its capital, the centre of its temporal power ; but the sanctuary, the centre of religious authority, was located elsewhere This needed rectification. Good government and reverence for religion demanded that the seats of temporal and religious power should be identified. The ancient tabernacle was settled at Nob till the destruction of that town and the cruel massacre of its inhabitants ; thence it was removed and carried to various places, finding at last a more stable rest at Gibeon (1 Chron xvi. 39). The Ark, divorced from its appointed receptacle ever since the ruin of Shiloh, was still enshrined in some temporary erection at Kirjath-Jearim [1] In order to complete the organization of the kingdom, it was requisite that this sacred memorial at least should be removed to Jerusalem. While the king was forced to acquiesce in the continuance of the public services at Gibeon under the authority of Zadok, the officiating high priest, he felt justified in establishing a more formal worship in connection with the Ark and his own tried friend Abiathar, hoping doubtless that some means would be found for terminating the double priesthood and uniting the worship of the whole nation in the metropolitan sanctuary. The removal of the Ark must be a national undertaking. So David held a consultation with the representatives of the people, stated his earnest desire for the centralization of religious worship, and demanded the co-operation of the chiefs. Nothing less than this would satisfy his wish, that notice should be sent throughout the land to all the inhabitants everywhere, and especially to the priests and Levites resident in the cities and villages, and that all should be invited to assemble together in order to countenance and assist at this important function. The chiefs readily agreed to

[1] See "Samuel and Saul," pp 56 ff.

their king's desire. They recognized the fatal neglect of religion which had characterized Saul's reign, and were now earnest in their intention of remedying this great defect in the national life. Thirty thousand[1] warriors gathered together for this purpose, a number sufficient to overawe any opposition of enemies and to give the ceremony a national character. Now was David's vow to be accomplished (Psa. cxxxii.).—

> "Surely I will not come into the tabernacle of mine house,
> Nor go up into my bed ,
> I will not give sleep to mine eyes,
> Or slumber to mine eyelids,
> Until I find out a place for the Lord,
> A tabernacle for the Mighty One of Jacob.

But where was the Ark? The poet says obscurely—

> "Lo, we heard of it in Ephrathah ,
> We found it in the field of the wood (Jaar)"

"The field of Jaar" is Kirjath-Jearim, where the Ark had rested for sixty years past and more, and Ephrathah is probably a name applied to the neighbouring district in consequence of its having been peopled from Bethlehem, originally called Ephrathah[2] To this place, distant about eleven miles in a south-westerly direction from Jerusalem, the great procession took its way. Arriving at Kirjath-Jearim, they proceeded to the house of Abinadab on the hill,[3] and received from his family the sacred Ark, "which," as the historian reverently adds, "is called by the Name, even the Name of the Lord of hosts, who sitteth upon the cherubim." The Levitical law had laid down strict rules for the removal and carriage of this hallowed coffer, which was to be touched by none but consecrated hands, and borne upon the shoulders of the appointed Levites[4] Whether these enactments had been forgotten in the lapse of time, or whether another mode of conveyance seemed more suitable under present circumstances, a new cart, as yet unused for

[1] 2 Sam vi 1 The Sept has "seventy thousand," as 1 Sam xi 8

[2] So Delitzsch See another explanation in "Samuel and Saul," p 58, note

[3] Not "at Gibeah" as in A. V. 2 Sam. vi. 4 See 1 Sam. vii. 1, where the translation is correct.

[4] Numb iii 29 ff, iv 15 , vii 9

common purposes, was provided, and the Ark was placed therein. Such method of transport had been employed by the Philistines in forwarding the Ark to Beth-shemesh (1 Sam. vi. 7 ff.), and the Phœnicians made use of such carriages in their religious ceremonies, but such customs were no precedents for the people of the Lord, who were bound to obey the requirements of their own law. The solemn procession set out, Uzzah and Ahio, the sons or grandsons of Abinadab, driving the cart with its team of oxen, David and a company of musicians, playing on various instruments, singing hymns, and dancing as they marched, heading the throng, the armed warriors bringing up the rear. All went well for a time, but when they arrived at a spot known as Nachon's threshing-floor, the oxen stumbled on the rough road, and Uzzah, fearing that the Ark might be shaken from the cart, seized hold of it, touching with profane hands the inviolable shrine. The act was immediately and awfully punished. Smitten by the anger of God, he fell down dead In dread surprise the procession was arrested. Music, song, and dance suddenly ceased. A fearful silence ensued throughout that vast concourse, so lately loud and jubilant. Why was the festive march so terribly checked? We can see the reason now, though at the moment the people stood in blank amazement, only half understanding the meaning and bearing of the unexpected calamity. It naturally recalled to the minds of those who knew the history of past times the fatal occurrences which had signalized the profanation of the Ark in the country of the Philistines and at Beth-shemesh. And here they were taught once more the exceeding holiness of Almighty God, of whose Presence the Ark was a symbol, and the great reverence due to all things consecrated to His service. Not with the best intentions might His enactment be violated. Uzzah ought to have been well acquainted with the injunctions regarding this holy shrine. Probably long familiarity had weakened the feeling of awe, and a solemn warning was required in order to recall both king and people to a proper sense of duty. Evidently the neglect of religious observances had become very general, and the Mosaic code in all its strictness was either ignored, owing to the distracted state of society, or was actually untaught and unknown. The severe lesson here given David took to heart. He was grievously vexed at the fatal interruption of his great undertaking, which upon reflection he could not but see was the result of his own unauthorized proceedings. At the first, his feeling was one of utter terror, he named the fatal spot where the Lord had, as it were, broken forth in sudden judgment, Perez-Uzzah, "Breach of Uzzah"; and in his perplexity he would not any longer prosecute his cherished enterprise, but had the Ark carried aside and deposited in the house of the Levite who lived nearest, one Obed-Edom, a Kohathite of Gath-Rimmon, a Levitical city in Dan. With subdued spirits the procession returned to Jerusalem, leaving unaccomplished the business for which such great preparation had been made.

Reflecting upon this event, David perceived where his error had been, and resolved to act in strict conformity with the Law if he should again see his way to completing his project. That way seemed to be opened by the news which reached him that the Lord signally blessed the house of Obed-Edom while the sacred symbol there abode. Josephus asserts that during this interval the guardian of the Ark had passed from poverty to opulence, and that all who saw his household or heard the report of his wealth were unanimous in considering him specially favoured by Heaven. Encouraged by the account of this prosperity, David rightly deemed that the fears which had led him to desist from his purpose were groundless, and that humble obedience to the Divine commands would ensure a blessing So after three months' delay he set forth to convey the Ark to the place which he had destined for it in Jerusalem. This time all was done in due and regular order, as the Chronicler (1 Chron xv.) relates at much length. There were summoned to assist at this ceremony the high priests Zadok and Abiathar, the heads of the six Levitical families with a large company of their relatives and dependents, and a numerous contingent from all the tribes of Israel A full choir was organized, music was arranged, special psalms and hymns were composed or appointed, and David himself, changing his kingly garb for the priestly ephod, joined heartily in the music and the solemn dance which was the usual expression of national thanksgiving. Covered with the appointed veil, and borne by its staves on the shoulders of the Kohathites, the Ark set forth No sign of Divine displeasure now marked its course, and when the procession had advanced six paces in safety, at David's command, a sacrifice of inauguration was offered, and one seven times as great at the conclusion of the function, in thanksgiving for the successful completion of the undertaking, "when God helped the Levites that bare the ark of the covenant" (1 Chron xv. 26). Thus with festive song, with trumpets, cymbals, harps and psalteries, the procession wound its way towards Zion. The dramatic hymn composed by David for this solemnity, and sung antiphonally by the choir, is extant, and thus it runs (Psa. xxiv.) :

> "The earth is the Lord's, and the fulness thereof,
> The world and they that dwell therein ;
> For He hath founded it upon the seas,
> And established it upon the floods.
>
> Who shall ascend into the hill of the Lord?
> And who shall stand in His holy place?
>
> He that hath clean hands and a pure heart ;
> Who hath not lifted up his soul unto vanity,
> And hath not sworn deceitfully
> He shall receive a blessing from the Lord,
> And righteousness from the God of his salvation.
> This is the generation of them that seek after Him,
> That seek Thy face, O God of Jacob.
>
> Lift up your heads, O ye gates,
> Yea, lift yourselves, ye everlasting doors,
> That the king of glory may come in.
>
> Who then is the king of glory?
>
> The Lord strong and mighty,
> The Lord mighty in battle.
>
> Lift up your heads, O ye gates,
> Yea, lift them, ye everlasting doors,
> That the king of glory may come in.
>
> Who is He, the king of glory?
>
> The Lord of hosts,
> He is the king of glory."

Many other psalms are connected with the event of this great day when, as it were, the Lord took up His abode in the sanctuary of Zion Perhaps it was now that first was heard the grand old hymn (Psa. lxviii)—

"Let God arise, and let His enemies be scattered";

and the simple teaching of how to approach God acceptably (Psa. xv.)—

> "Lord, who shall sojourn in Thy tabernacle?
> Who shall dwell in Thy holy hill?
> He that walketh uprightly, and worketh righteousness,
> And speaketh truth in his heart"

The Tabernacle proper was still at Gibeon, but David had erected a new and costly tent near his own palace, and hither with the utmost pomp and solemnity the Ark was conveyed, and temporarily deposited there in the Holy of holies. Burnt offerings and peace offerings followed in large profusion, and from the latter were distributed to all the people bread and flesh and raisins. This princely liberality raised the people's enthusiasm to the highest pitch, and the praises of the new monarch were celebrated throughout the whole land Before he dismissed the assembled multitude, he addressed them in loving words, and invoked upon them the blessing of Jehovah. But the day marked by such joy and happiness was not to pass without a cloud. At the conclusion of the solemnity, David returned to his own house to bless those of his family who had not been present at the public festival. Now Michal, the daughter of Saul as she is here significantly called, had no sympathy with this religious excitement; spiritual enthusiasm was a feeling which she could not comprehend; neither her father nor she had ever troubled themselves about the Ark and its honour, and she could not understand how a king could so forget his dignity as to discard his royal robes, assume the scanty and undistinguished ephod, and dance among the people like any common worshipper. She had watched his proceedings from her window as the procession marched onwards to the Tabernacle, and she despised her husband in her heart, and when he returned glowing and jubilant, she met him with reproaches "How glorious," cried she, ironically, "was the king of Israel to-day, who uncovered himself to-day in the eyes of the handmaids of his servants, as one of the vain fellows shamelessly uncovereth himself!" David's answer was impetuous and crushing What he had done he had done in honour of that Lord who had advanced him and had punished Saul, and in honouring whom there could be no degradation "And," he adds, "I will make myself even more contemptible in my own eyes, I will shrink from no humiliation in God's service; and if you honour me not, the maid-servants of whom you speak will have for me respect and reverence" For her arrogant sentiment Michal was punished by childlessness, the saddest fate that could befall a Hebrew woman [1]

The removal of the Ark to its home in Zion may well be called a turning-point in the history of Israel, as well as a great epoch in the career of her king. Henceforth the residence of the theocratic monarch and the presence of Jehovah were united in one centre; at any rate this was the first and most important step towards such a consummation. While the time-honoured Tabernacle and the great altar of sacrifice were located elsewhere, the unity of government and worship was not fully established, and a divided religious service was a necessity of the time. But, as we shall see, David had at heart a scheme for erecting a palace for Jehovah which should contain in itself all the accessories of divine service of ancient or of later date, and become the shrine for the worship and devotion of the whole people. But there was much to be done before this design could be accomplished. One work of primary importance was the reorganization of the priests and Levites, which was rendered necessary by the general decay of religion, and the confusion into which the affairs of the Levites had fallen since the time of the earliest judges. A succession of measures distributed over a number of years resulted in salutary reforms which, with certain modifications, continued in force throughout the whole period of Israel's national existence. The massacre at Nob had left the priestly community in a most depressed state, and although the solemnities of worship were performed in some sort at Gibeon, it was with maimed rites that they were carried on and with no active support or countenance from the royal authority. The Levitical arrangements originally established

---

[1] In 2 Sam. xxi. 8, "Michal" is evidently a clerical error for "Merab" (See 1 Sam. xviii 19) Some of the MSS of the Sept. and Vulg read Merab, and it is possible that the original reading was "Merab sister of Michal," the first two words having afterwards dropped out.

by Moses had in part become obsolete, and in part were unsuited to the circumstances of the present time. Details required alteration, fresh arrangements were necessary. The double priesthood must be acknowledged, and its duties regulated provisionally. Zadok, the head of the house of Eleazar, and his brethren were confirmed in the tenancy of their offices at Gibeon in Benjamin, where, in default of any Divine command for their removal, the Tabernacle and Great Altar still remained, while Abiathar and his son Abimelech, of the family of Ithamar, ministered in the Tabernacle at Jerusalem, though we have no intimation that they offered sacrifice there, and the first and only altar in the city was the one raised by David on the threshing-floor of Araunah some years later. It is probable that Samuel had intended or commenced some reform in the Levitical ministrations, and that David carried out and amplified the suggestions of the great seer.[1] Sacred music and song had been carefully studied at Ramah, and David had been always intimate with certain of the Levite families, some of whom, as we saw above, threw in their lot with him while still a fugitive from the court of Saul. The celebrated singers Heman, Asaph, and Ethan were specially appointed to conduct the musical portion of the solemnity which celebrated the introduction of the Ark into its new home; and after this inauguration, Asaph and others of their brethren were "left to celebrate and to thank and praise the Lord, and to minister before the ark continually, as every day's work required" (1 Chron xvi. 4, 37); while Heman and his family were appointed to lead the services at Gibeon, playing on musical instruments and singing when the sacrifices were offered morning and evening (1 Chron. xvi. 39-42) To this period is referred the introduction of that system of courses, afterwards further elaborated, whereby the whole sacerdotal body was divided into twenty-four classes, sixteen of which appertained to the family of Eleazar and eight to that of Ithamar, presided over respectively by Zadok and Abiathar These classes were designated by the name of their chiefs (as we read in Luke i. 5, of "the course of Abia"), who in our Lord's time were called "chief priests," and formed part of the great Sanhedrin. They executed their office week by week,

[1] See 1 Chron ix 22. I have gladly here availed myself of Dr Binnie's treatise on "The Psalms," new edition. The arrangements of David are narrated at length, 1 Chron. xxiii.–xxvi

their particular duty being apportioned by lot, it being also arranged that the family of Eleazar should take twice as many turns of service as that of Ithamar. The rest of the Levites, numbered from twenty years old and upwards at 38,000, were organized thus. Twenty-four thousand were apportioned to the twenty-four priestly courses to assist in the ministrations of the sanctuary; four thousand were set apart as musicians and singers divided into twenty-four courses, under the same number of masters or leaders, four thousand acted as guards and watchers; and the remaining six thousand, called "chief fathers," attended to matters away from the capital "pertaining to God and the king," performing the duties of officers and judges, probably also those of teachers and annalists. We shall see further on what provision was made for military matters; meantime we must note that David organized a spiritual force, regularly drilled and officered, which was as efficacious in building up and supporting the inner life of the state, as were the mighty men and valiant officers of the army in maintaining and extending the empire.[1] It was no mere school of music that he established at Jerusalem; rather, he transferred thither Samuel's prophetical college with all its accompaniments, musical, liturgical, educational As Dr. Binnie says,[2] reasoning from the language of 1 Chron. xxv, "the presidents of the Levitical families were not mere *artistes*, mere musical performers. They were men to whom God was wont to vouchsafe those supernatural motions of the Spirit which were witnessed in the Seventy Elders whom Moses ordained in the wilderness, and which attested the gracious presence of God in Samuel's school at Ramah" It is incredible that David should have omitted to avail himself of this institution which had so largely assisted the revival of true religion in Samuel's day. It was Heman, the old prophet's grandson, who, with Asaph and Jeduthun, was David's chief Levitical seer; and the writers of Psalms who were contemporary with him were all Levites belonging to families trained and dedicated to the music of the sanctuary. Such was the influence of these men, that their names were perpetuated till the latest times, and Psalms were attributed to Asaph and the sons of Korah many centuries after their voices had been silenced for ever.

[1] Weiss, pp. 190 f. [2] "The Psalms," pp. 67 f.

David himself composed many hymns especially for divine service, entrusting them to Asaph and his companions to set to suitable music. A familiar instance is the celebrated ode in 1 Chron. xvi. 8-36, portions of which are inserted in Psalms cv., xcvi., and cvi., wherein Israel, and heathendom, yea, and all creation, are invited to glorify the only true God. Other Psalms composed on various occasions in former days were adapted for liturgical use, so that in course of time every week-day and every festival had its own anthem. The melodies to which these Psalms were sung are sometimes noted in the titles ; and although of course it is impossible now to recover the airs, as they were preserved in no known notation, there is some reason to suppose that the old so-called Gregorian tones, or some of them, are derived from the music of the Jewish Temple, and embody strains which nearly three thousand years ago wafted the aspirations of the pious Jewish worshipper to heaven Certainly, the Spanish Jews, the most conservative people in the world, to this day chant the Psalter to simple melodies strangely like to, if not identical with, the primitive ecclesiastical tones

To support the voices of the singers, and to add solemnity to the service, David adopted the use of various instruments of music, viz., cymbals, harps of different pitch, and trumpets.[1] We have not sufficient materials to enable us to state with certainty the mode of service thus instituted ; but it is supposed that the worship began with a concert of harps ; this was followed by vocal and instrumental music interrupted by certain pauses, marked "Selah"; to this succeeded an interlude ($\delta\iota\dot{\alpha}\psi\alpha\lambda\mu\alpha$) played by instruments alone, while occasionally the congregation responded to the chorus of Levites, and added to the regular chant their "Amen" or "Hallelujah"[2]

The military organization established by David is known to us with considerable accuracy[3] The nucleus of the army was formed by the band of six hundred which had gathered round him in his exile, and which from their valour and military experience formed a model troop, and were called by the honourable title of *Gibborim*, "mighty men, heroes." They were mostly genuine Israelites, but among them were a few strangers, such as Uriah

---

[1] 1 Chron. xv. 19, 20, 21, 24, xvi. 5, 6 For later development, see 2 Chron v 12 f. [2] Weiss, p. 195
[3] Ewald, ii. 139 ff. Stanley, "Lectures," xxiii 91 ff Weiss, 173 ff.

the Hittite, and Zelek the Ammonite.[1] They were divided into three bands of two hundred each and smaller companies of twenty each. The smaller companies had each its own officer, thirty in all, advancement to these posts being the reward of special prowess. Over every two hundred with their ten officers was placed a commander or colonel, and at the head of all a general, who seems to have been later, if not at first, Abishai, the king's nephew. Thus this battalion consisted in all of six hundred and thirty-four men, to which doubtless was attached a numerous body of dependents and retainers. They had free quarters in Jerusalem and drew their pay from the king, being specially devoted to his service, and having no other duties than those connected with war. The exploits of some of these warriors have been handed down to posterity in the national annals. Of the three colonels, Jashobeam is celebrated for having withstood and conquered three hundred foemen with his single spear ; Eleazar at Ephes-dammim sustained unsupported the attack of a large body of Philistines smiting them till his hand clung to his sword, so that when at length his countrymen advanced to his relief they had nothing to do but to despoil the slain ; Shammah performed a similar feat, by his single arm saving a field of lentils from the devastations of the marauders and winning a great victory for Jehovah. Such almost incredible deeds of strength and courage were the fruit of national aspirations for liberty and a fiery emulation animated and supported by the innate feeling that God was on Israel's side. The main body of the army, called generally The Host, consisted of all males capable of bearing arms, estimated at 800,000 in Israel and 500,000 in Judah, over whom Joab was general-in-chief. These were called out only in case of necessity, and received no special training. But little reliance could be placed on this *landsturm*, which in any great emergency was too often found to deceive the expectations of its leader ; and in order to ensure an effective army there was formed a militia of twelve regiments, each twenty-four thousand strong, who were on duty for one month in the year under their own commander, either undergoing special training, or doing garrison duties in dependent cities and countries. As the six hundred mighty men were often employed at a distance from the court, and in their absence the king would have had no special household

[1] 2 Sam xxiii 37, 39

troops to defend his person and to execute his commands, in addition to these soldiers the monarch had his own body-guard, a survival of a similar force at the court of Saul, of which David himself had probably been commander. This had been finally organized during his residence at Hebron, was attached to his person, executed his commands, and was never sent on foreign service. It was originally composed of foreigners, the so-called Cherethites and Pelethites, who had been induced to take service with him when dwelling at Gath and Ziklag, and had been largely recruited since then from alien sources. They were commanded by Benaiah, son of the chief priest Jehoiada, and a principal man among the Gibborim, and may be paralleled by the Swiss and Scots in the pay of French monarchs, and the Varangians at the Greek court of Constantinople. Over such a body it was expedient to place not only a man of assured prowess and skill, but one who was a staunch friend of the king, free from restless ambition and self-seeking Such was Benaiah, who proved himself a trusty support both to David and his son, and succeeded Joab as Generalissimo of Israel The Cherethites are first mentioned (1 Sam xxx 14) in connection with the invasion of the Amalekites during David's sojourn at Ziklag. There they are evidently identical with the Philistines of the south; and the name has been connected with Crete, from which island the Philistines are supposed to have passed to the coasts of Canaan.[1] Another interpretation of the word would make it equivalent to "executioner," which indeed would describe one of their duties. Pelethite seems to be another form of Philistine, though here again some have found in the name an etymology which would give the meaning of "runner," a very appropriate title for Oriental attendants The Israelite king in taking as body-guard a band of foreign mercenaries followed the custom of Eastern monarchs, who were wont to entrust the safety of their persons to hired alien troops, bound to them by interested motives, and not liable to be diverted from their allegiance by dynastic or constitution l considerations. In David s case there was also the bond of strong personal affection, as well as the highest respect and

[1] It is suggested in the "Palestine Exploration" reports that Cherethite has nothing to do with Crete, but is derived from Keratiya, a place thirteen miles N N W from Beit-Jibrin (Eleutheropolis), where some Philistines from Egypt established themselves in old time, a hint of which circumstance may be found in Gen x 13, 14 "Memoirs," iii 260

reverence; and these feelings kept them faithful under all circumstances.

The Israelitish army was distinguished from those of surrounding nations by being wholly destitute of cavalry. We hear (2 Sam. viii 4) of a few chariots having been on one occasion retained from the spoils of a conquered nation, and of mules being used by princes and officers; but with these exceptions the force was altogether infantry Mosaic legislation discountenanced adventitious aids in war; personal bravery and trust in the Lord supplied the confidence and superiority which other nations found in chariots and horses.[1] Their offensive arms were spears and swords, in the exercise of the former of which weapons they attained wonderful dexterity. Bows and arrows, and slings, were less used, and seem later on to have been employed chiefly by the Benjamites, whose skill with them was notorious Probably they had been more universally distributed during the time of depression, when the Israelites were deprived of other arms by their Philistine conquerors, but fell into disuse as other more effective weapons became available. For defensive armour the great mass of infantry had nothing but shields, which were of round or oval shape, and were made of a framework of wood covered with leather, and sometimes edged or cased with metal. The large oblong shield covering the whole body was the peculiar appendage of kings and great chiefs, and was usually carried by an attendant. Helmet and coat of mail were also worn only by men of rank. These distinctions between the armies of Israel and those of surrounding nations emphasized their separation from the rest of the world and their dependence upon Divine guidance. Another peculiarity attended their military expeditions. They often took with them the sacred Ark,[2] thus giving to war a religious character, and showing that the enemies of Israel were the enemies of God and must be treated with the utmost severity.

In perfecting the military organization of the kingdom David did not consider that he had fulfilled all his royal functions; the national constitution and civil administration had still to be provided We are told briefly (2 Sam. viii 15) that he "reigned over all Israel, and executed judgment and justice unto all his people," and we have to gather details from various quarters to

---

[1] Psa. xx 7, [2] Comp 2 Sam, xi. 11.

fill out this scanty mention. He was no longer king of a tribe, but of a strong and united people, which had a regular organization at home, and entered into relations with other countries, and possessed an extensive dominion. Of the institutions which he established, and which continued till the final overthrow of the monarchy, we are enabled to give some account [1] While he himself was the head of all government civil and military, he did not supersede the time-honoured authority of the heads and elders of tribes. These still managed their own local affairs, and on great national occasions assembled in one body for deliberation and action, and by this system of home rule acted as a check on the despotism of the monarch. The king was also controlled by the co-ordinate authority of the prophets which, in the case of a pious prince, effectually prevented him from developing into an irresponsible tyrant. In order to conduct the government David associated with himself certain officers, who possessed his entire confidence and under him carried on the administration of the whole realm. He had his counsellors or "king's friends," at the head of whom was the Chancellor (*Mazkir*), "the Remembrancer," who had not only to commit to writing the chief events of the reign to be preserved among the public annals, but also to bring before the king the daily *agenda*, and all important questions that arose either at home or abroad. Then there was the Scribe (*Sopher*), "the Writer," a Secretary of State, who prepared all formal documents containing the royal commands, or concerned with public matters. Probably separated from the office of Scribe was that of the Collector of tribute, through whose hands passed all the accounts of the realm, the financial business, and the rating of the people. The royal revenues arose from various sources; there were free-will offerings, such as were presented to Saul at his election (1 Sam. x. 27), and without which no one thought of approaching a great man; there was tribute from subject nations; there was the portion of booty appertaining to the monarch, which consisted both of cattle and lands.[2] From these and such like sources, without oppression or injustice, the king's property continually increased, and officers were appointed to collect, preserve, and employ it to the best advantage.

It had long been the dearest wish of David's heart to erect a

[1] See 2 Sam. viii. 16 ff., xx. 23 ff., 1 Chron. xviii. 15 ff.; xxvii. 32 ff.
[2] See 1 Chron. xxvii. 25 ff.

permanent and substantial building for the reception of the holy Ark and the performance of Divine worship according to all the requirements of the Mosaic ritual. This wish became imperative when a pause in the constant wars in which he had been engaged gave him leisure to attend to the duties of external religion. It was further emphasized by the reflection that he himself had a sumptuous palace to dwell in, while the Ark of God dwelt within curtains. Now that Israel was firmly settled in her own land, and had one capital, the centre of government, and the holy symbol was set up there, it was not seemly that the abiding place of God's presence should be of this temporary and vagrant character; and it seemed to the king that the time had come for raising a magnificent temple, which should be a worthy expression of his faith in Jehovah, and a shrine at which could be offered the worship and devotion of an united people. As soon as the design was matured in his mind he communicated it to the prophet Nathan, who is here first mentioned, and who is celebrated as the chronicler of his reign. Nathan, speaking of his own motion, and without taking any steps to ascertain the Divine will in the matter, at once encouraged David in his pious project, and heard with satisfaction that he had imparted his intention to his friend Hiram of Tyre, who had already aided in the erection of the royal palace at Jerusalem. But God's thoughts are not as men's thoughts. In that very night a vision came to the prophet which completely altered his view of the project; and he was commanded to forbid the building at this time, and that on two grounds. First, it was an innovation not necessitated, and inexpedient. Hitherto a tabernacle had been sufficient for the requirements of the people; God had shown His presence there; with this, as the symbol of His favour, He had led them out of Egypt, and done many wonderful works, and raised David himself from the shepherd's lowly lot to be the ruler of Israel; and never had He ordered any prince or any tribe which for a time possessed the leadership to build a permanent temple in His honour. The wandering tent had been designed to give a truer idea of the spiritual worship of Almighty God than was conveyed by the magnificent structures of Egyptian idolatry. Too easily might the simplicity and purity of the religion of Jehovah be corrupted by the inconsiderate appliance of adventitious circumstances. Tied to one spot, and associated with one edifice of splendid appearance and aspiring pretentions, the service of religion would tend to become hard and sensuous, and its spirituality increasingly difficult of realization. And thus a breach would be made between the ancient and the present idea of religion, and the practical efficacy of the old Tabernacle would be forgotten and disparaged in the splendour of the new temple [1]

There was a second reason why David was disqualified from building a house of prayer. He had always been a man of war, he had shed blood abundantly ; and although he had fought in a good cause and under Divine direction, still this which was essentially a work of peace could not fitly be entrusted to the hands of one whose life had been one of turmoil and battle.[2] The incongruity was acknowledged by the ancients in classic times. Thus it enhanced the crime of Diomede and Ulysses that they touched the sacred Palladium with blood-stained hands ; and Æneas constrains his father Anchises to carry the sacred things when he escapes from Troy, because he himself being fresh from battle might not lawfully touch them [3]

But while he thus discouraged the execution of David's design, Nathan was commissioned by God to give him a comforting message, and an assurance of continued support and favour. He revealed a great future. Israel should be settled firmly in their own land, delivered from the thraldom of enemies, and should grow continually in prosperity and peace. Then the prophet tells him of the establishment of the kingdom

[1] According to Wellhausen and others, the chapter (2 Sam vii.) which contains the account of the vision and David's subsequent thanksgiving is a very late production, probably composed in Josiah's time. The writer is supposed to have known a long series of Davidic kings, and by markedly inserting "for ever" in verses 13 and 16, implies that he lived after the destruction of the northern kingdom. But all these guesses and suppositions are the outcome of a disbelief in the predictive element in the Old Testament. The wording of verse 12 ("I will set up thy seed after thee, which shall proceed out of thy bowels") denotes that Solomon was not yet born. The "rest" referred to in verse 1 may well be the interval after the defeat of the Philistines, before the next great wars were undertaken The clause is omitted in the parallel passage in 1 Chron xvii 1, both in the Hebrew and the Septuagint

[2] See 1 Chron xxii. 8, xxviii 3, which Ewald takes to be "later sacerdotal representations" of the fact that "the heavy wars in which David was constantly engaged hindered or delayed the execution of the scheme" ("History of Israel," iii. 130).   [3] Virg., "Æn." ii. 167, 717 ff.

in his family. He was not indeed permitted to erect a material house for the Lord, but God would make him "a house," would raise up seed for him, who should build a house to the name of God, and his throne should be established for ever. "I," says God, "will become a Father to him, and he shall be a son to Me. If he act perversely, I will chastise him with the rod of men; but My mercy will I not remove from him, as I removed it from Saul." And then the Lord repeats the gracious promise: "Thy house and thy kingdom shall be made sure for ever, thy throne shall be established for ever."[1]

Here was a glorious promise, an abundant compensation for the disappointment in not being allowed to perform the desire of his heart. The promise had in it three elements, each more exalted than the preceding. The house of David should reign for ever; the seed of David should erect a temple for the Lord who should take up His abode therein; and this seed should be raised to sonship with God, involving the chastisement of paternal love combined with everlasting mercy never again to depart from the chosen family. Who does not see that this supreme prediction looks far beyond the great son of David, Solomon, and the line of any earthly dynasty? The monarchs of that race were the heralds of its realization, but it could be ultimately fulfilled only in the Messiah, who for our sake suffered chastisement, who raised man's nature to the highest seat in heaven, and therein set up His eternal throne. And we know from revelation that a time will come when Christ shall tread all enemies under His feet, and the weary Church shall be triumphant, and, in the words of St. John (Rev xi. 19), there shall be "opened the temple of God that is in heaven, and there shall be seen in His temple the ark of His covenant"[2] How much of this promise David understood we cannot exactly determine. That he saw in it far more than an assurance of royal dignity to his son and his successors, is certain. St. Peter[3] declares that David well knew that "God had sworn

---

[1] 2 Sam. vii 11-16, 1 Chron xvii 10-14. Briggs, "Mess Proph" § 42.

[2] See Wordsworth on 2 Sam vii

[3] Acts ii 30 The R V, in deference to the chief uncials, reads "Of the fruit of his loins, he would set one upon his throne," but the intention is the same in both readings, the latter being more indefinite, the former clearly explaining the allusion See Liddon, "Bampton Lectures," ii p 122, ed. 1867, who, quoting Kennicott, interprets the obscure expression 2 Sam.

with an oath to him, that of the fruit of his loins according to the flesh, He would raise up Christ to sit on his throne." He must have recognized that previous predictions culminated in this one—the sceptre of Jacob was to be wielded by his own line, the great hope of Israel was to be fulfilled in his race. So the message brought by Nathan filled the king's heart with joy and gratitude. He thinks no more of the frustration of his cherished design; his regret is swallowed up by his delight at the fair prospect opened before him; his heart is so full that he cannot rest in his palace, and he goes forth to the sanctuary where the Ark was placed, that he may pour forth his soul to the Lord who had dealt so graciously with him. The prayer that he then uttered is preserved by the narrator (2 Sam. vii. 18 ff.), and consists of two parts—thanksgiving for the promise, and petition for its fulfilment. A solemn wonder is his prevailing feeling; he is astonished that God should select one obscure as he is for an abiding royalty, and for the possession of such great promises, and he prays that it may all be accomplished in God's good time, and he regards it as an act of undeserved grace. Years after this, at the very close of his life, David thought deeply on these hopes; they were the subject of his last utterances, the song of the dying swan.[1]

> "The God of Israel doth say to me,
> The Rock of Israel doth speak.
> A ruler over men—righteous,
> A ruler in the fear of God (shall arise);
> He shall be as the morning light when the sun ariseth,
> A morning without clouds,
> As when the tender grass springeth out of the earth,
> Through clear shining after rain
> For is not my house so with God?
> For He hath made with me an everlasting covenant,
> Ordered in all things and sure,
> Yea, all my salvation and all my desire,
> Will He not cause it to spring up?
> But the ungodly shall be all of them as thorns to be thrust away;
> For they cannot be taken with the hand,

---

vii 19, "Is this the manner of man, O Lord God?" as meaning, "This is, or must be, the law of the Adam," *i e*, this promise must relate to the ordinance made by God to Adam concerning the seed of the woman

[1] Weiss, 2 Sam. xxiii. 1 ff.

> But the man touching them
> Must be armed with iron and the staff of the spear,
> And they shall be utterly burned with fire in their place."

Before proceeding to recount more stirring events there is one pleasing episode which claims attention, and this is David's treatment of the surviving member of the family of his friend Jonathan. When a pause in his absorbing political duties gave him a time for reflection on the past, a yearning desire came over him to show kindness to any descendant of Saul's house who might survive. On inquiry it came out that the most likely person to be acquainted with the fortunes of the late king's family was one Ziba, an old house steward of Saul's, who had contrived to enrich himself notwithstanding, or in consequence of, his master's fall. This man informed the king that in the house of one Machir, a wealthy native of Lodebar, a trans-Jordanic town near Mahanaim, there was dwelling a son of Jonathan, named Mephibosheth.[1] The existence of this person had been kept secret, nor was it till Ziba was assured that the inquirer was animated by no hostile motive that he revealed his present residence. The youth had led a sad life. The death of his father at Gilboa had found him an infant; and his nurse, horrified at the news of the disaster, and flying, as she thought, for her life, had let the child fall and lamed him permanently. Thus rendered incapable of prosecuting his claim to the throne, or indeed of contributing to his own support, he had found an asylum in the neighbourhood where his uncle Ishbosheth had set up his mimic kingdom, and had there remained neglected and unknown till this time. David now sends for him, takes kindly to him, restores to him all the land that had belonged to Saul, and makes him an inmate of his own house with a constant place at the royal table, as if he had been one of his sons. And to assist him in the management of the estate thus granted, he made Ziba the tenant, with the stipulation that the latter should be answerable to his landlord for the produce.

[1] He is called (1 Chron. viii. 34, &c.) Meribbaal, and probably in 2 Sam iv. 4, &c., the name ought to be Meribbosheth, the words meaning "Baal," or, "the Shameful, contendeth." The word Baal may have been eliminated from the name for religious reasons, as we have seen above (p 83) Eshbaal changed into Ishbosheth.

CHAPTER VIII.

FOREIGN WARS.

War with Philistines—Moabites defeated and punished—War with Ammonites—Aramæan league against Israel—Hadadezer—Rabbah—Defeat of Syrians—Further operations—Aramæan cities reduced—Edom conquered—Psalms of victory—Extent of David's kingdom—Rabbah taken—Ammonites severely treated.

FROM the peaceful occupations of religion and communion with God we turn to the tumult of the battle-field and the horrors of war. He who sang so sweetly to the harp had to wield the sword in many a fight, and by many a bloody encounter to preserve the existence of Israel and fulfil its great destiny. The defeat of the Philistines which was effected in the earliest years of the reign left no long interval of peace; other enemies threatened the youthful kingdom, and required prompt and decisive action. The account of the wars which then ensued is contracted into very narrow limits, the sacred historian designing not to give exciting details and to chronicle worldly successes, but to narrate events only so far as they have a spiritual bearing and tend to the development of the kingdom of God. But enough is told to enable us to sketch an outline of the expeditions then undertaken, and to form an idea of the results obtained. We may regard these attacks of outward foes as types of the assaults of Satan upon the Christian, or like the temptation wherewith the devil assailed Christ after His Baptism. It seems as though the arch-enemy, regarding with envy and apprehension the various successes of David and the favour with which he was visited, stirred up opposition against him, and endeavoured to effect his overthrow ere his power was matured and consolidated.

DAVID.

The first campaign was a renewal of the war with the Philistines, which was remarkable for two reasons first, for the peril which David incurred in one of the battles, and secondly, for the important results which were then gained. At one of the engagements in which he took part David grew faint with his exertions, and a gigantic Philistine, Ishbi-benob, attacked him with the sword and thought to slay him, but his trusty nephew, Abishai, hurried to his rescue, and smote the foeman. Henceforward it was made the rule that the king should not personally take part in battle, "that," as his anxious friends said to him, "thou quench not the light of Israel."[1] At this time the war was carried into the enemies' territory, and garrisons were established in many of the chief towns Gath herself, formerly David's refuge, with her daughter cities fell into his hands, and became tributary unto him[2] With these important places subdued, the western portion of the Philistine territory would lie at the mercy of the Israelites; and indeed the spirit of this restless people was now finally broken, and they ceased to be troublesome.

It is impossible to fix with any accuracy the dates or sequence of these different wars, as they are not recounted with any attempt at chronological arrangement, but the expedition next mentioned was undertaken against Moab In the day of persecution, when his own country offered no secure asylum, David, as we have seen, entrusted his parents to the care of the king of Moab, with whom he was then on the most friendly terms What was the offence that provoked the war at this time we are not told. Jewish tradition asserts that the Moabite monarch treacherously murdered Jesse and his wife, and that it was to punish this crime that the attack was made. But it is more probable that by incursions and depredations these restless neighbours seriously impeded the prosperity of Israel, rendering life and property insecure, and endangering the national existence of the inhabitants of the districts in their proximity. It may be that they practised the cruelties of their

[1] 2 Sam xxi. 15 ff

[2] 2 Sam viii 1, A V., "David took Metheg-ammah out of the hand of the Philistines" R V, "Took the bridle of the mother city out of," &c 1 Chron xviii 1. "Took Gath and her towns out of," &c Gath could not at an earlier date be called the metropolis of Philistia, the chief of the five allied cities seems to have been Gaza, though the "king" of Gath appears to have a special dignity. See 1 Sam. xxvii 2, xxix. 2 ff.

cognate people, the Ammonites, who put out the right eyes of prisoners and treated women in the most barbarous fashion [1] It is possible, too, that they may have joined the Edomites, when they were at war with the Israelites, and treacherously have cut off stragglers after some temporary check to David's arms [2] The operations of David were completely successful, two sons of the Moabite king were slain by Benaiah, and the hostile army, outgeneralled and surrounded, fell nearly whole into the conqueror's power. Most Eastern monarchs in such a case would have put them to the sword without scruple David did not do this, but he inflicted a terrible punishment on them. He made the captives lie down on the ground, and then separated them by a measuring rod into three divisions, of which two-thirds were slain and only one-third permitted to live. Balaam's prophecy was indeed fulfilled the sceptre of Judah smote through the corners of Moab, and brake down the sons of tumult (Numb. xxiv 17). From that time the Moabites submitted to the position of a subject nation, and paid tribute for a century and a half, till they were able to throw off the yoke in the time of Ahab's successor Ahaziah. We do not know how the execution of the prisoners was carried out, whether they were treated as wheat to be threshed (like the Ammonites afterwards),[3] and were done to death by the trampling of horses and the pressure of armed rollers, literally, according to the saying in the Book of Proverbs:

> "A wise king winnoweth the wicked,
> And bringeth the threshing wheel over them;"

or whether they were slain like any other criminals; in any case to modern minds David seems to have been guilty of revolting cruelty. To escape this conclusion explanations have been offered which are strained and inadmissible The plain fact remains that these prisoners were executed in cold blood. But if we put ourselves in David's place, and do not import modern notions and Christian opinions into other times and circumstances, we shall take a juster and more lenient view of his conduct. David was a man of his time, superior indeed to contemporaries in being guided by highest motives, but

[1] See 1 Sam xi 2, Amos 1 13
[2] Psa. lx and "Speaker's Comm" there.
[3] 2 Sam. xii. 31, Prov. xx. 26, Ewald, iii. 150.

adapting his policy to the spirit of the age. What was the Mosaic ordinance respecting conquered heathen cities? If a foreign city refused to surrender when summoned, and was taken by siege or by assault, all the males were to be put to death, the women and children led into captivity, and the place was to be sacked; but if the city appertained to any of the seven Canaanite peoples, the whole population, male and female, was to be put to the sword. Regarded then as the executor of Divine vengeance and the enforcer of the stern Mosaic law, David erred on the side of mercy. He punished not all the inhabitants with death; only those taken with arms in their hands were dealt with, and of these one large portion was spared. The use of war, the public spirit, the popular feeling, demanded this severe proceeding, and David had not the desire, and, probably, not the power to oppose it. No charge of cruelty could be laid against one who carried out, and that leniently, law and custom which were universally recognized as binding.

The war with the Moabites was followed by another, having very serious consequences and leading to various campaigns, which ended in establishing David's dominion over that wide extent of territory which prophecy had defined in patriarchal times. It was no lust of conquest that led to these results. As the Hebrews displayed little of the missionary or proselytizing spirit in religious matters, so they were not aggressive or ambitious in the wars which they waged and the conquests which they made. Their wars were either thrust upon them by wanton attacks, or were undertaken to secure their independence; and conquered regions were retained for safety's sake and to insure the fruits of victory. Their amicable relations with the Phœnicians, whom they left in undisturbed possession of their maritime cities and their strip of sea-board, sufficiently prove the non-aggressive character of their policy. The long succession of foreign wars which now ensued sprang from a paltry insult offered by a petty tyrant.[1]

Soon after the subjection of the Moabites, and while their

---

[1] We consider, with Ewald and Weiss, that the passage in 2 Sam. viii. 3 ff. summarizes the longer account in chaps x -xii , and that the wars there mentioned are dependent upon that with the Ammonites, which is recorded at greater length on account of its connection with Bathsheba and the dark train of events which followed.

defeat and signal punishment were fresh in all men's memories, Nahash, the king of the Ammonites, died, and was succeeded by his son Hanun. This Nahash was probably the son of the monarch who was defeated by Saul at the beginning of his reign. He had proved friendly to David in the days of his exile, and, like the kings of Moab and Gath, countenanced him as the enemy of Saul. Hearing of his death, David sent a friendly embassy of condolence to the new prince. Such messages, whether of sympathy or congratulation, customary enough in modern times, were quite usual in those days. Thus Hiram sent an embassy to Solomon on his accession to the throne, and Berodach-baladan despatched envoys to congratulate Hezekiah on his recovery from sickness.[1] An unpleasant and unexpected result followed from these friendly overtures The Ammonites had seen the treatment of their allies and connections, the Moabites : they, like other neighbouring peoples, viewed with jealousy the rising power of the Israelites, and easily persuaded their young king that David's conduct arose from no desire to cultivate amicable relations, but sprung from interested motives, and that the messengers were sent really to reconnoitre the royal city Rabbah, that he might know how best to attack it on the first opportunity The prince listened to these representations, seized the ambassadors, and in a kind of insolent pleasantry offered them, and through them their master, the direst insult by shaving off one side of their beards and cutting off the lower half of their garments, and dismissing them in this disgraceful plight. Where the beard is cherished as man's chief ornament and prerogative, and where costly, long flowing garments represented the dignity of the wearers, such treatment was a grievous outrage, and could be atoned for only at the cost of bloodshed. David received early intimation of the matter, and as the envoys could not appear in public till their beards had grown, he considerately ordered them to wait for the present at Jericho, the first Israelite city on their homeward route.

Hanun had not offered this wanton insult to the Israelites without counting the cost. He well knew that they would endeavour to avenge it speedily, and he proceeded to prepare himself for the struggle which was impending and which he desired to provoke. He first appealed to the Syrians of Zobah

[1] 1 Kings v. 1 , 2 Kings xx. 12.

whose assistance he purchased at the price of a thousand talents of silver; then other tribes were induced to join the league, from Beth-rehob, Beth-maachah, and Tob. The auxiliaries thus collected amounted to 32,000, with a strong force of cavalry and chariots, to which the Israelites had nothing to oppose but their usual infantry. Some of these nations had already felt David's arm, and all were inspired by the ambition of avenging previous defeats, or crushing this young aspiring kingdom before it became more formidable The contest was at first on David's part a struggle for existence. Hadadezer, the king of Zobah, was a dangerous antagonist, possessed of great power and military skill. Zobah,[1] itself a place of small importance, which only claims notice as the temporary capital of this prince, lay in the region between Damascus and the Euphrates; and here Hadadezer had established a kingdom which extended from Hamath on the Orontes to the Great River, and had obtained dependencies even in Mesopotamia. The other little Aramæan states which are mentioned as taking part in the war were situated to the south-west of Zobah, Rehob being in, or close upon, the possessions of Asher, Maachah beyond the waters of Merom, and Tob, the scene of Jephthah's exile, to the south-east of the Lake of Gennesaret.

The first action of this formidable coalition was the siege of Medeba (*hod.* Madeba), a strong Reubenite city, about twelve miles to the eastward of the north end of the Dead Sea, and situated on the great road through Moab. As soon as David heard that the Syrians were entered upon this campaign, knowing that Medeba could stand a siege without immediate danger of capture, he determined to carry the war into the enemies' country and so effect a diversion Accordingly he despatched Joab with his most trusty forces against Rabbah the Ammonite capital. This was a well-fortified place in a very strong position, some twenty miles east of the Jordan, on the banks of the southern of the two streams which when united form the river Jabbok. "For picturesqueness of situation," says a traveller in these regions, "I know of no ruins to compare with Ammon. The most striking feature is the citadel,

---

[1] In an inscription of Assurbanipal (Smith, "Assurb.," p. 259) mention is made of a city Subiti=Zoba in a list of Arameo-Kanaanite tribes next to Edom, Ammon, &c. Elsewhere the name occurs in lists of Syro-Phœnician cities. Schrader, "Keilinschr.," pp. 121, 183.

which formerly contained not merely the garrison, but an upper town, and covered an extensive area. The lofty plateau on which it was situated is triangular in shape; two sides are formed by the valleys which diverge from the apex, where they are divided by a low neck, and thence separating fall into the valley of the Jabbok which forms the base of the triangle, and contained the lower town. Climbing up the citadel we can trace the remains of the moat, and crossing it find ourselves in a maze of ruins. The massive walls—the lower parts of which still remain, and which, rising from the precipitous sides of the cliff, rendered any attempt at scaling impossible—were evidently Ammonite"[1] To meet the attack of the Israelites, the Ammonites had massed their forces in front of the walls of their city, and feeling themselves secure, exulted in the belief that they had caught their enemies in a trap from which there was little chance of escape. For the Syrians, hearing of the march of the Israelites towards the capital of their allies, broke up from Medeba and followed them, so that when Joab arrived before Rabbah he found not only the Ammonites drawn up in his front, but at his rear the Aramæan army ready to overpower him. The situation was hazardous, but Joab's invincible courage and military skill were equal to the occasion. He divided his troops into two bodies, taking under his own immediate command a chosen band of his most tried soldiers to oppose the Syrians, and committing the rest of the army to his brother Abishai with orders to hold the Ammonites in check and to prevent them from affording aid to their allies. An agreement was made that if either division was in danger of defeat, it should be succoured by the other. Then, as if he had learned the spirit of his master, Joab appeals to the faith and patriotism of his comrades. "Be of good courage," he cries, "and let us play the men for our people, and for the cities of our God; and the Lord do that which seemeth Him good." Fired by this address, and confident that the Lord was with them, the Israelites attacked the Syrians with the greatest energy, the cavalry and chariots offered no efficient resistance to their brave onslaught; the enemy turned and fled, and, before the eyes of the Ammonites who were unable to come to their support, suffered a disastrous defeat. Dispirited and terrified, the Ammonites retreated within their walls and prepared for a siege.

[1] Oliphant, "Land of Gilead," p. 259 f.

Joab wasted some time in an endeavour to capture the town, but finding it too strong to be taken by assault, and possessing no military engines, the time of the year likewise being unfavourable for warlike operations, he withdrew his forces and returned to Jerusalem with the large booty which he had gathered in his late victory.

Whether Hadadezer was himself engaged in this first campaign is uncertain. But in the following year he headed the expedition, combined the Aramæan kingdom in one league, drawing in even Damascus, which had hitherto stood aloof, and obtained contingents from Mesopotamia and the confines of the Euphrates, whither he had extended his conquests. Pursuing the tactics of an active and energetic general, David determined to anticipate the attack of this formidable antagonist, and march with all his available forces to meet him ere he could enter the Israelite territory. Accordingly he put himself at the head of the army, the adventure being too critical to be entrusted to any lieutenant, and crossing the Jordan to the north-east, encountered the combined forces of the enemy at a place named Helam, the position of which is unknown, but which is supposed to have been far northward in the direction of Hamath.[1] Here the Syrians suffered a crushing defeat, their general Shobach was slain, 700 chariots were captured, and some 7,000 horsemen and 20,000 foot soldiers fell or were made prisoners.[2] But the victory must be completed by the subjugation of the kingdoms which had joined the hostile league. Damascus first felt the arm of the hero-king. Powerful and rich in resources, it could not stand against his irresistible onslaught; 22,000 of its defenders perished in the battle, and this great city was added to David's conquests, received an Israelite garrison, and paid tribute to the victors. Pursuing his triumphant march, David speedily overran the smaller Aramæan districts which had assisted Hadadezer, and reduced them to vassalage. Toi, the Canaanite king of Hamath, whose dominions lay between Lebanon and Anti-Lebanon, and who had felt the weight of oppression at the hand of the Aramæan tyrant, sent warm congratulations to David, accompanied with rich presents of brass,

---

[1] 2 Sam. x. 16, 17; 1 Chron. xviii. 3.

[2] The numbers in the accounts vary, and cannot be satisfactorily reconciled. Comp. 2 Sam. viii 3 ff. with 1 Chron. xviii. 4; and 2 Sam. x. 18, with 1 Chron. xix. 18.

silver, and gold. Opposition was seen to be no longer possible, and the whole country up to the Orontes submitted to the Israelites and became tributary.

In these expeditions an immense amount of booty had been taken, some of the Syrian troops even being equipped with shields of gold A large portion of this was stored up at Jerusalem to be employed hereafter in the erection and adornment of the proposed Temple But there was some spoil which could not be thus dealt with. Captured chariots and horses were the subject of special enactment in the old Law. A prince was forbidden to multiply horses, lest he should be tempted to lean too much on material appliances, and lose trust in the Lord.[1] In accordance with this direction, David destroyed all the chariots, except a hundred, which were preserved for purposes of state, and as monuments of victory, and retained only horses sufficient to draw them, rendering all the rest useless by houghing them.

While David was thus employed in the North, the restless and always hostile Edomites, seeing the South denuded of troops, and excited to action by the vindictive Ammonites, invaded Judah with a large force They had given some trouble to Saul in the early part of his reign, but hitherto had not molested his successor. The danger in this quarter could not be disregarded. Joining with the Amalekites and other warlike tribes of the desert, the Edomites might inflict serious damage, and the victories over the Syrians would be dearly bought by the ruin and desolation of Israel. Joab and Abishai were immediately despatched to the South with a portion of the army, and with orders to treat the enemy with the utmost rigour. They found that the Edomites had already caused wide distress, and were now retiring to their own territories at the approach of the Israelites. Sending on Abishai with the main body of the army, Joab occupied himself some little time in giving decent funeral to the many whom these barbarians had slain and left unburied[2] Meanwhile his valiant brother turned to the work of vengeance. Marching along the west shore of the Dead Sea he encountered the enemy in the Valley of Salt, at the southern extremity, and inflicted on them a severe defeat with the loss of 18,000 men. A war of extermination ensued. But Idumæa was a difficult

[1] Deut. xvii. 16, Josh xi 6, 9   [2] 1 Kings xi. 15.

country to subdue. Its mountains, and defiles, and caves, offered refuges which could not easily be searched or stormed; and it took six months to reduce the people to submission, and to establish garrisons in the conquered districts. All who were taken with arms in their hands were put to death, but a great many escaped, and waited with watchful care for an opportunity of revolt. The royal family for the most part perished; one of the princes, however, Hadad by name, made his way to Egypt, and found great favour with Pharaoh, who gave him his sister-in-law in marriage, and aided him to harass Solomon some years later. The dangerous position in which David was placed by this outbreak in his own country, while he was struggling for existence with his Syrian opponents, is expressed in the Sixtieth Psalm, which the inscription attributes to this conjuncture:

> "O God, Thou hast cast us off, Thou hast broken us down;
> Thou hast been angry, O restore us again.
> Thou hast made the land to tremble, Thou hast rent it:
> Heal the breaches thereof, for it shaketh. . . .
> That Thy beloved may be delivered,
> Save with Thy right hand, and answer us. . . .
> Moab is my wash-pot,
> Upon Edom will I cast my shoe;
> Philistia, shout thou because of me.
> Who will bring me into the strong city?
> Who will lead me unto Edom? . . .
> Give us help against the adversary,
> For vain is the help of man.
> Through God we shall do valiantly,
> For He it is that shall tread down our adversaries."

The exultation of the conquering king, with a distinct Messianic reference, is expressed in Psalm cx.:

> "The Lord saith unto my lord, sit thou at My right hand
> Until I make thine enemies thy footstool.
> The Lord sendeth forth the rod of thy strength out of Zion:
> Rule thou in the midst of thine enemies. . . .
> The Lord at thy right hand
> Doth smite through kings in the day of His wrath.
> He judgeth among the nations,
> He filleth the field with dead bodies,
> He strikes through the chiefs over a wide land.
> He drinketh of the brook in the way,
> Therefore doth he lift up his head."

This great crisis, too, may well have given birth to the Second Psalm, when the nations raged and the peoples imagined a vain thing, and the kings of the earth set themselves together against the Lord and against His anointed; while through all the danger and the tumult gleamed the sure promise:

"Yet have I set My king
Upon My holy hill of Zion. . . .
Ask of Me, and I shall give thee the nations for thine inheritance,
And the uttermost parts of the earth for thy possession.
Thou shalt break them with a rod of iron,
Thou shalt dash them in pieces like a potter's vessel."

On his return from Syria, David joined his victorious generals, and with them entered Jerusalem in triumph, the ample spoils which he had taken, the golden shields, the rich armour, the costly vessels, the hundred chariots and horses, adding to the splendour of the procession, and attesting the completeness of the victory.

Never in all his life had the son of Jesse thus triumphed; no such day ever again dawned upon him. This was the zenith of his glory We must not be induced to minimise these victories by the little stress laid upon them by the sacred historian, and the meagre account of them which he affords. The Bible does not pander to the thirst for details of great battles and thrilling achievements with which modern histories are filled, and these wars are recorded only because they trace a fulfilment of the promise made to Abraham a thousand years before, repeated in Mosaic times, and show how the sway of the chosen seed was extended from the river of Egypt to the Euphrates, from the Red Sea unto the sea of the Philistines, from the Desert unto the River, from the wilderness, and from Lebanon, from the River unto the uttermost sea. In other words, the Hebrew dominion at this time reached to the Ælanitic Gulf of the Red Sea, and to Thapsachus on the Euphrates, having for its western boundary the Mediterranean, and for its southern the Arabian wildernesses of Shur and Paran, and in the north embracing Syria even unto the river Orontes.[1] This was a wonderful result of a terrible struggle. The once down-trodden and insignificant people of Israel takes its place among great

---

[1] Gen. xv. 18, Deut. xi. 24, Exod xxiii. 31, and "Speak. Comm." there.

nations; with no idea of universal conquest, forced by circumstances to extend its sway far and near, it has arrived at a position of power and influence which could only have been achieved by reliance on the protecting arm and in obedience to the guiding counsel of Jehovah. David's own feelings are expressed in that noble psalm of thanksgiving (Psa. xviii.), which the historian has enshrined in his pages (2 Sam. xxii.), and which not only reflects his experience, but introduces therein gleams of Messianic lustre, which, by the teaching of the Christian era, we can readily acknowledge. The dangers that menaced him, his marvellous escapes, the establishment of his throne, the wide extent of his dominion—if these topics are concerned with the circumstances of David's earthly life, they have a certain reference to the acts of "the son of David" and the results of His spiritual war. Thus in the day of his exultation the sweet Psalmist sings:[1]

> " By Thee I run through a troop,
> And by my God I leap over a wall. . . .
> The God that girdeth me with strength,
> And maketh my way perfect, . . .
> He teacheth my hands to war,
> So that my hands do bend a bow of brass;
> Thou hast also given me the shield of Thy salvation,
> And Thy right hand hath holden me up. . . .
> Thou hast girded me with strength unto the battle,
> Thou hast subdued unto me those that rose up against me, . . .
> Thou hast delivered me from the strivings of the people,
> Thou wilt make me the head of the nations;
> A people whom I have not known shall serve me,
> As soon as they hear of me they shall obey me;
> Strangers shall fawn upon me,
> Strangers shall fade away from their strongholds.
> The Lord liveth, and blessed be my rock,
> Yea, exalted be the God of my salvation,
> Even the God that taketh vengeance for me,
> And subdueth peoples under me,
> Who rescueth me from mine enemies,
> Yea, He lifteth me up above them that rise against me;
> From the violent Thou wilt deliver me
> Therefore I will give thanks unto Thee, O Lord, among the nations,
> And will sing praises unto Thy name.

---

[1] See Briggs, " Mess. Proph " 143 ff.

> Great salvation giveth He to His king,
> And showeth loving-kindness to His Anointed,
> To David and to his seed for evermore "

There was one enemy still unsubdued, the original cause of these serious wars, the Ammonites, whose strong fortress had hitherto defied the power of David, or perhaps, in the multitude of more engrossing engagements, had not been assailed with vigour and perseverance, but was simply blockaded. This dilatoriness was now to be remedied. The allies whom the Ammonites had enlisted in their quarrel were either conquered or tributary, and no further help could be expected from them. The men of Rabbah had no one to look to, and must bear the brunt of the onslaught as they could. This was made in the spring of the following year When military operations could safely be carried on, David sent Joab, with certain commanders of eminence and a large army, into the Ammonite country. The region was undefended, and lay at their mercy, the enemy having concentrated all their troops for the defence of the capital. The Israelites worked their will throughout the district, plundering towns, destroying crops, enslaving captives ; and so made their way to Rabbah. This fortress was then attacked with determined energy. The spoils of the late wars had given the Israelites effective arms, and the experience then gained enabled them to conduct an assault with better hope of success than heretofore. The city, as we have seen, was divided into an upper and a lower town, the former being the citadel, the latter —the "city of waters "—lying on the stream, which was probably here dammed so as to form a lake. It was felt that the capture was an arduous undertaking, but a result that was to be attained at any risk. Every preparation was made for a successful attack To arouse the enthusiasm of the army, and to have at hand the means of inquiring of the Lord, the unusual step was taken of sending the Ark with the host. Thus equipped, the Israelites, after a severe struggle, got possession of the lower city. The capture of the acropolis was now certain. The water supply was in the hands of the besiegers; and although the huge walls, overlooking precipices on two sides three hundred or four hundred feet deep, rendered any attempt at scaling impossible, the surrender of the fortress was a matter of time only, as neither provisions nor water could now be replenished. Seeing this, and wishing to bring his royal master under an obligation to him, Joab sent a message to David, expressing the need of immediate reinforcements, and urging him to head the troops himself that he might have the honour of being the captor of this redoubtable city, "lest," as he puts it, " I take the city, and it be called after my name." Hereupon David, with a body of fresh troops, crossed the Jordan, stormed the capital, and completed the conquest of the land, securing an immense amount of booty, among which is mentioned the crown of Malcam,[1] the national idol of the Ammonites, an ornament enriched with precious stones, and estimated to be worth a talent of gold,[2] or £10,000 of our money. This was offered to the king as his part of the spoil, and it, or the central gem extracted from it, was worn by him in triumphal procession, and afterwards upon important occasions, in spite, it seems, of the prohibition of Deut. vii 25, which, in the course of foreign wars, had become a dead letter. On some of the captive inhabitants, both of this and the other towns, a terrible punishment was inflicted, such as had befallen their friends, the Moabites, in the former war. They were cut to pieces with iron saws or axes, they were put under the sharp teeth of threshing-drags, and as they had made their children pass through the fire to Moloch, so they were burned in brick-kilns.[3] It was a barbarous age. Even Mosaic legislation had enacted, " an eye for an eye, and a tooth for a tooth ; " and the Ammonites were notorious for inhuman cruelty and pitiless animosity, and could be taught by nothing but by savage acts of retribution. The infliction of such punishment showed them and neighbouring peoples that Israel could not be touched with impunity, and that the dream in which they had indulged of

[1] "The crown of their king," R.V. (2 Sam xii. 30), Hebrew, "the crown of Malcam." The same uncertainty in rendering is found in Zeph. 1 5. The word is here a proper name ("Molchom," Sept). Had Hanun been intended, he would doubtless have been mentioned, as above.

[2] The words here are usually translated, "The weight whereof was a talent of gold " This would make the diadem weigh some 120 lbs. Uneasy indeed would be the head that wore such a crown , and it is most likely that the expression in the text refers to value, not weight.

[3] Attempts have been made to soften the barbarity of this punishment, by interpreting the text of severe servile work, "put them to saws," &c , but there is no sufficient ground for so explaining the original expressions

annihilating the chosen nation would not be fulfilled. The severity extended only to the military, and perhaps only to those of them taken with arms in their hands, the other inhabitants being left in peaceable possession of their lands A brother of King Hanun certainly retained his high position, and at the time of Absalom's revolt came to David's assistance with provisions and beds and other articles for the accommodation of the fugitive host.

Thus ended the Ammonite campaign, the last great war in which David was engaged, and he and his army returned in triumph to Jerusalem, and thus, in the course of some eighteen years from the time when he was crowned king at Hebron, he had completely destroyed the power of the enemies that surrounded his native country, firmly established the Hebrew monarchy, and raised it to a commanding influence among Oriental nations.

CHAPTER IX.

SIN AND ITS CONSEQUENCES.

Polygamy—Adultery with Bathsheba—Vain attempt to implicate Uriah—Uriah virtually murdered by Joab's connivance—Nathan's parable—David's repentance—Death of his child—Solomon born—Amnon's incestuous outrage—Absalom in revenge murders Amnon, is kept in banishment—Joab's stratagem effects his return—Three years' famine for the slaughter of the Gibeonites by Saul—The atonement—Rizpah

ORIENTAL opinion regarded the multiplication of wives as a necessary exhibition of the magnificence of a ruler. Each wife had a separate establishment, and the number of these afforded to the vulgar mind a test of the sovereign's power and resources. It is true that Mosaic legislation [1] distinctly discountenanced polygamy in the case of the theocratic monarch of Israel, not only forbidding alliances with women of foreign nations lest they should pervert the faith of their husband, but also extending the same disapprobation to marriages with persons of Hebrew descent if unduly multiplied. But the strictness of this rule could not be enforced, and a certain laxity was tolerated by public opinion, and tacitly allowed by ecclesiastical authority. David, as we have already seen, had a plurality of wives even in his exile; and when he was established at Jerusalem, he added to this number, "taking unto him more concubines and wives." The consequences of this license were serious. While the perpetrator thought only of his own pleasure or political interests, he was preparing for himself infinite sorrow and trouble. The harem was the scene of perpetual heart-burnings, jealousies, and quarrels; the happy home life had no existence

[1] Deut. xvii. 17.

SIN AND ITS CONSEQUENCES.

there, and hatred and envy reigned among the various branches of the divided family. Of the legitimate consorts which David possessed we have received the names of only seven, viz. two married in the wanderings, and five at Hebron; those at Jerusalem are not recorded Besides these, are mentioned sixteen concubines, whose children are not named. Of the wives' children the following are recorded Amnon or Jehiel, Chileab or Daniel, Absalom, Tamar, Adonijah, Shephatiah, Ithream, Ibhar, Elishua, Nogah, Nepheg, Japhia, Elishama, Eliada, Eliphelet, Jerimoth, sixteen in all. To this number, as we shall see, some further additions were made in the course of time. Now these various establishments, if they added to the magnificence of the kingdom, also introduced a luxury and a worldliness which tended to assimilate the habits of David's Court and the sentiments of the courtiers to those of other Oriental potentates. To the king himself, now at the height of his glory, the temptation to abuse his absolute power came with fatal force. What could be denied one whose successes had been so wonderful? Was there anything that was unlawful to so favoured a ruler? The sensual element was strong in David's emotional character; but this hitherto had been regulated by the laws of immemorial custom, and had led to no violation of private rights. The temptation to which David now succumbed was the occasion of grievous crimes, and its fatal consequences darkened the whole of his after-life. The account has been omitted in the pages of the Chronicler[1] from a mistaken idea of saving the reputation of the ideal theocratic king, but in the earlier Book the guilt is plainly revealed, and the great lesson against presumption on the one hand, and teaching the way of repentance on the other hand, is plainly set forth for all time.

It was after his great victories, and while Joab was engaged in the siege of Rabbah, that David, having concluded his midday siesta, was walking in the cool of the evening on the roof of his newly-built palace From this height he overlooked the houses in the neighbourhood, and in the open courtyard of one of these he saw a woman bathing herself She was very beautiful, and her charms appealed to the sensuality of his nature. He was in an idle, listless mood, when a man is most exposed to temptation; and instead of turning away his eyes

---

[1] The section contained in 2 Sam xi 2—xii 29 is omitted in the corresponding passage 1 Chron xx.

from a forbidden sight, he gazed with an eager curiosity, till a passionate desire filled his breast, and, accustomed to find means to accomplish any plan upon which he had set his heart, he determined to gratify his lust. He may have thought at first that the woman was unmarried, but on sending to make inquiries about her, he was informed that her name was Bathsheba, or Bathshua, the daughter of Eliam, or Ammiel, who was the son of Ahithophel, a trusted counsellor, and that she was the wife of Uriah the Hittite, one of the band of "mighty men" now serving with the army before Rabbah. This intelligence ought to have checked the disorderly passion at once. The marriage vow was regarded universally with the utmost reverence, and none of the chiefs of the people, as far as we know, had ever attempted to violate it. The head of the nation was bound to set an example of obedience to law and respect for the rights of his people, most of all, was it his duty to guard inviolably the families of the brave men who were jeoparding their lives in his service. But all such considerations were feeble barriers against the gratification of an overmastering passion. Lust conceived and cherished brought forth sin. David makes no endeavour to avoid the strong temptation; he sends for the woman, he overcomes her scruples; he uses his position to influence her to yield to his wishes; he finds her perhaps only too ready to acquiesce in his sophisms; and he takes her into his house. This is the first scene in the tragedy. Attempts have been made to shift a large proportion of the blame of this evil transaction upon Bathsheba. She is accused of vanity in displaying her charms before the king's eyes, of immodesty in bathing in a place where she was liable to observation, and of a weak compliance where refusal would have been easy and no violence was to be feared. There may be truth in some of these allegations (though, as the royal palace was only lately erected she may not have realized the fact that it overlooked her courtyard, and she may have misconceived her power to resist the solicitations of so mighty a prince), but however this may be, the sin of David is evident and admits of no palliation. At the end of this evil day, observing the ceremonial law,[1] while she scrupled not to break the moral, the dishonoured wife returned to her house. Some weeks passed, and finding that the consequences of their sin could not be hidden,

[1] Lev. xv. 18.

SIN AND ITS CONSEQUENCES.

she sent word to David that she was with child. Here was a terrible complication. Adultery was punishable by the death of the guilty pair.[1] Something must be done, and that immediately, to conceal the sin and to misdirect public opinion. Fruitful in expedients, David saw that the safest way to hide the crime was to contrive that Uriah should spend a night at his own house, and should thus be regarded as the father of the child that should be born. Accordingly he forwarded a message to Joab desiring him forthwith to send to him Uriah; and on the arrival of the soldier he made many inquiries respecting the progress of the siege of Rabbah, and the doings of the army After hearing all the news he dismissed Uriah, bidding him go home and refresh himself after his long journey, and sending a portion of food from his own table, which would be regarded as a special honour. Whether Uriah had any suspicion of his wife's connection with the king we know not ; but he did not fall in with the plan proposed, instead of going to his own house, as was natural, he spent the night in the palace with the rest of the royal servants, eating his portion of meat in the common hall, and sleeping where the domestics slept. Next morning, uneasy in conscience, David asked for his guest, and heard with disgust and inward foreboding that he had not visited his own house during the preceding night. Asked why he had acted in this manner, Uriah answered that it would ill become him to enjoy the comforts of home and the society of his wife, while the ark of the Lord was in the field and his comrades were engaged in active military service. The high sense of duty and the self-restraint of the Gibbor are here displayed, and afford a painful contrast to his lord's sensuality and absence of self-command and dissimulation David detained Uriah one more day in the hope of making him break his resolution. He feasted the soldier at his own table, and made him intoxicated ; but even under these circumstances Uriah was not induced to do as David desired. "At even he went out to lie on his bed with the servants of his lord, but went not down to his house" Thus if any question were to arise respecting the parentage of Bathsheba's child, her husband might appeal to the king's household to testify to his wife's adultery David saw this ; and he saw that a further and a horrible crime was needed to conceal the original transgression. He did not

[1] Lev xx 10.

shrink from the alternative. Having embarked on this awful voyage he will continue it unto the end. He seemed to feel that to turn back now was impossible Uriah must be got rid of; and this end must be accomplished in some crafty way which would leave no suspicion of foul play, and be considered simply as one of the ordinary casualties of war. But to do this, it was necessary to take Joab partly into his confidence, and to use the commander's authority for the execution of this evil design. So he sent a letter to the camp—making the unconscious messenger carry his own death-warrant—couched in these terms: "Set ye Uriah in the forefront of the hottest battle, and retire ye from him, that he may be smitten, and die" No reason for this order was given. Josephus indeed asserts [1] that the king declared that the man had committed a crime worthy of death; but the sacred narrative gives no hint of such an accusation, nor would Joab have required any such justification of the fatal order conveyed to him. Besides, had Uriah been lawfully condemned, there would have been no need for accomplishing his destruction in this insidious manner. Joab saw that there was some secret motive for the injunction, and though he may not have fully known its purport, he was none the less willing to execute it. Rather, he rejoiced to receive it and to carry it out. The king was thus putting himself in his power; he could no longer reproach his nephew with the treacherous murder of Abner, now that he was equally guilty. By making Joab his accomplice in the crime he deprived himself of the right of objecting to any of the latter's violent proceedings, and afforded ground for grave doubts as to the sincerity of his religion, and a growing suspicion that he was at heart as lawless and unscrupulous as Joab himself. In contriving this scheme against the life of his trusty servant did David think of the similar plot laid against him by Saul, and of the Providence which then defeated the design? Did he realize the depth to which the Lord's anointed was descending, the abyss into which he was plunging? Ah, bitter indeed must be the return to light, heart-piercing the sorrow that shall countervail the sin!

Joab carried out the king's wishes; Uriah was put at the head of an attacking party, and, with others, fell a victim apparently to his own rashness in venturing too near the enemy's fortifications. "As I leant over" the precipitous sides

[1] "Ant." vii. 7. 1.

of the cliff, says Mr. Oliphant, "and looked sheer down about three hundred feet into one wady, and four hundred feet into the other, I did not wonder at its having occurred to King David that the leader of a forlorn hope against these ramparts would meet with certain death, and consequently assigning this position to Uriah The only possible point from which that officer could have advanced was at the apex, where the low neck connects the citadel with the high plateau beyond, but even here he would have had to charge an almost hopeless escarpment. . . . Portions of the colossal gateway and the massive wall flanking it, at the point where the low neck joins the apex of the triangle, still remain to attest the truth of this narrative, and to identify the spot where Uriah met his fate"[1] News of the event was at once sent to David, who received the information with much composure, returning a message to Joab that he should not be disheartened at this failure, "for the sword devoureth one as well as another," but should prepare immediately for a more effective assault. Thus meanly he tries to throw a cloak over his proceedings. Bathsheba, who possibly knew nothing of the machinations of which her husband had been the victim, passed the customary seven days of mourning, and then was taken into David's harem and became his wife, the marriage being thus indecently hastened in order, if it were possible, to hide her shame. But, doubtless, the truth leaked out, the king's position was such, that his actions were closely observed, the glare of publicity was turned upon his private life Cruel and keen must have been the disappointment with which the knowledge of these events was received; such crimes shocked the moral sense of the nation, and made men fear that the idol which they had so highly prized and honoured was of very common clay. The historian adds with sad significance, "The thing that David had done displeased the Lord"

It was soon after this marriage that Joab, as we have seen above, urged David to come in person and complete the reduction of the city of Rabbah The severities, which we have noticed, exercised on the military inhabitants, coincide with his state of religious declension, when his love of God was chilled and weakened, and an uneasy consciousness of guilt rendered him morose, irritable, and unforgiving. Hence, too, arose his

[1] "Land of Gilead," p. 260.

eager acquiescence in Joab's request, and readiness to seize the fame of his general's operations. Restless and dissatisfied with himself, he silences thought by excitement; and conscious of being an object of suspicion to his subjects, he is glad of an occasion for showing the old valour and skill which had endeared him to his countrymen. And he seemed to have succeeded in quieting his own conscience, and in appeasing any disaffection that may have arisen. Returning at the head of a victorious army, lauded to the sky by his fond soldiers, bringing with him vast booty of infinite value and variety, David was tempted to think that his sin was forgotten, the scandal would pass away, and all would go on as of old in peace and quietness. He had yet to learn that sin has consequences as certain as death, that you cannot commit transgression and be none the worse for it. Was David happy in this interval? Had he succeeded altogether in lulling conscience to rest? Could so good and pious a man have sunk into such callous indifference without many an inward struggle? Was his soul so engrossed with unholy passion, that the better thing within him stirred not to lead to unrest and amendment? Nay, we may be sure that he had many a qualm, many a misgiving, many an anxious hour. The feelings of this time are expressed in a few verses of Psalm xxxii.:

> "When I kept silence, my bones waxed old
> Through my roaring all the day long.
> For day and night Thy hand was heavy upon me:
> My moisture was changed as with the drought of summer."

It needed only a little external stimulus to unlock the floods of penitence, and to open the way to full confession and humblest abasement. And this encouragement the mercy of God supplied.

This year of sin was drawing to its close, and the wedded adulteress had borne a son in the royal palace, when the prophet Nathan was commissioned by God to reprove the king for his grievous offences, and to exhibit in its full hideousness the evil of his heart. Skilfully, though sorrowfully, the Divine messenger approaches the subject. Under the pretence of asking David's judgment on a story of wrong-doing,[1] he makes

[1] Some MSS of the Sept., together with the Complutensian and Aldine editions, make Nathan introduce his parable with the words, "Decide for me this case." The clause seems to be required by David's answer,

the royal sinner pronounce sentence on himself. Two men, he says, were dwelling in one city, one rich and prosperous, possessed of flocks and herds innumerable ; the other, poor, having only one little lamb which he had brought up in his house and loved as a daughter. There came a traveller to the rich man ; and having to entertain the stranger, he grudged to take one of his own sheep or oxen to prepare a meal for him, but seized the poor man's lamb, and dressed it for the guest David sees not his own likeness, or the reflection of his own deeds in the little narrative himself, the rich robber ; his lust, the traveller; the poor man, Uriah ; the ewe lamb, Bathsheba—the application is at the moment hidden from him ; he is highly incensed at the dastardly transaction, and not only will demand the fourfold restoration which the Law enacts,[1] but in the heat of his indignation he condemns the offender to death, as if he had been guilty of the crime of man-stealing or murder. Unconscious of the application, he gives the verdict; and startlingly on his ear falls the prop iet's solemn announcement, "Thou art the man. Thou art the robber who has done this wrong, and art worthy of a malefactor's end" Astonished, horrified, half self-convinced, the king stands silent , then Nathan proceeds to bring home to his heart the greatness of his fault, its ingratitude, its blackness "Thus saith the Lord," the prophet sternly announces, "I anointed thee king over Israel, and I delivered thee out of the hand of Saul ; and I gave thee thy master's house, and thy master's wives into thy bosom, and gave thee the house of Israel and of Judah ; and if that had been too little, I would have added unto thee such and such things Wherefore hast thou despised the word of the Lord to do that which is evil in His sight ? Thou hast smitten Uriah the Hittite with the sword, and hast taken his wife to be thy wife, and hast slain him with the sword of the children of Ammon." Conviction streamed in upon the guilty man's soul as he heard these words ; the criminality, the cruelty, the baseness of his conduct, became clear to him But yet he spoke not , and the prophet completed the denunciation by declaring the punishment that awaited him in the future. The retribution was to be twofold ; the murder of Uriah should be avenged by bloody deeds in his own family ; the sword should never depart from his house ; the adultery with Bathsheba should be requited

[1] Exod. xxii. 1.

by the public dishonour of his own wives. Now at length the full light penetrated his soul; he saw what he had made himself; the moral aspect of his late actions was revealed to him in all their hideousness; his abasement followed, no palliation or excuse was offered. Simply he cries with heart-broken earnestness, "I have sinned against the Lord." So sincere and utter was this confession, that immediately it received the gracious intimation, "The Lord hath put away thy sin; thou shalt not die as thou hast deserved to do." God knew the reality of his repentance, and acknowledged it by His pardon. We may learn the same by the utterances of his soul in penitential psalms,[1] which, while they show his deep abasement, show also his faith, once dimmed, never lost, and ready to be revived at the breath of the Spirit, show the gleam of hope emerging from the depth of misery and humiliation.

"Have mercy upon me, O God, according to Thy lovingkindnesses,
  According to the multitude of Thy tender mercies blot out my transgressions·
Wash me throughly from mine iniquity,
And cleanse me from my sin,
For I acknowledge my transgressions,
And my sin is ever before me . . .
Purge me with hyssop, and I shall be clean;
Wash me, and I shall be whiter than snow;
Make me to hear of joy and gladness,
That the bones which Thou hast broken may rejoice. . . .
I acknowledged my sin unto Thee, and mine iniquity have I not hid.
I said, I will confess my transgressions unto the Lord,
And Thou forgavest the iniquity of my sin . . .
Thou art my hiding-place, Thou wilt preserve me from trouble,
Thou wilt compass me about with songs of deliverance. . . .
Many sorrows shall be to the wicked,
But he that trusteth in the Lord, mercy shall compass him about."

The punishment denounced was not delayed; it immediately

---

[1] See Psalms xxxii and li The former is generally allowed to belong to this period, the latter is by some critics attributed to exilian times owing to some expressions at the end, e.g, "Build thou the walls of Jerusalem." But these last verses may be a later addition, or they may refer to the still uncompleted fortification of the city, and embody a prayer that God will not visit the offences of the ruler upon the innocent people. There can be no doubt that the heading of the psalm is fully confirmed by the rest of the contents.

SIN AND ITS CONSEQUENCES.

began to work. The child that had lately been born was struck with sickness. David's crimes had become more or less known abroad, and unbelievers, both among the heathen and the Israelites themselves, had scoffed at the religion whose professors thus violated their own principles, and whose God favoured and supported an adulterer and murderer. To remove occasion for further blasphemy this child must die. The father recognized in the infliction of this illness the penalty of its parents' sin. To see the mother grieving over the sufferings of her infant sent a terrible pang to the king's affectionate heart; but to know that these sufferings were the retribution of his transgression, that the innocent was bearing the punishment of the guilty, added fresh torment. Though the prophet had said that the child should die, he thinks the judgment may be averted by penitence, prayer, and fasting; he goes into his chamber, he pours forth his soul in earnest supplication, he takes no food, he lies all night upon the earth. His confidential servants come about him, urging him to rouse himself from his penitential devotion, and to eat bread; but he turns a deaf ear to their persuasions, concentrating his thoughts and energies on the one object that God would grant the life of the boy, and thus give him a token of restoration to favour. But this was not to be. After a long week of suffering the child died; and the attendants feared to tell the father the truth, expecting that the announcement would only increase his anguish. But their looks and whispers led him to suspect the fact, and on inquiry he was told that his prayer had been in vain. On hearing this, instead of abandoning himself to unmitigated distress, as his friends anticipated, he arose from the earth, washed and anointed himself, and changed his apparel, and humbly accepting the dispensation, turned his steps to the tabernacle to worship, and at his return took bread and did eat. This proceeding, which seemed so strange to his servants, he explained reasonably. While there was life there was hope, when that was extinct, nothing was left but submission to the will of God and expectation of reunion hereafter. "Can I bring him back again? I shall go to him, but he shall not return to me." The resignation was perfect, as the repentance was absolute and unrestricted. That this latter was the case we see by the expressions in the psalm quoted above, and in the fact that it was delivered to "the chief musician," *i.e*, intended to be used in the Temple service, a standing memorial of his sin and humiliation from which contemporaries and all posterity might derive warning and instruction.

When these days of mourning were over, David returned to his home life, and comforted his beloved wife, Bathsheba ; and in the course of time she bore another son, whom the king, seeing in this a proof that his penitence was accepted and his peace made with God, called Solomon, "Peaceful." A further assurance of this reconciliation he received from the prophet Nathan, who was commissioned to impose on the child the name Jedidiah, "Beloved of the Lord,"[1] from which the father gathered the assurance that this son should not die prematurely, and that he should be endowed with abnormal qualities. Bathsheba became the mother of other sons, Shimeah, Shobah, and Nathan (whose name appears in the genealogy of our Lord), but Solomon was the dearest of them all, as he was destined to be the most celebrated.

Shortly after the birth of Solomon,[2] as if to prevent David from forgetting his lapse, and to carry on the retributive punishment, a terrible outrage was perpetrated by his eldest son. This, too, was a result of that debasing custom of polygamy which was answerable for so many quarrels and crimes. The luxurious life of the harem, the sensuality which was there made so prominent, tended to introduce dissoluteness of morals among the younger members of the families. David's own example

---

[1] Klostermann gives some forcible reasons for maintaining that Jedidiah was the name given to the dead child, not to Solomon He would transpose verses 24 and 25 of 2 Sam xii , and the clauses of verse 24, so that it would run : "And he called his name Jedidiah, according to the word of the Lord, which He had sent through the prophet Nathan " He sees in this name a token that "Jehovah judges," in agreement with the sentence of verse 14, that the child should surely die.

[2] The number "forty" in 2 Sam xv. 7 ("it came to pass after forty years") is almost certainly an erroneous reading, and ought to be "four." Thus Josephus ("Ant " vii 9 1), and the Syriac and Arabic versions. Some ten years elapsed between Amnon's outrage and Absalom's rebellion, and the latter event took place about ten years before David's death. Ewald, "History of Israel," iii 170, note 1 Absalom was born in David's first year at Hebron, and would have been some sixteen years old at the time of Uriah's death , and as we may reckon that he murdered Amnon when he was twenty, and two years after the outrage, so the crime of Amnon happened in Absalom's eighteenth year, i e., the second year after David's fall (Weiss),

encouraged laxity ; he was now to see his own sin reflected in another's misconduct. Amnon, the son of his first wife, Ahinoam, conceived a guilty passion for his beautiful half-sister, Tamar, the uterine sister of Absalom, and the daughter of David's third wife, Maacah. This Amnon was a man of violent disposition, a wanton profligate, unaccustomed to restrain his desires and impeded by no scruples in their gratification Giving way to his wanton imagination, he fell quite sick and pined away because he could not at once satisfy his evil appetite The restrictions of the Mosaic law (Lev. xviii. 9, 11), which forbade all such incestuous connections, had no correcting influence ; and the separation of the royal families who lived in different houses under their own mothers' supervision, tended to minimize the ties of consanguinity ; but there were other obstacles that barred the way. There was the strict seclusion of the Oriental home which rendered any approach to the maiden difficult ; there was the girl's own modesty which shrank from the thought of dishonour ; added to this, the expression (2 Sam xiii. 2), "for she was a virgin," seems to imply that either of her own accord, or by her parent's wish, she had taken a vow of chastity. In the face of these impediments Amnon despaired of success, and the disappointment, daily brooded on, affected his bodily health. But he had a friend, one Jonadab, son of his uncle Shimeah, a cunning, heartless, unscrupulous parasite, who, noticing his altered appearance, wormed from him the cause, and suggested a plan by which he might obtain the object of his desire. He was to feign sickness and take to his bed, and when, as was sure to be the case, his father came to inquire about his malady, he was to use a sick man's privilege and pretend that he had taken a fancy for some cakes prepared by his sister Tamar's own hand in his presence He at once fell in with the villanous plot, and all happened as his rascally counsellor had foreseen. Tamar, who was known to be skilful in the culinary art, was sent by her father to Amnon's house, and prepared before his eyes the food that he had longed for, and gave it to the servants to offer to him. But he refused to eat or to receive it at their hands , and, as though he could not bear the presence of his attendants and needed perfect quiet, he directed all to leave the chamber but Tamar, and besought her to minister to his sick appetite. The gentle maiden thinking no ill, brought the food to his bed-side, when the monster seized her by the hand, and made an infamous proposal to her. Horrified she shrank away, entreating him to cast aside this wicked thought, and by her words reminding him of a patriarchal warning: "Nay, my brother; no such thing ought to be done in Israel: do not thou this folly."[1] And in the confusion of her mind, or wishing to temporise, or thinking that the king had power to annul the operation of the Law, she cries: "Speak, I pray thee, unto the king; for he will not withhold me from thee." All was in vain; in spite of her opposition, he accomplished his purpose. And then a sudden revulsion of feeling comes over him; the love, such as it was, is suddenly changed to violent hatred, and he brutally bids her to go. Uselessly she pleads that this dismissal is worse than the first wrong, as it will make her shame known, and brand her as an infamous woman who herself had been the tempter. This is just what the unprincipled ruffian desired; so he called an attendant, and ordered him roughly to turn this person out of the chamber, as though her presence were pollution; and the poor victim was cast forth without compunction to life-long sorrow and ignominy. She could not conceal the shameful occurrence; rending the long-sleeved robe which the king's young daughters wore, and sprinkling herself with ashes, and with her hand laid upon her head in token of grievous trouble,[2] she went weeping to her brother's house. Absalom heard her sad tale, but dissembled the rage that filled his heart, intending to wait for a fit opportunity of avenging the dishonour of his sister. He bade her to be silent and not to take the thing to heart—advice easily given, but not so easily practised; and the poor maiden remained in seclusion, her life for ever darkened by the crime of her betrayer. And was not this wretch called to account for his wickedness? No; Absalom spake not to him a word either good or bad, biding his time. And though his father was very wroth, he did not punish the evil-doer, as it was his duty to do. His own hands were not clean. It is true that the sacred law enjoined the penalty of death for such an offence;[3] but David had himself incurred the same punishment, and could not condemn in another that which he had condoned in his own case. The Greek translators, followed by the Latin Vulgate, give another reason for his inertness: "But he vexed not the spirit of Amnon, his

---

[1] Gen. xxxiv. 7.   [2] Comp. Jer. ii. 37.   [3] Lev. xviii. 9, 29.

SIN AND ITS CONSEQUENCES. 149

son, because he loved him, because he was his first-born"[1]
This weakness had fatal consequences. It rankled in Absalom's
mind, and gave a fresh impulse to the fell purpose of revenge
which he had conceived. That his sister, one of royal descent
on both sides, should be treated like a common prostitute by
one whose mother was of plebeian extraction, and that the
audacious offender should go unpunished, suffering neither in
person, nor position, nor reputation—this the haughty youth
could ill endure. Amnon deserved death, and Amnon should
die. Revenge coincided with ambition. Failing the first-born,
he himself might look to the throne; for the second son,
Chileab, was probably dead, or else was a quiet man who took
no interest in public affairs, and would not stand in the way of
his brother's preferment. Neither David nor Absalom ever
thought of the wrong being repaired by marriage; evidently
the idea of such an union was abhorrent and inconceivable in
the holy land. The brother felt that, in the father's negligence,
it lay with him to avenge the honour of his sister, and that the
disgrace could be atoned only by the blood of the violator, even
as Simeon and Levi punished the wrong of their sister Dinah by
the murder of the Shechemites, and as at this day, if an Arab
maiden is wronged, it becomes the duty of her brethren to pursue the seducer to death.[2]

For two years Absalom nursed his wrath, the lapse of time
not weakening his intention, though it lulled to sleep any suspicion that might have been entertained of a murderous retaliation. Now he sees a mode of getting Amnon into his power
away from the protection of the royal palace. He possessed
an estate at Baal-Hazor, once a centre of idolatrous worship, and
always a conspicuous landmark, rising with its grey summit
more than 3,000 feet above sea level. It is now known by the
name of Tell Azur, and is situated a few miles north of Bethel
and about twelve from Jerusalem. Here he was about to hold
a sheep-shearing, which, as we have seen in the case of Nabal,
was always the occasion of a joyous festival; and he invited his
father and the chief courtiers to honour the feast with their
presence. David excused himself on the ground of being un-

---

[1] We see David's immoderate partiality for his sons in other instances,
e.g., 2 Sam. xix. 1; 1 Kings i. 6.

[2] Gen. xxxiv. 25 ff. Ewald refers to his notes on Cant. i. 6, viii. 8, in
"Dichter des A. B."

willing to burden his son with the expense of so large a company; but on Absalom persisting in his desire to have at his table, if not the king, at least the heir-apparent and his brothers, David, wholly unsuspicious of treachery, and satisfied in his own mind that no ill-feeling remained between these near relations, gave his consent to the acceptance of the invitation. This was all that Absalom wanted, and he made his preparations, ordering his attendants to break in upon the feast, and, when Amnon was off his guard and his heart elated with wine, to fall upon him and slay him. His wishes were carried out to the letter. The seducer was ruthlessly murdered at the festive board. The princes, dreading a like fate, in the utmost consternation rose from the table, and mounting their mules fled with all haste towards Jerusalem. Speedy as they were, rumour outstripped them, and carried to David the exaggerated story that Absalom had slain all his brethren. The tale gained credence for a time, and the horror-stricken father rent his clothes, and lay mourning on the earth, a prey to the most terrible sorrow. But Jonadab, who had guessed or was privy to Absalom's secret design, comforted the king with the assurance that Amnon alone was killed; and this assertion was soon confirmed by the appearance of the rest of the princes who were seen riding in hot haste towards the city. At their arrival the exact truth was known, and David had to grieve only for the loss of his first-born; but this was a very bitter blow, and one for which he felt his own conduct was answerable. This feeling, too, prevented him from pursuing the murderer with determination. Absalom, indeed, had fled for refuge to his mother's father, Talmai, the king of Geshur; but this petty monarch could not have withheld the fugitive had his surrender been formally demanded. But no such requisition was made. The treacherous plotter of Uriah's death could not bring himself to pursue the avenger of a sister's wrong, and he contented himself with virtually pronouncing sentence of banishment against the offender, for whom, in spite of his cold-blooded cruelty, impiety, and insubordination, he still cherished an unreasonable affection.

This state of things continued for three years, in which time David had recovered from the shock of Amnon's death, who had never been very near to his heart, and had begun to feel keenly the void caused by the absence of his favourite Absalom. The

SIN AND ITS CONSEQUENCES.   151

weakness of the parent contended with the severity of the judge,
while every motive of policy and justice combined to make it
expedient to keep aloof from the court and out of people's sight
this clever, unscrupulous criminal, who could be no fit successor
to the theocratic throne, the king's partiality urged him to recall
the exile and to receive him again into favour, penitent and
pardoned. Joab, the banished man's secret friend, marked the
struggle in the father's soul, and thought to use it in order to
effect a reconciliation. The welfare of the kingdom had little
influence in this determination; he wished to induce his lord
to do that which he knew was secretly desired, and he hoped
thus to secure the favour of the heir-apparent, whose ambitious,
daring character found a responsive echo in his own disposition.
But he was not very confident of his own standing with the
king, who since the murder of Abner had held him at a distance,
and he thought it best to approach his object by a stratagem.
Like Nathan, he wished to surprise David into a verdict which
was applicable to the case in hand. Such *ruses* are common in
antiquity. A matter is introduced by an example on which the
opinion of the judge is obtained, and the sentence thus given is
adroitly turned to the real subject, and quoted with telling effect
as an irrefragable decision. Joab availed himself of the services
of a wise woman of Tekoah, a village a few miles south of his
own town of Bethlehem, and celebrated in after years as the
birth-place of the prophet Amos. Instructed in her part by the
wily general, dressed in the garb of mourning, she comes before
the king, who, in the capacity of judge, was accessible to all his
subjects She falls before him with a cry for help, explaining
that she had been left a widow with two sons, that these had
quarrelled in the field, and that one had slain the other. Now
the whole family demanded the death of the offender in accordance with the law of blood-vengeance, and if she surrendered
him there would be no heir to continue her husband's name, and
her sole remaining coal would be utterly extinguished. The king
listened to the appeal, and, impressed with the case, promised
to give orders for her son's protection. The woman then, with
the cunning pretence of drawing back, and hinting that she knew
that the offered impunity was illegal, prayed that if the conces-
sion was not right the fault might be visited upon her and not
upon the king. After some further conversation she extorted
an oath from David that it should be as she wished. Having

thus in the most emphatic manner obtained from the king the precedent of an exception to the general rule, and the great truth that there was something higher and more Divine than a blood-feud, she proceeded with boldness, yet respectfully, to execute the important and most difficult part of her mission. She could not openly denounce her listener, as the prophet Nathan had done; she could only, as it were incidentally, and without mentioning a name, apply the matter to the case of Absalom, and intimate that the treatment which he received was not consistent with the leniency extended to her son In somewhat ambiguous language she represented that, as her relatives wanted to deprive her house of its heir, so he was depriving his people of the heir-apparent, which must be against the interest of the nation. Life was short, revenge was not satisfying. "For," she goes on, "we must needs die, and are as water spilt on the ground, which cannot be gathered up again We should act as God Himself; He does not take away life at once in punishment of crime, but is merciful and gives a way for repentance." In conclusion, as if her reference to the king's affairs had been only an interlude, she craftily reverts to her own case, and says that she can now go home happy, for the king was like an angel of God, listening to every just complaint and granting aid to the afflicted; and she prays with the utmost fervour that Jehovah may be with him. David could not help perceiving the drift of her petition, and at once divined that this had been her real object; and knowing Joab's predilection for Absalom, he suspected that the whole matter had been arranged by him. Finding on inquiry from the woman that this was the case, he sent for Joab, and gave him leave to go to Geshur and bring home the banished prince. With much pleasure Joab performed his commission, and Absalom once more appeared in Jerusalem. But though he thus far condoned the offence, David did not at once receive the sinner into favour; his sense of justice would not permit him to treat him as though he had committed no heavy transgression. The young man was allowed to dwell in his own house, but was strictly forbidden to appear at court, neither would his father see him, or allow him to enjoy any of the privileges of the king's son and heir This state of things continued for two years In vain he chafed at these restrictions, and endeavoured to get Joab to intercede for him The latter saw danger in the complete restoration of this ambitious, unprincipled youth, and resolutely refused to attend the summons when urged to grant an interview. Determined to gain his end, Absalom ordered his servants to set fire to a barley-field of Joab's, calculating that the owner would come to complain of the outrage, and when it so fell out, he used the occasion so adroitly, that he persuaded Joab to go to the king and implore a full pardon. The acute general saw that half-and-half measures were a mistake. The culprit should either be completely forgiven or capitally punished; this virtual ostracism did not vindicate the claims of offended justice, and only irritated the sufferer. He went to the king, and urging these and the like considerations, prevailed at length on David to receive the banished prince into favour, and to give him the kiss of peace. Thus in weak obedience to doting affection, and in infatuated reliance on his own unguided judgment, David prepares for himself the greatest trouble of his life, and gives this evil-minded son the opportunity for which he had long waited. Before relating the momentous events that arose from this circumstance, we must for a short space turn to another transaction which took place somewhere about this time, if not much earlier.[1]

There fell upon the land a grievous famine which lasted three years. Whatever may have been the secondary causes that occasioned the visitation, drought, or blight, or unfavourable seasons, David ascribed it to its author; he knew that nations are thus punished by temporal calamities, and his chief care was to discover the transgression which had led to the affliction. Accordingly, when year after year brought no relief, he inquired of the Lord in the appointed way whether the sin lay at his door or was a legacy from the late king's reign; and he was told in answer that the punishment was sent "for Saul, and for his bloody house, because he slew the Gibeonites." These people had craftily secured protection from Joshua at the time of the

---

[1] The actual date of the famine is uncertain. We know thus much: it took place after the advancement of Mephibosheth, and while Saul's crime was still fresh in people's memory, the persons devoted to death in expiation were all unmarried, or, at least without families; Shimei refers to this destruction of Saul's descendants (2 Sam. xvi. 7, 8). From these facts we gather that the event occurred before Absalom's revolt, and in the earlier half of David's reign at Jerusalem. The account is placed in 2 Sam. xxi. not in its chronological order, but as a kind of appendix relating the final ruin of the house of Saul. See Josephus, "Ant." vii. 12. 1.

conquest,¹ and had ever since lived peaceably in a subordinate condition among the Israelites, but Saul in a fit of zeal had been guilty of a breach of faith, and had tried to exterminate this remnant of the original inhabitants, or had treated them in some cruel way, which left in their breasts a rankling feeling of injury and a thirst for vengeance. The indignation occasioned by this barbarous violation of a solemn compact was very general, and sympathy for the sufferers prevailed largely among the Israelites themselves. The particular transaction to which reference is made finds no record in the sacred pages, and we can only conjecture its nature and its occasion. It may have been that many of the Gibeonites, who were employed as hewers of wood and drawers of water for the sanctuary, were cut off in the massacre at Nob;² or Saul may have attacked the four Canaanite cities, Gideon, Caphira, Beeroth, and Kirjath-Jearim, at the time when he exterminated witches and sorcerers. Ewald³ has suggested that when the tabernacle was placed for a time at Gibeon after the massacre at Nob, a dispute arose on the matter between Saul and the citizens, who resisted the introduction of an emblem of Hebrew worship, as an infringement of the religious liberty guaranteed to them by Joshua, and the former with characteristic recklessness, and, in his unspiritual conception, thinking to atone for his impious outrage at Nob by zeal against the traditionary enemies of the God of Israel, commenced a war of destruction against the Gibeonites. There is an intimation⁴ that the inhabitants of Beeroth (a suburb of Gibeon) were driven into exile to Gittaim, from whence, as we have seen above (p 93), came the two chieftains who assassinated Ishbosheth. This migration was doubtless caused by the violence with which they were treated. If we consider the event to which the account refers to be thus ascertained, there are still other difficulties which need solution. It is asked why, when the sin was Saul's, the punishment should fall upon David and his people, who had no share in the crime. The answer is, that the unity of prince and subjects renders both answerable for the action of one. Saul committed the offence, not as a private individual, but as king and representative of Israel which acquiesced in his proceedings. The breach of faith was national, therefore the nation must be involved in the atonement. It is not at all im-

---

¹ Josh ix 3 ff   ² See "Samuel and Saul," p 184.
³ " Hist of Israel,' iii 135 f.   ⁴ 2 Sam. iv. 3.

SIN AND ITS CONSEQUENCES.

probable that the lands and property of the dispossessed or murdered Gibeonites were bestowed upon the courtiers, so that in this respect also the people were implicated in the guilt, and winked at the violation of the old compact. David, too, had been supine in the matter; he was powerful enough to see justice done to the injured; but occupied with other concerns he had paid no attention to the claims which made no clamorous appeal, and he was now to be taught the continuous responsibility of a nation and that lapse of time does not annul the guilt of transgression. A national sin must be atoned for by a national reparation, which could be enforced only by some general calamity. But then, why was the blow so long delayed? Many years had elapsed since the massacre, why had vengeance not overtaken the perpetrators and accessories long ago? We may say, that Saul had so many sins to answer for, that during his lifetime special prominence could scarcely have been given to this offence, nor the Divine displeasure markedly emphasised; and in later times, when Israel was struggling with mighty enemies for bare existence, the lesson of the famine would not have been read. It was in a period of peace and comparative security that the visitation would be most especially observed, and its significance investigated. It may have been too that this act of discipline was now needed to prevent similar deeds of retaliation or breaches of national contract.

The ultimate cause of the calamity having been divinely determined, how was it to be appeased? The idea of retributive justice was inseparable from the ancient view of the moral government of the world; and Mosaic enactments confirmed the general sentiment. Blood must be atoned by blood, the guilt of a land would be washed away only in the blood of the perpetrator or his representatives, or in some cases by an equivalent payment in money. As to the exact measure of justice to be required, this lay with the nearest of kin, what satisfied them was supposed to be sufficient atonement. In the present case, David inquired of the Gibeonites what satisfaction they demanded, and was answered that they would not accept blood-money or any return of appropriated possessions, nothing would compensate for the wrong done, but the power to inflict the punishment of death upon seven of their oppressor's sons. These they required David to give over to them that they might crucify or impale them in the very home of the murderer, in Gibeah of Saul, before the high-place which was there. The scene of the execution would show that the offence was his; and the perfect number, seven, indicated that the atonement would be complete. It was not in accordance with Mosaic law to exact the penalty of death from the relations of a murderer; but Oriental custom sanctioned such an infliction, and the solidarity of the family rendered it natural that the sins of fathers should be visited upon children. The demand appeared to David nothing unusual, and though he had personally treated the family of his predecessor with a leniency that no Eastern monarch would have displayed, he could not resist this claim, and he consented to deliver the required victims into the hands of the Gibeonites. The selection was left to him. Accordingly, sparing Mephibosheth, the son of his lamented friend Jonathan, he took two sons of Rizpah, Saul's concubine, a woman of foreign extraction, and five sons of Merab, Saul's eldest daughter, whom she bore to Adriel, the son of Barzillai of Meholah,[1] and gave them over to the avengers, who, after putting them to death, probably by strangulation,[2] hung the bodies up before the Lord at the sanctuary of Gibeah. And here a touching scene was enacted. Rizpah, the mother of two of the victims, could not stay the execution, and might not remove the corpses of her children for decent burial, but she could prevent their becoming the prey of the vultures and jackals which act as the scavengers in the land. It was now the season of the barley harvest, about our April, and the country was still suffering from the long-continued drought. The devoted mother took sackcloth, and spread it as a couch or tent for herself on the bare rock where her sons'

[1] He is thus distinguished from Barzillai, the Gileadite of Rogelim who entertained David after Absalom's revolt (2 Sam xix. 31) The name "Michal" in 2 Sam xxi 8 is, as already mentioned, a clerical error for "Merab." See 1 Sam xviii 19, and 2 Sam vi 23.

[2] It was the custom among the Jews not to impale or crucify criminals alive, but first to put them to death, and then to make a public exhibition of their bodies on cross or stake (Numb xxv 4) The modes of death were stoning, strangulation, beheading, and burning. To say that David acquiesced in the demand for these persons in order to rid himself of Saul's descendants, is to attribute to him a meanness of which he never showed the least trace. Such a suggestion could be made only by that scoffing criticism which can sympathize with nothing high and noble, and delights to blacken the character of God's heroes, and to attribute to them the basest of motives.

bodies were fixed, and here she remained, driving off the foul birds and beasts of prey, till heaven's wrath was appeased and rain fell once more. The Hebrew law indeed ordered[1] that the bodies of criminals should be interred on the day of execution, but the Gibeonites maintained the custom of their own countrymen which knew no such reservation, and insisted on the expiatory sacrifice being exposed till a token was given that it was accepted. In due time the welcome showers were poured forth, and David, deeply impressed by the courage and affection of Rizpah, hastened to relieve her of her melancholy watch. He seized this opportunity to send and collect the bones of Saul and Jonathan from their temporary grave at Jabesh-Gilead, and, taking down the seven bodies of the crucified, buried them all in the ancestral sepulchre of Kish at Zelah, a town in Benjamin a few miles south of Bethel. "And after that God was intreated for the land," the drought ceased, and the penal famine was removed.

[1] Deut. xxi 22, 23.

CHAPTER X.

ABSALOM'S REVOLT.

Absalom's ambitious design—He steals the affections of the people—Causes of disaffection—Absalom at Hebron—Ahithophel—The insurrection breaks out—David leaves Jerusalem, sends back the ark and the priests—Hushai—Ziba—Shimei's insult—Ahithophel's evil counsel adopted—His further plan defeated by Hushai—David informed of the movement in Jerusalem, arrives at Mahanaim, is supported there by friends—End of Ahithophel—Battle of Mahanaim—Defeat of rebels—Absalom slain by Joab—News brought to David—His grief for Absalom—Joab rouses David to action—The ten tribes submit to David—Judah also invites his return—Shimei, Ziba, and Mephibosheth—Barzillai—Dissension between Israel and Judah—Revolt of Sheba—Amasa made commander, murdered by Joab—Sheba slain—Joab reinstated

THE leniency with which Absalom had been treated by his fond father soon began to produce disastrous results. He was now in the position of eldest son and natural heir to his father's throne. The measure of punishment dealt and the favour now accorded to him had effected no change in his turbulent, ungrateful character, and he had already conceived designs as audacious as they were base and disloyal. He had brooded on these during the years in which he had been debarred from the associations of the Court, and compelled to live obscure and retired. Now that all this was changed, he began to see his way to realize his ambitious aspirations. He may at one time have hoped that his father would associate him with him in the kingdom, but he soon saw that there was no such intention, and his aim now was to bring himself into notice, making himself the most prominent and the most popular person in Jerusalem. Nature wonderfully favoured this design. The mob are ever influenced by appearances; and Absalom was exceedingly beautiful, faultless from head to foot, his head graced with luxuriant locks, the weight of which, when cut once a year, is noted as something extraordinary Thus handsome in person, he was no less winning in manner, courteous, affable, and of honied speech, and was regarded by general acclamation as one in every way fitted for sovereignty Richly supplied with resources by his injudicious father, he began to make such a display in the city as had never before been seen. He imitated heathen monarchs by setting up a grand equipage, had chariots and horses for daily use, and never stirred abroad without having fifty runners to attend him David's unpretending style of living was quite eclipsed by the pageantry of his brilliant son, and fawners and flatterers flocked round this rising luminary, and encouraged his extravagant aspirations. Soon he proceeded to undermine his father's hold on the regard of his people The king's duties were very arduous, and involved great personal attention and labour He was the supreme judge of his subjects; he had to sit and try every cause that might be brought before him; and as the kingdom was now of wide extent, and accordingly the cases which came for decision became yearly more numerous and important, it often happened that suitors were unable to get a hearing, or suffered long delays, or departed dissatisfied with the royal verdict Absalom took advantage of this state of things in order to spread abroad a feeling of discontent, and a vague desire for change. He posted himself at the gate of the palace, and met the applicants in the most friendly manner, would not suffer them to make the customary prostration, but took them by the hand and kissed them He pretended to have the warmest interest in all who came in his way, inquired into their position, residence, and business, listened to their complaints, assured them that their cause was just, insinuating at the same time that they would not get justice done, as the king could not attend to all such matters himself, and had deputed no one to act for him, and always taking care to express a wish that he had the authority which his father mismanaged, for that things would then be very different In this hunt after popularity he spared no trouble, was at his post in the early morning hours, with an ear always open, with a sympathy always ready, and an affability that was absolutely unheard of. No wonder that "he stole the hearts of the men of Israel;" no wonder that there was a large party prepared to follow his lead for good or ill, though there were other causes, as we shall see, beside his popularity and insidious plotting, which favoured his views.

After preparing the ground assiduously for four years,[1] he thought the time for action had arrived. We can note some of the reasons which led him to consider that a revolution might now be successful. He reckoned of course on the support of the young and restless members of the community, who had grown up with him, had been dazzled by his outward magnificence, had profited by his extravagances, and hoped to reap further benefits from a political commotion. But there were deeper and more powerful causes at work, there were materials for a great conflagration which needed only a spark applied by a skilful hand to kindle into flame. David had reigned about thirty years, and had arrived at the age of sixty; he was probably at this time suffering from some severe disease;[2] at any rate his early vigour had forsaken him; he was a depressed, sorrow-stricken man. All his light-heartedness, his spirit of enterprise, his enthusiasm had fled. He no longer took people's affection by storm, and won the favour of the fickle crowd by deeds of daring courage and self-devotion; and though no impartial observer, who knew his difficulties and his honest struggles to do his duty thoroughly, could have justly found fault with his rule, there were defects in the internal administration of the kingdom which innovators thought might be remedied by a change of government. The imposts, rendered necessary by the expenses of foreign wars, and the maintenance of authority in distant and numerous dependencies, were felt to be peculiarly burdensome by a people still mindful of their ancient liberty and indisposed to make sacrifices for the public benefit. A new generation had sprung up to whom his earlier prowess and successes were known only by hearsay, who looked upon his government as old-fashioned, and thirsted

[1] The present Hebrew text (2 Sam xv. 7) gives, "after forty years," but this is plainly an error, as the term suits neither Absalom's age, nor the reign of David. The Syriac and Arabic versions give "four," which number is confirmed by the "Itala," and Josephus, "Ant." vii. 9, 1. See also Theodor. "Quæst." 28 in 2 Sam

[2] See certain expressions in Psalms xxxviii., xxxix., xli.

for a more stirring and ostentatious administration, fretting under the restrictions imposed by the piety of a theocratical monarch. Many right-minded persons, too, had been grievously scandalized by David's actions in the matter of Uriah and Bathsheba, his weakness in letting the murder of Amnon pass unpunished, his infatuated affection for his guilty son, they contrasted the glorious reputation of his earlier years with the dark deeds of the later, and were disposed to transfer their allegiance from one who had already lost their affection and respect In the case of the tribe of Judah, which was the stronghold of the disaffection, other causes were at work This tribe had resented the adoption of Jerusalem as the capital of the kingdom to the disparagement, as they thought, of the ancient sanctuary of Hebron David's energetic attempt at the unification of the tribes had met with but sullen and unwilling acceptance on the part of Judah, which could not forget its promised prerogatives and its claims to the hegemony of the country.[1] The hereditary jealousy between itself and the other members of the community was only slumbering for intervals, and was always ready to break out into overt action The northern tribes had their own special grievances respecting the discipline introduced by David and the administration of justice, and were not unwilling to form a temporary alliance with other malcontents in the expectation of gaining some material benefits thereby.

Of these various motives for a desire of change Absalom took advantage He determined that the attempt should be made at Hebron, the time-honoured capital of Judæa, and a place where the disaffected could readily be collected, not too far from Jerusalem to render his preparations there unavailable, nor yet too near to be liable to inconvenient observation. Trading on his father's well-known piety, and knowing how gladly he would welcome any token of religion in his son's heart, Absalom went to David with the story, that, when an exile at Geshur, he had vowed to offer a sacrifice at Hebron if ever he came home again. The time for fulfilling this vow was now arrived, and he prayed his royal father to allow him to go to Hebron and make the promised offering at his own birthplace. David was utterly unsuspicious of any treachery, he had perfect confidence in his son's loyalty. The prince's plans

[1] Gen. xlix 8 ff, Deut xxxiii.

had been kept scrupulously secret, and even Joab, a man keenly alive to his own interests, knew nothing of the conspiracy. So the permission was cheerfully given, and Absalom proceeded to Hebron, taking with him two hundred of his friends whom he had invited to grace the sacrificial feast, and who might serve as hostages in case of any serious opposition to his plans in Jerusalem. He had not informed these men of his design, but he knew that they were devoted to his interests, and would be ready to follow his lead whithersoever it might take them. Meantime he had sent trusty emissaries among all the tribes to sound the sentiments of the people, and, where they found these favourable, to warn them that, when they heard the trumpet alarm sound from town to town, they should proclaim that Absalom was anointed king in Hebron. Another great point was to exhibit on his side a personage of importance, whose espousal of the cause would not only be in itself beneficial, but would win for it acceptance at the hands of others. Such an adherent was found in Ahithophel, the grandfather of Bathsheba, whose son Eliam had been a friend and comrade of the hapless Uriah. This man had been David's most trusty counsellor, so highly valued was his advice that men regarded it as an oracle of God, and long had the king profited by his wisdom and experience. But Ahithophel had now for some time ceased to frequent the court though without any open rupture, he had taken umbrage at the dishonour brought on his family in the matter of Bathsheba and at the treacherous death of Uriah, and had retired in disgust to his native city Giloh, a place about seven miles north of Hebron. Hence he was summoned by Absalom; and entering heart and soul into the conspiracy, became the chief mover of the whole enterprise, and gave it method and prestige. Such a clever, calculating man would not have been led solely by private feeling to espouse a doubtful cause; he evidently considered that the usurper would win the day; his public policy chimed with his private grudge; in gratifying his personal malice he deemed that he was upholding the side that would eventually triumph in the approaching struggle. Some days had been spent in performing sacrifices and attending to the consequent festivities; and thus time had been given for extending the movement and gathering support; and doubtless the solemn occasion had been utilized to pledge the **guests to favour their entertainer's** cause. The excitement spread rapidly; everything seemed to favour the undertaking; multitudes, who in calmer moments would have seen good reason to adhere loyally to the old *régime*, carried away by the contagion of the general disturbance, flocked around the pretender, and swelled his forces to a body formidable indeed in numbers if not by reason of military experience Of all that had been going on David had remained in utter ignorance. With a noble confidence in his son, trusting him as the heir to the throne with full freedom of action, he had seen nothing in the late proceedings to make him suspect disturbance or disaffection. There was no system of police to spy out political secrets or to convey information of hidden dangers, so that when suddenly the news of the insurrection was conveyed by alarmed messengers to the king, the intelligence was as unexpected as it was overwhelming. Report doubtless exaggerated the extent of the movement, but there was enough in the reality to make immediate action necessary. Without hesitation David at once resolved to leave Jerusalem. Many motives contributed to this determination. The capital was not prepared to stand a siege, and he could not bear to be the cause of indiscriminate bloodshed in the streets, if it were captured after resistance. He too himself might be made prisoner and lie at the mercy of an infuriated mob. Time would thus be gained for the commotion to subside, and the strength of the two parties to be more accurately gauged. He could not know how far the conspiracy had spread in Jerusalem itself, and feared the presence of treachery within its walls. Causes such as these combined to make flight expedient; but under all lay the consciousness of guilt, the feeling that the retribution threatened by Nathan, the evil rising from his own house, was come upon him, and that it became him to bend meekly to the blow. Hence he makes no pretence at resistance; this was part of his chastisement; he must bear it, and wait God's good time for its removal.

Immediate orders were given for a retreat beyond Jordan amid the Eastern tribes, in whose cause he had fought so bravely and successfully, and whose gratitude might be supposed to have resisted the seductions of the young pretender. The removal was conducted in an orderly manner None of the king's household or officers of state shrank from accompanying their master. His wives and children he took with him, leaving on'y ten concubines as custodians of the palace in his absence. The bodyguard, and his veteran warriors, the six hundred Gibborim, with the gallant Ittai of Gath and his comrades, cheerfully followed his fortunes, and would have proved a formidable obstacle to a pursuing force, though the presence of the women and children rendered defence difficult, and made it advisable to place the deep valley of the Jordan between himself and danger as soon as possible. Ittai, indeed, as an alien and one who had only lately taken service with him, David thoughtfully advised either to return to his own countrymen, or to seek advancement at Absalom's hands; but the noble Philistine declined both alternatives, making an answer which is justly celebrated for sincere and uncompromising loyalty : " As the Lord liveth, and as my lord the king liveth, surely in what place my lord the king shall be, whether for death or for life, even there also will thy servant be." This was cheering certainly, but offered a painful contrast to the conduct of the son, beloved, cherished, pardoned, and now an ungrateful traitor, a parricide at heart. The fugitives set forth; but at the last house [1] on the eastern side of the city, before passing the Kidron, a halt was called and a hasty review was held. Then the order of march was arranged. The bodyguard led the van, followed by the Gibborim; David and his household brought up the rear. In this array they crossed the brook, and once more came to a halt by the first olive-tree at the foot of Mount Olivet in the spot afterwards known as the Garden of Gethsemane, the scene of the agony of the "son of David" on a more momentous occasion. Weeping and lamenting the people accompanied their beloved monarch, who with bare feet and covered head, in token of profoundest sorrow, wended his melancholy way. It was some comfort amid the misery of the position to receive these signs of sympathy and affection from subjects of a higher class than those who had thoughtlessly upheld the usurper's cause. Another great and important support, which was offered by the ministers of religion, in his humility he voluntarily refused. The two priests, Zadok, and later on [2] Abiathar, had

---

[1] A. V. (2 Sam xv. 17) gives, "A place that was very far off." R. V, "Beth-Merhak," margin, "The far House." It may have been a fort erected in the suburbs to guard the usual passage across the brook.

[2] The expression, 2 Sam. xv 24, "and Abiathar went up" (after the mention of the presence of Zadok and the Levites), seems to point to some

brought forth the Ark from the city, and with a large body of Levites had stationed themselves at David's side while the fugitives defiled before him. The presence of this holy symbol would have invested the king's cause with a sacred character in the eyes of all good men, he would be seen to have put himself under the protection of Jehovah, while its absence from the adversary's camp would have testified that the party of Absalom was not favoured by heaven. But the pious king would not avail himself of this adventitious aid. He may have thought of the disastrous issue of such an use of the Ark in Eli's days, and trembled at the idea of incurring a similar calamity. His mind was recovering from the depression which had first affected him; he began to take a less gloomy view of the situation. The holy Ark had been placed in Zion; with great solicitude he had prepared a place for its abode, and Jehovah had signified that there was His dwelling-place and that He had a delight therein. It was not for His servant to disturb this arrangement If the Lord prospered him, he would be brought out of all his troubles safe again to Jerusalem without the aid of the Ark, if he was to be rejected, the symbol could not save him; he would bow with submission to the chastening hand, and say. "Behold, here am I, let the Lord do to me as seemeth good unto Him" So he desired Zadok to carry the Ark back to its place. And he showed how he and his brother might do him good service by sending information of the usurper's plans. He would not be molested as guardian of the tabernacle, and he might in his capacity of high priest be consulted by Absalom.[1] At any rate he would have every opportunity of knowing what was going on, and might communicate with David by means of his own son Ahimaaz or his nephew Jonathan. These arrangements being completed, the ascent of Olivet was commenced, the first stage on the march to the wilderness of Jordan. It was a sad procession that took its way up the slope. "All the country wept with a loud voice." The people sympathized with their afflicted ruler, thus in his old age driven from

tardiness or unwillingness on his part, and we know that later he espoused the cause of Adonijah and was punished for his defection (See 1 Kings 1. 7, 11. 26 f.

[1] The expression in 2 Sam. xv. 27, rendered, "Art not thou a seer?" may be translated, "Seest thou?" or, "Thou art a seer." It may well be explained as above.

home and throne by an evil-minded son and a body of unprincipled conspirators, who had forgotten the incalculable benefits which the discarded monarch had conferred upon the country. Well might he and his people lament over the blindness and ingratitude which had rendered support to this senseless rising. Irresistibly are we reminded of the time when the blessed Jesus from this same spot, whence the view of Jerusalem is most imposing and beautiful, beheld the city and wept over it, because it knew not the time of its visitation. And as His heart was darkened by the knowledge that among the chosen Twelve one was a traitor, so it was a bitter pang to David to hear that his trusted counsellor, Ahithophel had joined the enemy it was a grief to him to pray God to "turn his counsel into folly." His feelings with regard to this Judas are expressed in the Fifty-fifth Psalm:

> "It was not an open enemy that reproached me;
> Then I could have borne it,
> Neither was it he that hated me that did magnify himself against me;
> Then I would have hid myself from him;
> But it was thou, a man mine equal,
> My companion, and my familiar friend.
> We took sweet counsel together,
> And walked in the house of God with the throng."

When David arrived at the top of the hill, where was a Bamah or high-place, and whence the last sight of the city was obtained before the descent towards the valley commenced, it seemed as though an answer had been sent to his late prayer for the frustration of Ahithophel's counsel. As he offered up his supplications in this hallowed spot, he was joined by an old and trusty friend, Hushai, of Archi (Ain Arik), a town on the borders of Ephraim and Benjamin, six miles west of Bethel. This good man met him with his clothes rent and dust upon his head, in token of grief at the public calamity, and expressed his firm determination to share the fortunes of the fugitive monarch. But David would not allow this Restored to his usual equanimity, and able now to take a calmer view of contingencies, the king saw that his friend could do him better service at Jerusalem than by attending him in his flight. So he bade him go to the city, and pretend to side with Absalom, while he used his utmost endeavours to defeat the counsel of Ahithophel; and desired him to send intelligence by means of the two youths, the sons of Zadok and Abiathar. This delicate mission Hushai willingly undertook : and, as we shall see, the scheme was quite successful. As David now turned his face resolutely to the desolate march that lay before him, he was overtaken by a party led by Ziba, the crafty steward to whom had been entrusted the management of Mephibosheth's estate. This person brought two asses for the use of the king's household, and a goodly store of bread and wine and dried fruits, for the refreshment of the fugitives ; and when questioned as to Mephibosheth's proceedings, why he had not come with his steward, he falsely affirmed that his young master had stayed behind at Jerusalem in the hope that in the present confusion the royal power would fall again into the hands of Saul's family On this, the king, disgusted at the prince's ingratitude, which seemed to him the natural corollary of the conduct of his own son Absalom, and making no further inquiry, somewhat hastily presented the traducer with all the property which belonged to Mephibosheth As the company proceeded on their way, a vexatious interruption occurred, which offered a confirmation of the sentiments attributed by Ziba to the family of the late king. They had reached the little town of Bahurim, where David proposed to rest for a while, when they were met by one of the inhabitants, Shimei, son of Gerar, a cadet of the house of Saul, who advanced towards them, cursing and throwing stones, upbraiding David with his cruelty to the family of Saul, especially in the case of the victims handed over to the Gibeonites, and rejoicing in his present calamity which was only a just punishment of his crimes. We know how little David's treatment of his predecessor's relatives deserved this censure ; but Shimei had that mean nature which exults in trampling on the fallen The jealousy which had always slumbered in the bosom of all connected with the house of Saul burst forth here in open violence, and showed itself in gross insolence and venomous invective. " Begone," he shouted across the ravine that separated him from the king's company, " begone, thou man of blood and man of Belial ; the Lord hath returned upon thee all the blood of the house of Saul, in whose stead thou hast reigned ; and the Lord hath delivered the kingdom into the hand of Absalom, thy son ; and, behold, thou art taken in thine own mischief, because thou art a man of blood " As he thus reviled David in the presence of his attendants, Abishai, that hasty warrior, urged the king to let him go and take off his head. But David will not consent to this; he has learned meekness under rebuke; he who needs mercy should show mercy; he who was even then suffering under the retributive sentence of Jehovah might well bear with patience the insults of this mean instrument of deserved vengeance. "My own son," the sad king says, "is seeking my life; how much more may this Benjamite do it! Let him alone, and let him curse; for the Lord hath bidden him." And he adds a pious hope that the Lord will requite him with good for the evil which he is patiently bearing. So the insolent reviler was allowed to vent his curses unchecked, and the interrupted march was resumed. After a weary journey of some fifteen or twenty miles, the pilgrims encamped on the plains of Jordan, safe for a time from surprise.[1] Here they had determined to wait for news from the city before continuing the flight. While his tired company slept around, David awoke in the early morning and poured out his soul in a psalm of hope and trustfulness (Psa. iii.):

> "Lord, how are mine adversaries increased!
> Many are they that rise up against me . . .
> But Thou, O Lord, art a shield about me;
> My glory, and the lifter up of my head. . . .
> I laid me down and slept,
> I awaked, for the Lord sustaineth me.
> I will not be afraid of ten thousands of the people,
> That have set themselves against me round about. . . .
> Salvation belongeth unto the Lord;
> Thy blessing be upon Thy people."

Meantime Absalom with his friends had arrived at Jerusalem only a few hours after the flight of David, and had been received by the fickle populace with every demonstration of delight. There was no enemy to oppose his entrance, and he proceeded at once to the palace to receive the homage and congratulations of adherents. Among those who came to greet the usurper appeared the crafty Hushai, playing the part

[1] The name of the place where the fugitives rested seems to have dropped out of the text, unless the word rendered "weary" ("they came weary," 2 Sam. xvi. 14), *Ayephim*, be a proper name. The word "there" at the end of the verse implies the previous mention of some place. Josephus ("Ant." vii. 9. 4) says that they reached the Jordan before encamping

assigned to him, and in reply to Absalom's natural inquiry why he deserted his father, roundly asserting that he felt it his duty to obey the sovereign whose claims were confirmed by success, he would be the trusty servant of the reigning king, whoever he was; as he had served the father, so now he would serve the son. Absalom, who at first had felt the incongruity of this good man's presence amid his godless supporters, was easily persuaded by these professions which vastly gratified his vanity, and he welcomed Hushai's cry, "God save the king," as a hearty expression of devotion to himself. Such a stratagem as this of Hushai was quite allowed by the verdict of the age; it had been suggested by David himself, and, indeed, has been practised by partisans in most Christian countries; and although we may consider it base and disreputable, and take our stand upon the high principle that God's cause is never served by men's lies, we must judge of actions by the light vouchsafed to the doers of them, and not measure them by a standard of morality as yet unknown.

The question now arose, What was the best course to pursue in order to make good the present position, and secure the fruits of the bloodless victory? There was no thought of seeking counsel of God; the sacred ephod would have ill beseemed the company there gathered together. It was the wisdom of this world that the prince desired, and accordingly he asked first the opinion of the astute Ahithophel. This wily counsellor, well aware that to win the wavering and to assure the actual conspirators some compromising action which made retreat impossible was needed, advised his master at once to assume public possession of his father's harem, and to treat the concubines left in the palace as his own. The advice, however revolting to our notions, was quite in accordance with Oriental principles. The harem of the predecessor passed on to the successor, the women having no voice in the matter, and being treated as mere chattels; and it was understood that this proceeding sealed the transference of the throne to the new incumbent. In the present case the outrage was pre-eminently atrocious, and rendered the breach between father and son irreconcilable. David in weakness or love might have overlooked the rebellion, but he could never forgive this outrageous insult to himself as king and father; and those who supported Absalom must see that no middle course was left, and that the contest

between the old and the new government was internecine. With
this crafty but abominable advice the prince immediately
complied. A tent was spread on the roof of the palace—the
very spot where David had admitted to his heart that fatal
temptation which had such terrible issues—and in the sight of
all Israel, and, as Nathan had declared, "in the sight of this
sun," he assumed possession of the royal concubines, and thus
consummated the irremediable rupture between himself and his
father

But Ahithophel was too acute not to see that other measures
were necessary to ensure the success of the conspiracy. Accordingly he counselled Absalom to let him this very evening
pursue David with a picked body of twelve thousand men, and
fall upon him while weary and dispirited , and he promised the
prince to win an easy and a bloodless victory The people with
David would be unable to resist the sudden onslaught of a
superior force ; they would flee without striking a blow , and he
would find no difficulty in seizing and despatching the old king.
With his death all opposition would collapse, and the whole
nation would submit itself to the new monarch. The counsel
was sagacious, and commended itself at once to the heartless
usurper and the assembled chiefs. By adopting it useless bloodshed would be spared, the success of their schemes would be
secured, and the transference of the royal power would be
effected at the least possible cost So prudent and feasible was
the proposal, that it seemed impossible for it to be defeated by
any rival plan. But Hushai feared that, if carried out, it might
be fatal to his friend, and he used his utmost art to prevent its
adoption. On Absalom inviting him to express his opinion, he
at once counselled delay. His secret idea was, that not only
would time be thus given to David to recover from the fatigue
and despondency of the flight, and to make preparations for
defence, but that the pause would afford an opportunity to the
people generally to reflect with calmness on the situation, and
allow the tempest of revolution by which they had been thoughtlessly carried away to subside. His speech was skilfully adapted
to the character of the vain youth whom he was addressing He
enlarged on the bravery and prowess of David and his followers ;
they were now bitterly exasperated, like a bear robbed of her
whelps, and would fight with the utmost desperation The king,
too, would not be with the troops, but safely concealed in some

cave or other hidden refuge. If the enemy had at first even
a partial success (which might well happen with such tried
warriors), a report would immediately be spread of a great
defeat, a panic would ensue, and the cause would be wofully
endangered, if not wholly lost. Let another plan be adopted.
Let all Israel be gathered together from Dan to Beersheba; let
Absalom place himself, as became him, at the head of the
assembled host; thus victory might be made absolutely certain;
they would fall upon the fugitives like dew upon the ground, and
utterly destroy them; or, if these had found refuge in some city.
the people should take ropes and draw it into the river, and not
one stone should be left upon another. Such was Hushai's
counsel, and it pleased the deluded prince. Whether he was
somewhat jealous of the vast influence of Ahithophel, and
wished to assert his own independence, or whether he was at
the moment satisfied with the capture of Jerusalem, and desired
to enjoy for a season the sweets of repose and the pleasures of
his high position, for some reason he preferred the last speaker's
advice to that of Ahithophel His followers took the same view.
The sacred historian sees in this the work of an overruling
Providence answering David's prayer (chap xv. 31) "For
the Lord had appointed to defeat the good counsel of Ahithophel, to the intent that the Lord might bring evil upon Absalom"
It was necessary for David's safety that he should be at once
informed of the resolution at which the insurgents had arrived,
and of the plan which had been first proposed. Absalom might
awake to the folly of his present decision, and act upon wiser
advice At any rate the loyal party must be warned to put the
river between itself and the rebels as soon as possible. So
Hushai sent a message to this effect to the high priests, who, in
spite of the strict watch kept over their movements, found
means to forward the intelligence to their sons, Jonathan and
Ahimaaz, with a direction to convey it at once to David. The
young men had remained hidden at Enrogel, the spring, afterwards known as the Fountain of the Virgin, which lies close
under the hill Ophel, south-east of the city. Here they waited
for the expected errand. On receiving their commission they
immediately set out on their journey; but a spy had observed
them, and betrayed them to Absalom, who forthwith sent men
on horseback to effect their capture The youths meantime had
arrived at Bahurim, and, ere the pursuers came up, were safely

hidden in a dry well in the court of a friend's house. The mistress of the house had placed the lid on the well's mouth, spreading over it a cloth covered with corn to dry; and, when the spies made inquiries about the fugitives, she directed them on a wrong track, whence, unsuccessful, they returned to Jerusalem. The young men carried the tidings safely to the king, who forthwith acted on the advice given, and led his company across the Jordan, making his way eventually to Mahanaim, the stronghold where Ishbosheth had formerly established himself, and which might well endure a siege without much fear of the result which Hushai had promised to the vain usurper. The expectation of support which had led David to select the Eastern district as a refuge proved to be well founded. Three Gileadites of high social position, and possessed of ample means, at once ranged themselves on his side, and gave him material assistance. These were Shobi, the brother of the Ammonite king Hanun, to whom David had assigned the property, though not the throne, of his brother, Machir, who had fostered Mephibosheth in his house at Lodebar; and Barzillai of Rogelim, the venerable man for whom David entertained sincere affection. They brought welcome contributions for the support and comfort of the king and his troops—mattresses, household utensils of metal and earthenware, wheat, barley-meal, flour, parched corn, beans, lentils, honey, butter, sheep, and fatted oxen. Such tokens of loyalty in this time of distress awoke a confidence in the royal poet's heart which found expression in the words of Psalm iv. .

> "Answer me when I call, O God of my righteousness;
> Thou hast set me at large when I was in distress,
> Have mercy upon me and hear my prayer . .
> Know that the Lord hath set apart him that is godly for Himself;
> The Lord will hear when I call unto Him . .
> In peace will I both lay me down and sleep,
> For Thou, Lord, alone makest me dwell in safety."

Besides these wealthy citizens of Gilead, a large body of the inhabitants, who had not been seduced into rebellion, joined the king at Mahanaim; and, of the other tribes, many on reflection had seen cause to doubt the expediency and success of the revolution, and, returning to their old allegiance, came and swelled the ranks of the royal army, which thus, in the course of a few weeks, mustered many thousand men.

ABSALOM'S REVOLT.

Meanwhile Absalom had been solemnly anointed king[1] at Jerusalem, and had used his authority to gather all Israel together, collecting a huge, if somewhat unmanageable, army, sufficient, it would seem, by mere force of numbers to crush all opposition. But he had lost his chief counsellor Ahithophel. That crafty and ambitious man, who had his own ends to serve in supporting the usurper's cause, when he saw his advice overruled and his influence shaken, at once concluded that all was lost. In bitter disappointment he hastily left the court, returned to his own city, put his worldly affairs in order, and, like his antitype Judas, deliberately hanged himself. It remained now to appoint a general to command the host. Joab and Abishai were with David; in default of them, Absalom selected one Amasa, who bore the same relation to David as they, being the son of Abigail, Zeruiah's sister. His father was an Ishmaelite, named Ithra or Jether.[2] A well-known and experienced warrior, Amasa, by his relationship to the royal family, added to the confidence with which he was generally regarded, and no better commander-in-chief could have been chosen. Whether, as some have supposed, this man occupied Gilead and besieged David at Mahanaim, cannot be determined, as the accounts that have reached us are abridged and indefinite. It is clear, however, that the siege was raised before the decisive engagement took place, as David was able to choose his own ground, and commenced the attack. Some two or three months had passed in preparations on both sides. At the end of this time Absalom marched from Jerusalem at the head of an imposing force. While all his troops were on foot, he ostentatiously rode a gaily-caparisoned mule, wearing his flowing locks like a Nazirite, though very far from imitating the pure, ascetic life of a devotee. The huge, unwieldy army crossed the Jordan, and made for Mahanaim. While still some miles south of this city, they were met by the opposing force near a locality called the Forest of Ephraim, the name probably recalling an event in the time of the Judges, when the Ephraimites, invading Gilead, suffered a severe defeat at the hands of Jephthah.[3] David's army, number-

[1] 2 Sam. xix. 10.

[2] In 2 Sam. xvii. 25 he is called in the Hebrew "an Israelite" (which is unmeaning), and in some MSS of the Sept., "a Jezreelite" (which is a conjecture). In other Greek texts he is called "an Ishmaelite," which is the reading confirmed by 1 Chron. ii. 17.

[3] See Judges xii. 1 ff. One MS. of the Sept. gives, "in the forest of

ing some twenty thousand men,[1] was divided into three equal battalions under the command respectively of Joab, Abishai, and Ittai. The king himself had desired to head the troops in person, but his generals would not consent to this infringement of the rule made some years before, that the monarch should not risk his life in actual fight; he could keep a reserve in the city, and aid them there should they be driven back. To these representations he was obliged to yield, and he took up his position at the town-gate to review the troops as they marched forth in due order, arranged in their hundreds and thousands. To all the columns and their leaders he gave one special command, showing that he had no fears of the result of the coming battle; his one word was, "Deal gently for my sake with the young man, even with Absalom." Having perfect confidence in the justice of his cause, knowing that the God of Israel would never give final success to the impious rebels who were striving to drive the Lord's anointed from his throne, he looked forward to certain victory, and only begged the chieftains in the hour of triumph to spare the misguided usurper who, in spite of all that had passed, was still so dear to him. It was a richly wooded district where the two armies met in conflict, covered with trees growing in clumps, which impeded the concerted movements of a large force, but materially assisted the desultory attacks of smaller bodies who knew the country, and chose their time for assaulting the enemy while embarrassed by the difficult ground. The undisciplined rabble that Absalom brought into the field were no match for the warriors of David's army, who were not only more experienced, but were fighting by the side of the invincible Gibborim, and emulous of their approval. The result was obvious. The insurgents were routed with great slaughter; many were lost in the neighbouring morasses; and the number that fell was estimated at twenty thousand men. Absalom made no attempt to rally his panic-stricken troops. Seeing the battle lost, he took to flight. No one attended him or guided his movements in this dark hour. Deserted by all who so lately had fawned upon him, he plunged madly into the forest, only eager to escape, and caring little whither his mule bore him so that it was away from the disastrous battle-field. Fate overtook him

Mahanaim," and this reading is adopted by Klostermann. An Ephron in Gilead is mentioned, 1 Macc v 46. There can be no doubt that the battle took place on the east of Jordan. [1] See 2 Sam. xviii. 1–3.

as he fled. Hurrying thus recklessly onward, and endeavouring to avoid a party of the enemy whom he saw in the vicinity, he rode into the thickest part of the wood, and his head, with its mass of hair, becoming entangled in the arms of a huge terebinth tree, while he struggled with his hands to disengage himself, the mule went from under him, and left him hanging between heaven and earth a helpless prisoner. In this condition he was discovered by one of David's soldiers, who forbore to kill him, remembering the king's injunction, but went to Joab with the tidings. No such scruples deterred the general. In Absalom's death he saw an end to the present disturbances and security in the future for himself. If the prince were saved, and in due time occupied the throne, the commander who had opposed his cause and inflicted upon him this severe defeat, could never hope to be received into favour or advanced to high place. In view of his own interests the king's command weighed little with him, so, after chiding the messenger for being so unnecessarily conscientious, he went himself to the spot, and, either with his own hand or by the hands of his attendants, despatched the unfortunate prince. The mutilated body was cast into a pit in the midst of the forest, and over it was raised a huge heap of stones, not like the cairns of northern countries raised to honour a hero, but in token of hatred and abhorrence of a great criminal, whose punishment was such as befitted a rebellious son taken and stoned beyond the walls of his city [1] Such was the end of the career of this unprincipled youth, who had abused the high endowments with which nature had adorned him, and had turned them to his own destruction His miserable fate offered as great a contrast to the promise of early days as did the horrible pile in the melancholy depths of the dark forest to the fair marble monument with its pompous inscription, which, on the death of his three sons, he had reared for a memorial of himself in the King's Dale beneath the walls of Jerusalem.

On the death of Absalom, Joab gave the signal for stopping the pursuit, and allowed the defeated rebels to disperse as they could The news of the victory had to be conveyed to the king, waiting anxiously at the gate of Mahanaim. Ahimaaz, son of Zadok, a notoriously fleet runner, who had already brought David intelligence of the insurgents' movements, offered himself as the bearer of the happy tidings. But Joab was loath to

[1] See Deut. xxi. 21, Josh vii 26, viii 29.

entrust to a personal friend of the king a message which contained in it the painful element of the death of Absalom. The sad intelligence which the envoy would have to communicate would, he knew, affect the bereaved father with the most poignant sorrow, and make him regard with disfavour the bearer ; and Joab, though not a soft-hearted person, was unwilling to place Ahimaaz in this position. Besides this, he was far from easy about his own share in Absalom's death, and feared the youth might make compromising disclosures in the matter. For many reasons it was advisable that the report should be made by a simple official not connected by personal ties with the royal family, and one whom he did not scruple to expose to the possible punishment of a bringer of evil tidings. So Joab called an Ethiopian slave [1] of his own, and bade him run to Mahanaim, and tell the king what he had seen. The man bowed his head in obedience, and set forth, taking his course direct for the city But Ahimaaz was not to be put aside. When the other had departed, he again urged his request ; and though Joab warned him that he was undertaking a thankless office, he at last gained his point, and started on his errand. Not like the slave, who had taken the shortest but most difficult and impeded route, the young priest swerved aside from the direct way, and ran for a time along the level and smooth turf of the Jordan valley, making such good progress that he reached his destination before his competitor. Meantime the aged king sat between the outer and inner gates of the city wall, waiting anxiously for tidings Suddenly the sentinel on the roof of the gate-house proclaimed that he saw a man running alone, and David at once concluded that he brought news. In a few minutes a second runner came in sight , and as there were no signs of others appearing in flight or distress, it was plain that this man was also a messenger. By this time the watchman had recognized the foremost of the two as Ahimaaz, and communicated the fact to the king, who received it as a happy omen. " He is a good man," he said, "and cometh with good tidings" On arriving near the gate, the runner shouted aloud, " All is well," and then, kneeling before the king, he announced that God had given victory to

[1] "Cushi" in 2 Sam xviii should doubtless be rendered "the Cushite " The name is found with the article throughout the chapter except in one place, where it is accidentally omitted.

their cause, and that the rebels were completely defeated. The father's anxiety showed itself here. Before he uttered his gratitude for this announcement he asked after his misguided son's welfare. " Is the young man Absalom safe ? " The answer of Ahimaaz was ambiguous, but calculated to arouse apprehension. "When I was sent," he replied, " I saw a great tumult, but I knew not what it was " The king bade him stand aside while he awaited the arrival of the Cushite. Putting the same question to this messenger, he received a reply which he could interpret only in a disastrous sense. " The enemies of my lord the king, and all that rise up against thee to do thee hurt, be as that young man is " The slave had endeavoured to soften the blow by suggesting that Absalom had deserved his fate, and that his death had relieved the State from a formidable danger ; but such considerations were at that time wasted on that stricken parent's heart. His beloved son was dead ; nothing could alter that lamentable fact ; private sorrow obscured all thought of public concerns ; he could listen to no further details ; the sovereign was lost in the father, the victory over the rebels, the recovery of the kingdom, the prospect of peace, were utterly disregarded in the presence of this crushing calamity. The annalist narrates the incident with touching simplicity . " The king was much moved, and went up to the chamber over the gate, and wept , and as he went, thus he said. ' O my son Absalom, my son, my son Absalom ! would God I had died for thee, O Absalom, my son, my son !'"

The king's grief affected the people, the general rejoicing was suddenly checked by the sight of their monarch's behaviour, and there was much murmuring and discontent at this untoward interruption of the universal jubilation They could not enter into David's feelings, they did not realize the grounds of his poignant sorrow ; they had no sympathy for the forbearance of the father whose love outweighed all considerations of patriotism and policy ; they saw not the misery of having a son cut off in his prime without time for repentance, without a cry for forgiveness from him whom he had so cruelly wronged ; they failed to recognize that David was owning the smart of retributive justice which visited the sins of the fathers upon the children ; and therefore they murmured, and were inclined to disaffection and mutiny Joab was soon made aware of what was going on ; he beheld the people's lowering looks, he saw how they slunk into the city, not like victorious soldiers returning from a successful battle, but rather as a defeated rabble, downcast and disheartened, and though it was a painful, and might be a dangerous, task to approach him whose son he had murdered, yet in the interests of the kingdom he determined to make an attempt to rouse the monarch from his selfish sorrow. He breaks in upon his lamentation, and bluntly puts the position before him. David was endangering his restoration, and losing the goodwill of his subjects; he must show himself to the troops, and return them thanks for their brave efforts: he must not let them suppose that the rebel Absalom's life was in the king's eyes worth more than the safety of his loyal army; unless he altered his conduct, and spoke in grateful and friendly guise to the people, they would desert his cause, and leave him unsupported and desolate. This remonstrance could not be safely neglected. A crisis plainly was at hand; it behoved the king to lay aside personal feelings and attend to public interests. Putting a great restraint on himself, he came forth from his retirement, concealed the bitter grief in his heart, sat in his accustomed seat at the city gate, and as the troops at his command defiled before him, he spoke a few words of thanks and encouragement, which were received with general favour, and had the desired result of keeping the disaffected to their allegiance.

Once aroused from his prostration, David grasped the state of affairs, and took measures to recover his authority. There was no need for immediate action. The Western tribes who had joined in the revolt and anointed Absalom as king had indeed to be reduced or conciliated; but David saw that compulsion was not required. Public opinion was fast veering round; he had but to make use of the movement, and wait for a favourable opportunity, and he might return in peace. Now that the puppet whom they had blindly followed was dead, and his cause hopeless, the Israelites bethought themselves of the merits of the king whom they had displaced; they considered his public services, his skill in war, his wise administration, his amiable character; they began to see the injustice, the ingratitude, and the impolicy of their behaviour; and a desire for his restoration became general. The only portion of the people which held back at this crisis was the tribe of Judah. The others had already sent a deputation to Mahanaim conveying their submission, but David's own tribe had taken no part in the matter. This was a source of great annoyance to the king, who of all things dreaded disunion among his countrymen, and he set himself at once to overcome the disaffection which was thus displaying itself, and to induce Judah to participate in the movement. The late insurrection had not destroyed the tribal organization, and overtures could be made to the elders who held the chief authority, as in more peaceful times. He accordingly sent the two high-priests Zadok and Abiathar to remonstrate against their unnatural conduct in exhibiting such coldness to one who was of their bone and their flesh. And in order to secure the support of the tribe, he forwarded a special message to Amasa, who was now the foremost man among them, condoning his rebellion, and promising to appoint him general in Joab's place. The latter had, as we have seen, incurred his lord's heavy displeasure by acting in wilful disobedience to an express command, and was daily growing in self assertion and independence. David had long wished to free himself from the restraint of this unscrupulous man's influence; and now an opportunity of effecting this deliverance offered itself, and was eagerly seized. Whatever might be the result of this step in the case of Joab himself, who was no contemptible enemy, the policy acted favourably on the minds of the Judæans. They saw that their rebellion was pardoned; they recognized the unusual generosity of their ill-used monarch, and repenting of their disloyalty, with one accord invited him to return. From sullen hostility they passed to intemperate zeal; a solemn deputation was despatched to meet him at the passage of the Jordan; and David left Mahanaim with all his followers, and commenced a triumphal progress to Jerusalem. Arriving on the bank opposite to Gilgal, he found that Judah had provided the means of transport, and made every arrangement for his honour and comfort, without consulting the other tribes or inviting their co-operation. It was too late to remedy the omission, and David was forced to fall in with the present plan, though quite opposed to his grand idea of united action. Among those who put themselves prominently forward at this juncture were Shimei and Ziba. The former, who naturally feared that he would now meet with the punishment which his late atrocious conduct deserved, came cringing to the king, humbly suing for pardon, bringing with him a thousand of his

Benjamite tribesmen, and representing that he was heartily sorry for his crime, and had hurried the first of all the house of Israel to offer homage. Abishai, with rough justice, desired at once to despatch him, but David, at this supreme moment, would not forego the kingly attribute of mercy, and granted the abject suppliant his life. The harsh character of his nephews was especially repugnant to the clement spirit of the son of Jesse, whose magnanimity and superiority to Eastern prejudices were never more strikingly shown than in his treatment of the conquered. "What have I to do with you, ye sons of Zeruiah,' he indignantly exclaims, "that ye should this day be adversaries to me? Shall there any man be put to death this day in Israel? for do not I know that I am this day king over Israel?" Ziba wished by his apparent zeal in the royal cause to be confirmed in the possession of the estate of which by his slanders he had defrauded Mephibosheth. But he was nearly losing all. For the lame prince himself appeared at the Jordan, and showed how treacherously Ziba had dealt with him, taking from him the ass which he intended to ride, and without which he could not accompany the king's train, and then asserting that he stayed behind in the hope of succeeding to the throne , whereas it was his earnest wish to follow David's fortunes, and in token of grief at late events he had not cut his nails, nor dressed his beard, nor washed his clothes, since the sad day when the king left Jerusalem His excuse was plainly truthful as far as it went, but David apparently was not so entirely satisfied of his freedom from tacit complicity in the rebellion, as to restore his possessions to him in their entirety, but directed that they should be equally divided between himself and Ziba. It was a necessary policy to refrain from making an enemy of Ziba, a man of great eminence among the Benjamites, who, as we shall see, were very lukewarm supporters of the present dynasty Mephibosheth, who had no skill in the management of an estate, and was glad to be spared the trouble and care that come with large property, at once replied that Ziba might take all; he wanted nothing for himself now that he had been allowed to witness the happy restoration of the king. Another meeting was of a more agreeable nature. The good old Barzillai, who had so bountifully supplied the royal party with necessaries at Mahanaim, came with his family to convoy the king over Jordan. David would willingly have kept this stanch friend near him, and tried to induce the Gileadite to take up his abode at Court; but Barzillai respectfully declined the invitation; he was too far advanced in years to care for any of the pleasures which a royal palace might offer, and was resolved to die in his own city, and be buried among his own people. The overtures which he refused for himself he gladly accepted for his son Chimham, whom David took with him to Jerusalem, and treated with the utmost consideration. Thus, after a long and affectionate embrace, David and Barzillai parted, never again to meet in this world.

Having crossed the river, David halted at the celebrated Gilgal, which was in the immediate neighbourhood. Here an untoward event occurred, which marred the joy of triumph, and threatened disastrous consequences. Representatives from the ten tribes had arrived at this moment, and were greatly incensed to find that they who had been the first to acknowledge the king had been allowed to take no part in the restoration, while Judah, which had long stood aloof, had assumed the lead in escorting David home, and would reap a rich reward for their selfish zeal in the royal cause. Thus the slumbering jealousy between the two sections of the people was roused to fury. The men of Israel complained that the men of Judah had stolen the king away for interested motives; the latter replied that the king was of their kin, and that this was the cause of their action, and not any expectation of special honour and privileges. But the Israelites retorted that they had ten parts in the kingdom for Judah's two; theirs also was the birthright,[1] and they were fully justified in resenting the contemptuous way in which their co-operation had been disregarded. Judah was not inclined to conciliation, and retaliated with fierce and exasperating words. David could not censure the proceedings of his own tribe, and the quarrel thus begun was augmented into a serious schism. One Sheba, an ambitious and artful Benjamite, saw his opportunity in this state of matters, and raised the standard of revolt. He is called "son of Bichri," which implies that he was of the family of Becher, the son of Benjamin, from which stem Saul also was descended. The transference of the sovereignty from the house of Saul still rankled in the minds of the Benjamites,

[1] 2 Sam. xix. 43. "We have more right in David than ye." The Sept reads, "I am firstborn rather than thou," Josephus ("Ant." vii. 11. 5), "We are older than ye." The assertion would be true of Reuben

and when Sheba blew the trumpet, seditiously proclaiming, "We have no part in David, neither have we inheritance in the son of Jesse," the national cry, "Every man to his tents, O Israel," was followed by a general secession of the northern tribes, who left Judah to escort the king to Jerusalem and withdrew, some in sullen disaffection to their own homes, others in the train of this new pretender.

Arrived at Jerusalem, and once more settled in his palace, David found time to arrange the future life of the ten concubines so dishonourably treated by his unworthy son. They were placed in confinement in a separate dwelling, ineligible for marriage, and condemned to joyless widowhood. Then he turned his attention to more important affairs. The movement of Sheba was gathering strength and must be at once checked, if it was not to produce more disastrous effects than the revolt of Absalom. Amasa, therefore, who had now superseded Joab as commander-in-chief, was commissioned to assemble within three days the levies of Judah, and to present himself at the end of that time for final orders. The interval passed without his appearing; either he was dilatory in his movements, or the people were indisposed for a new military expedition, or unwilling to accept him as leader; and David, fearing that the insurrection might reach formidable dimensions, as a measure of precaution and not with any idea of displacing Amasa, directed Abishai[1] to take the body-guard, and Gibborim, and any troops present at Jerusalem, and pursue Sheba at once, lest he should get possession of some strong fortress and be in a position to defy the power arrayed against him. The king entrusts the expedition to Abishai, as he had by no means restored Joab to favour and declined all dealings with him. But the two brothers understood one another; and Joab, with a select body of his own troops, accompanied the party nominally as a volunteer, but ready to exercise the office of commander as occasion might allow. The little army had marched no further than Gibeon, a few miles north of Jerusalem, when they were met by Amasa at the head of the levies which he had collected. The meeting, we are told, took place by a certain great stone, which, from the bloody event there occurring, was rendered

[1] There is no need to read "Joab" for "Abishai" in 2 Sam. xx 6, as is done in the Syriac and in Josephus, "Ant" vii 11 6 David's conduct is quite intelligible, and no alteration of the text is required.

ever memorable. Joab, who was dressed in his long military cloak, with his girdle outside in which he wore a short sword, advanced towards his cousin in friendly fashion. As he hurried forward, his sword apparently by accident fell from the scabbard Picking it up with his left hand, he went on, and took hold of Amasa's beard with his right, as the custom was among friends, to kiss him on the cheek. Amasa, suspecting no treachery, and thrown off his guard, received a deadly thrust from his unscrupulous relation, who thus took the earliest opportunity to rid himself of a dangerous rival, following the atrocious precedent which he had set in the parallel case of Abner. The hapless Amasa was left on the road side wallowing in his gore; but finding that the troops were dismayed at the murder of their leader and hesitated what to do, one of Joab's officers removed the corpse from sight, and calling on all those who wished to serve with Joab and to side with David, to follow Joab at once, persuaded the troops to accept their old commander. The pursuit was then commenced in earnest. Meantime Sheba, who had but few forces and possessed no military talents to compensate for lack of strength, was driven from station after station, making a stand nowhere, and retreating ever northwards, till at length he took refuge in Abel Bethmaachah, a strong town some miles north of the Lake Merom, where some of the inhabitants of the Benjamite city of Beeroth had founded a colony of Berites.[1] The dwellers in this place, who knew little of the late occurrences in the distant south, compassionately received the fugitive, though by no means identifying themselves with his cause or having any settled animosity against David. Joab soon arrived before the city, and commenced operations by raising a mound of earth from which the walls could be battered and the defenders harassed, and would soon have reduced the place, had not a wise woman called for a parley and remonstrated against this destruction of "a city and mother in Israel," that is, a metropolis with many dependent villages, an important portion of the Lord's inheritance. Joab declared that he had no desire to destroy this old and loyal city, he was in pursuit of the rebel Sheba, and that if he were delivered up, he would at once raise the siege. The woman promised that this should be done, and the citizens being easily persuaded to save themselves at Sheba's

[1] 2 Sam. xx. 14

expense, the wretched traitor was decapitated, and his head thrown over the wall to the besiegers. Upon this, Joab at once withdrew his troops, and the rebellion being completely quelled, he returned in triumph to Jerusalem. He had proved himself indispensable in military affairs, and in spite of his insubordination and his crimes, David felt himself obliged to confirm him in his supreme command. It was a humiliating position for the king thus to truckle to his own wicked servant; but he must have regarded it as a phase of the punishment of his sin, and as a constant memorial of the darkest hour of his life which it was good to keep near him. At the same time, it must be observed, that Joab was not only the most influential subject in the whole state, but that with all his ferocity and self-will, he had his lord's interests always at heart, and had proved himself a most useful servant. Doubtless, it was part of the discipline needed for David's perfection that constrained him to tolerate the presence and tyranny of Joab, but they were a grievous burden to him, and clouded all his happiness.

CHAPTER XI.

THE CENSUS.

Administration of the kingdom—The census ordered; its guilt; its progress and completion—Gad's message to David—Three days' pestilence, stayed at Jerusalem—Purchase of Araunah's threshing-floor on Moriah —An altar raised there

THE suppression of the two rebellions left the country at peace, and permitted David to reorganize the constitution, and arrange the executive in a more complete fashion than had been possible in times of war and commotion. Foreign nations had not been able to take advantage of Israel's internal troubles in order to invade her territories The insurrections had occupied so short a period that enemies had scarcely received news of the disturbances ere they were ended. Whatever painful consequences the revolts had left on the king's reputation and position, they had served to strengthen his government and to lead the people to trust to him as ruler, if they had lost some of their respect for him as a man. Accordingly, the remaining years of his life, with one remarkable interruption, were passed in peace and prosperity. The chronicler (2 Sam. xx) gives a list of the chief officers at this epoch, which, compared with the previous catalogue (chap. viii), shows that some changes were made both in persons and offices. But we need not linger on this, save to remark that no mention is now made of the king's sons as chief rulers, late experiences having proved the danger of entrusting power to such hands, and that the subjugation of foreign states had rendered a collector necessary, who is said to be "over the tribute."

The kingdom of Israel had now arrived at a high pitch of

perfection; its organization was complete, its army numerous, well commanded, and quite equal to coping with the troops of the great powers on the Nile and Euphrates; foreign peoples respected it and sought its alliance; and David, if regarded merely as an Eastern potentate, might well be pardoned for feeling elated at the happy progress of his people, and their enrolment among the great nations of the earth. This very prosperity led to the sin which darkened the close of his life, and brought a heavy calamity upon his country. The offence consisted in taking a census of the people. That this was a grievous sin is proved by the terms in which the account is introduced: "The anger of the Lord was kindled against Israel, and He moved David against them to say, Go, number Israel and Judah;" or, according to the Chronicler. "Satan (*or*, an adversary) stood up against Israel, and moved David to number Israel"[1] Its sinfulness is concluded also from Joab's repugnance to undertake the business, from David's own confession, and from the punishment with which it was visited The special guilt of the transaction has been greatly debated. Wellhausen and his school see nothing in the matter, but the taking of a census for military purposes, which happened to be followed by a terrible plague that was regarded by the superstitious people as a punishment of the king's pride. The whole chapter in these critics' eyes is legendary, and they allow no moral connection between the census and the plague. We are content to take the religious view, and, putting ourselves in David's place, consider wherein the guilt of his action consisted. The numbering of the people was not in itself sinful. Moses himself had twice held such an inspection; and though it was ordained that atonement money was to be taken from all who were numbered, this was only a temporary enactment, and its omission could not be considered in the light of a heavy transgression.[2] Some, acquitting David of a mere childish curiosity to know the number of his subjects, have deemed that he took the measure in order to see what amount of taxation, additional or otherwise, the people could bear, and thus increase his own treasure, a measure which would contravene the enactment that forbade the ruler to multiply to himself gold and silver.[3]

[1] 2 Sam xxiv. 1, 1 Chron xxi 1.
[2] Exod xxx 12 ff, see Numb 1, xxvi., Josephus, "Ant." vii. 13. 1.
[3] Deut. xvii. 17.

But there are absolutely no grounds for the supposition, and it is plain from the returns that the inquiry had a military reference. Nor was it merely in a proud, self-glorifying spirit that he counted his numbers, relying on the arm of flesh, and estimating his power not by the Divine favour and support which he enjoyed, but by the material resources of his kingdom Such a view of national prosperity would have contradicted the whole tenour of his life, which was chiefly remarkable for a perfect reliance on God's support and faith in His leading. Nor if the fault was his alone can one understand the justice of the penalty falling so heavily upon his subjects. It was, we must conclude, an ambition wholly alien from the spirit of a theocratic king which constituted the evil in this transaction. David looked around, and saw other empires, with natural resources not greater than his own, become mighty and celebrated by foreign conquests, why should Israel not be as one of these world-powers? Why should she not play a more important part in the earth, and assume a position among the chief of nations? Schemes of conquest floated before his imagination; he might make the name of David feared in distant lands, and by the victories which he won hand down his fame to future generations It was a grand dream, but how opposed to the very idea of the chosen people! They had been placed in Canaan that they might be secluded from contact with other nations, they were debarred from the use of chariots and horses that they might not be tempted to undertake distant expeditions; they had been taught to rely not on numbers, or weapons, or skill, but on the God of the armies of Israel, who could save by many or by few. They were to go forth in war, not at the promptings of ambition or lust of power, but at the voice of the prophet, at Divine direction. And the children of Israel should be multiplied as the stars of heaven only if they served the Lord and did His will; otherwise they would be cut off. The fault of David was analogous to that of his countrymen in later days, when they obstinately looked for a great temporal prince in the Messiah, expecting a victorious earthly conqueror, and refusing to recognize Him who was to come in the lowly Jesus Therefore at this time punishment was inflicted to recall Israel to its duty, and to check in the most decided manner the worldly and profane spirit which was eating away the true life of the theocratic people. God allowed the king to be tempted to this transgression that He might thereby convey a salutary lesson, and by a sharp infliction teach His vicegerent that he must live for God and not for himself.

Having determined on the census, David entrusted its execution to Joab and other chiefs, directing them to go through all the tribes from Dan to Beersheba, and to take the number of the people. The commission did not please the councillors, and Joab as their mouthpiece remonstrated with David against the measure. They may have been affected with the vulgar notion that a keen investigation into the amount of one's possessions always resulted in loss and disaster. Whatever may have been the laxity of Joab's principles, and the keenness of sight for his own interests, he was a true patriot at heart, and looked to the good of his country. His prudence and sagacity were seldom at fault, and in trying to dissuade David from his purpose he was animated by motives of general expediency. The numbering was not necessary and would answer no good purpose, nay, it might lead to renewed murmuring and discontent; the king's purpose was not religious, but dictated by an ambition which was plainly contrary to God's will; the people were all his subjects, and the Lord could increase them at His pleasure, what use was this vain display? No good would come of it, and his most trusty friends were opposed to the plan. "Why then doth my lord the king delight in this thing?" Remonstrance was vain; David was not to be dissuaded, and the enumerators set forth on their expedition, carrying out the design with great regularity and precision, and taking a list of all males of military age. They commenced their task on the east of Jordan, in the tribe of Gad, at Aroer, a place now called Aireh, situated on the right bank of the Wady Shaib between Beth-Nimrah and Ramoth Gilead. Thence they proceeded northwards to Gilead and the foot of Mount Hermon, thence to Dan, the most northern city of the Israelites. Fetching a compass, they next turned westward to Sidon and down the coast to Tyre, which cities were leagued with Israel for military purposes, visited the towns in Naphtali, Zebulun, and Issachar, the district called Galilee in later days, and numbered the central tribes and those on the south as far as Beersheba, where their labours were brought to a close. The census had taken nearly ten months to execute, and was even now not complete, the tribe of Levi and that of Benjamin being excluded from the

THE CENSUS.

computation, unless the latter is counted in the population of Jerusalem. It seems that the sudden outbreak of pestilence put an end to the business, as it also prevented the numbers from being accurately counted, and entered in the royal archives.[1] Hence arises a discrepancy in the accounts gathered from oral tradition and preserved respectively in the Books of Samuel and Chronicles, the former estimating the fighting men of Israel at 800,000, and those of Judah at 500,000, the latter assigning 1,110,000 to Israel, and only 470,000 to Judah. If these numbers are even fairly correct, the population of the country must be reckoned to have amounted at this time to six or seven millions, and David might have reason to be proud of his people's progress, and to appreciate highly the military resources which lay in his power.

But there was sin in this matter, and in some way David before the census was finished became deeply conscious of his fault. We know not what means God had taken to awake his slumbering conscience. He seems to have seen the folly and iniquity of his conduct certainly without a Nathan's parable this time. When the results of the census, so far as it had gone, were brought before him, he reflected within himself on the motives which had led to the undertaking and the use which he had thought to make of it; he compared his worldly ambition with the theocratic idea which had hitherto controlled his conduct; he weighed his action in the balance of religion, and his heart smote him; in profound humiliation he confesses his sin: "I have sinned greatly in that I have done," he says; "and now, I beseech Thee, O Lord, take away the iniquity of Thy servant; for I have done very foolishly." Yes, God would pardon his transgression; but he must first suffer for it. As the shadow follows the substance, so punishment follows sin; guilt may be removed, the penalty must be paid. After a night of poignant sorrow, his old friend, the prophet Gad, comes to him with a stern message of chastisement, offering him a choice of three evils, viz., three years of famine,[2] three months' sub-

[1] 1 Chron. xxvii. 23 f.
[2] The Hebrew text of 2 Sam. xxiv. 13 gives "seven years," but in 1 Chron. xxi. 12 it is "three years," and this is the reading of the Greek in both passages, and seems best to harmonize with the context, though it is possible that the original "seven" has been altered to "three" on this account.

jugation at enemies' hands, or three days of pestilence. Two of these scourges he had already experienced ; he had fled for three or more months before Absalom ; he had suffered three years of famine in retribution for the slaughter of the Gibeonites ; what should he now choose ? " I am in a great strait," he answers ; then his faith in God's care decides the question : " Let us fall now into the hand of the Lord : for His mercies are great ; and let me not fall into the hand of man." He chose not war, for he knew the cruelties and hardships inflicted therein by man on man, and he shuddered now, under his better feelings, to think whither his ambition unchecked might have led. He chose not famine, for that would have fallen upon his people, while he himself would have been spared the infliction ; and he either selected the pestilence as the punishment, in which his danger was as great as that of the lowest of his subjects, or he left the choice between famine or plague, the special stroke of God, to the Lord Himself. And God sent the pestilence. With unexampled virulence, such as proved it to be a supernatural visitation, it fell upon the land ; and though it did not continue for the whole of the three days,[1] yet in the short time of its prevalence seventy thousand died. Thus was rebuked pride of power, trust in the arm of flesh, ambitious dreaming. He who could make Israel as the sand on the shore for multitude, could at a blow bring its number down, could change the voice of exultation to the cry of despair, could sap the power of the mightiest nation and turn its strength into weakness. The plague which had marched through the country ravaging far and wide, had hitherto spared Jerusalem : but now it approached the capital, and to David's eye was revealed a wonderful sight. As in fearful consternation he awaited the inevitable stroke, he saw in the heavens an awful angel hovering over the city, with a sword drawn in his hand as in the act of striking. And beholding the vision, David lifted up his voice and cried aloud : " Lo, I have sinned, and I have done perversely , but these sheep what have they done ? Let thine hand, I pray thee, be against me and against

---

[1] The words in 2 Sam xxiv 15 rendered, " even unto the time appointed," are unique and variously explained The end of the third day can scarcely be meant, as, according to ver. 16, the Lord repented of the evil and stayed the plague earlier It seems best to take the expression, as Jerome advises, as meaning the time of the evening sacrifice.

my father's house, and not on thy people that they should be plagued." Thus in his humiliation cries the king, taking all the blame on his own shoulders. But truly the people shared the guilt. Their late rebellion was a grievous crime; they had been too readily seduced from the path of duty; in their prosperity they had forgotten God, and doubtless shared in their monarch's ambitious projects and worldly pride. Thus they were deservedly rebuked. But in the midst of wrath God remembers mercy; He stays the destroying angel's hand, and suffers him not to smite the holy city. As a thousand years before an angel on Mount Moriah withheld the hand of Abraham when the knife was raised to slay his son, so in this same spot David saw the angel disarmed and the victim people saved. For it was at the threshing-floor of Araunah on the hill of Moriah that the heavenly visitant appeared. This place was outside the city on the eminence that rises on the east, separated from Zion and the city of David by the Tyropœon Valley, at that time some hundred feet deep, though now hardly to be distinguished from the neighbouring surface. The owner Araunah, or Ornan, as he is called in Chronicles, was a Jebusite chieftain who had been permitted to remain when the stronghold was taken. Some say that he had been king of Jerusalem, at any rate he was a man of ample means, and, if not a proselyte, well acquainted with the Hebrew religion, and a personal friend of David. And now Gad was sent to David with another message. He was bidden to order David to raise an altar on the spot where the angel had been seen, and to offer sacrifices there. David with his attendants immediately sets forth to execute the Divine command. It was now wheat-harvest, when the summer temperature made the plague most especially virulent, and Araunah was engaged in threshing when the king approached. On the Jebusite inquiring the reason of this royal visit, David informed him that he had come to buy the threshing floor, that thereon he might build an altar of propitiation. Araunah at once with the generosity of a noble heart offers to give him as a present not only the floor, but the oxen with which he was treading out the corn, and the implements also, that no time might be lost in providing victims and fuel for the intended sacrifice. But David, enunciating a great principle, that one should not serve God with that which costs one nothing, will not take the liberal offer, but purchases land, beasts, and tools at a fair price. An altar of earth was soon raised, the appointed sacrifices were made, and consumed by heaven-sent fire; the Lord was entreated for the land, and the pestilence ceased its ravages as suddenly and mysteriously as it had broken out, thus showing its supernatural character, and constraining men to look behind secondary causes, and see the moral bearing of such visitations. The sanctity affixed to this locality by this transaction, added to the ancestral respect paid to it for Abraham's sake, pointed it out as the most appropriate site for the worship of the people when the Temple came to be built.

CHAPTER XII.

CLOSING YEARS.

Quiet times—Preparations for building the Temple—David's declining health, last song—Adonijah's conspiracy, supported by Joab and Abiathar—Conspirators at Enrogel, proclaim Adonijah king—News brought to David—He has Solomon proclaimed king, anointed, and enthroned—The conspirators disperse—Adonijah spared—David's last injunction to Solomon respecting religion—Advice concerning Joab and Shimei—Care of Barzillai—Plans and details of the Temple—David's last public address—Solomon's second anointing—David's death, funeral, tomb.

WE have arrived at the closing years of David's life. The evening of his days set in peace; the storm, the tempest, the external tumult, the fiery passion, were calmed; in the stillness of a placid old age he was sinking to his rest. Of the acts of these latter days we have but scanty notice. There was indeed no stirring event to chronicle. The people had learned to trust their ruler. They had seen that deviation from ordained paths brought signal punishment; that their safety and prosperity depended upon strict adherence to theocratic principles; and they were content to await patiently any progress or development that might be forthcoming, and not to forestall events or to introduce improvements for which the times were not ripe. No foreign wars disturbed the peace of this period, and David could turn his attention to domestic matters, perfect the machinery of his government, and correct evils which had grown up unchecked amid the crash and jar of great occurrences. One of the chief points to which he directed his attention during these last ten years of his life, was the collection of materials for the erection of the Temple which his son was to build. In this he was largely assisted by the good will of his subjects, whose religious impulses had been strengthened by late circumstances, and who had learned to take warm nterest in the centralization of Divine worship at Jerusalem with its orderly ritual, its service of song to which their king so largely contributed, and its stately array of ministers who, when not engaged in the special duties of their office, carried the knowledge of the Lord into the remotest districts of the land. The chronicler[1] gives a full account of the preparations made for the House of God, which were so ample and complete that Solomon was able in the first year of his reign to commence the execution of the great design. The contemporary annals in the Books of Samuel and Kings indeed are silent concerning this large accumulation of materials, but they give evidence for the existence of such treasures, and confirm the probability of the details given. The king's own resources were extensive, comprising large agricultural estates, vineyards, olive and fig orchards, flocks and herds, then there were the annual tributes from subject nations as well as the taxes of countrymen; there was likewise the spoil taken in war. Also free-will offerings were largely made by the wealthy among the people. From these and such-like sources David was enabled to provide the enormous sum of 100,000 talents of gold, and 1,000,000 talents of silver. Besides this amount of the precious metals he collected immense stores of copper, iron, cedar, and other wood, marbles and precious stones, and engaged stone-masons and artificers of every kind, both native and foreign, to prepare these materials for their future employment. Still further, from the accumulations of his own private fortune he dedicated to the same purpose 3,000 talents of gold, and 7,000 of silver If we reckon the talent of gold as worth £5,000 and that of silver at £350, the amount of the whole contributions seems to our modern notions incredible, though the commentators remind us that Pliny[2] credits Cyrus with having gathered in the course of his Asiatic wars 34,000 pounds of gold, and 500,000 talents of silver.

We have come to the fortieth year of David's reign and the seventieth year of his life. The infirmities of age had crept upon him and enfeebled his body, though his mental vigour was

[1] 1 Chron. xxviii , xxix, [2] "Nat Hist." xxxii 15.

CLOSING YEARS. 195

still unimpaired, and the song of faith and praise still sounded from his aged lips. Many men, warriors and statesmen, are vigorous and active at his age. But David's life had been abnormally trying; both body and spirit had passed through extraordinary labours; the hardships of the early days of exile, the military toils of later years, and the terrible mental conflicts which he had experienced, affected his bodily constitution, and during the last months of his earthly existence he was confined to his couch. The Jews indeed at this time seem to have been not a long-lived race. No Jewish monarch after David, as far as we know, excepting Solomon and Manasseh, exceeded the age of sixty years.[1] David was so prematurely exhausted that he could not be kept warm, and his friends and physicians consulted how best to nurse him under these circumstances. In accordance with the medical science of those days they provided him with a young maiden to act as companion and nurse, one Abishag of Shunem in Galilee, whom subsequent events raised to some notoriety This girl cherished the old man in her bosom, and with her strong vitality restored warmth to his decaying frame, and gave him strength to execute the task that still remained for him to do Before, however, we relate the closing scenes of this eventful life, we must just refer to what are called "the last words of David," the dying song of "the man who was raised up on high, and anointed by the Lord to be the sweet psalmist of Israel"[2] The words of this beautiful poem have already been given,[3] and they are to be remarked because they have a bearing far beyond the actual condition of things to which they primarily refer. As his end approached, the vision of a great future grew clearer; amid disappointments and failings he comforts himself with Messianic promises; "he pictures the righteous God-fearing ruler shining forth like the dawn and springing up like the tender grass after a shower. He expresses his confidence in the firm, sure, and everlasting covenant of God, that He will cause all His salvation and delight to spring up in due time, and that He will utterly destroy all the wicked adversaries"[4]

Though David had long ago determined to appoint as his successor Solomon, the son of his beloved wife, Bathsheba, no public announcement of this selection had been made, and the

[1] "Speak. Comm " on 1 Kings 1 1.   [2] 2 Sam xxiii 1–7
[3] See above, Chap VII p 119 f.   [4] Briggs, "Mess Proph " 132.

eldest surviving son, Adonijah, thought himself justified in assuming royal airs and acting as the future occupant of a throne about to be vacated. The mother of this prince was Haggith, and as he was born during his father's reign at Hebron, he must have been at this time about thirty-five years old. His personal appearance was strikingly similar to that of the hapless Absalom, but he was not his equal in ability or capable of maintaining a settled purpose against contending circumstances. He had been indulged all his life, and suffered little restraint at his parents' hands, so that he had grown up proud and wilful, and prone to gratify his wishes unchecked by any higher considerations. Taking advantage of his father's weakened condition, which, as he thought, incapacitated him for government, or would prevent any serious opposition to his pretentions, Adonijah gathered a party round him, set up, like his brother, a quasi-royal state, with chariots, horses, and running footmen, and prepared to make a public demonstration of his claims. He was joined by Joab and Abiathar the priest. The defection of these two persons is very remarkable. Doubtless the designation of Solomon was more or less known at Court, David having probably imparted it to some of his trusty councillors when the will of God concerning this son was made known to him,[1] and Joab may have thought this to have been unfair to the elder born, or he may have seen that in the character of Adonijah which appealed to his sympathies, and promised more to his ambition than he could expect from the man of peace. But he had long been estranged from his old master; added years had only widened the interval between them, and he saw in this revolution an escape from an irksome restraint, and a new field for restless self-interest. Abiathar's desertion of his old friend is still harder to understand. The son of that Ahimelech who had perished in the massacre at Nob, he had proved his devotion to David's cause through all the latter's chequered career, attended him in his outlaw life, served him as priest at Hebron, and later at Jerusalem, proposed to accompany him in his flight from Absalom and was with difficulty induced to forego his purpose, and had always been one of his most trusted counsellors and companions. Some have thought that Adonijah was generally looked upon as the heir to the throne, and that the conspiracy to confer the succession on Solomon was contrived

[1] 2 Sam. xii 24 f , 1 Chron xxii 8 ff

by Benaiah and Zadok. But the record that has reached us conveys quite another impression ; and, as far as we know, there was at this time no legal prescription concerning the right of inheritance, so that the king might designate as his successor whomsoever he willed The only plausible solution of Abiathar's defection is derived from the idea that it sprung from jealousy of Zadok, who, as being the descendant of the elder line of Eleazar, was somewhat unduly favoured by David. In support of this conjecture we may observe that whenever the two priests are mentioned together Zadok is always put first. A sudden step taken by Adonijah, or forced upon him by his partisans, brought matters to a crisis. Misconceiving the public feeling, and deeming his position much stronger than it was, he invited his adherents, including in the invitation all his brethren except Solomon, to meet him at a solemn banquet in the neighbourhood of Jerusalem for the purpose avowed or implied of proclaiming him king. The spot chosen for this demonstration was at the spring Rogel, south-east of Jerusalem, by the stone of Zoheleth, which is probably the cliff Zahweileh on the east side of the valley of the Kidron opposite the Pool of Siloam which derives its supply of water from Enrogel (The Fountain of the Virgin). At the sacrificial feast here celebrated Adonijah was proclaimed king, and matters seemed tending to secure his success. But though the commander-in-chief and other military officers favoured the usurper, the stanch Benaiah with the veteran body-guard remained true to his allegiance, and was well fitted to cope with the incipient rebellion. The great prophet Nathan also was Solomon's firmest supporter, as he had from the first favoured his succession and been privy to, or inspired David's private designation of this son to the throne. Hearing of the gathering and the transactions at Enrogel, without delay he sent Bathsheba to David to remind him of his promise to nominate her son Solomon as his successor, and to acquaint him with Adonijah's proceedings. During her interview with the sick monarch Nathan himself came in, telling the same tale and urging the king to take some decided step by which the present difficulty might be settled once for all. David immediately roused himself to meet the emergency, exhibiting a promptness and decision for which the conspirators had not given him credit. The call of duty, the sight of factious opposition, excited the old hero's soul, and with an emphatic oath, "As the Lord liveth, who hath redeemed my soul out of all adversity," he swore that Solomon should be enthroned on that very day. Zadok, Benaiah, and Nathan were summoned to his bed-chamber, and commissioned to execute his orders, which were to this effect. They were to take Solomon, set him on his own royal mule which he had always ridden on public occasions, conduct him to Gihon[1] (a place on the north of the city, and therefore distant enough from Enrogel to prevent any danger of collision with the opposite party), and there proclaim him king. All was done as David commanded. The young prince was escorted by Benaiah and the faithful body-guard to Gihon, and there he was solemnly anointed by the priest and prophet, with the holy oil preserved in the tabernacle, and amid the blast of trumpets and the acclamations of the assembled multitude proclaimed king. Conducted with much pomp and rejoicing back to Jerusalem after the ceremony, he was seated on his father's throne, and publicly recognized as monarch in David's place, though the latter retained the dignity of the crown till his death It was a politic measure to ordain that the ceremony inaugurating the young ruler should be performed outside Jerusalem. The procession that marched from thence to the city, with the three great chiefs heading it, and which was composed of the tried veterans of David's army, easily affected the minds of the people , they flocked around with cries of "God save King Solomon," playing, and dancing, and shouting till the earth rang again All the chief officers assembled in the palace to congratulate the old king on this happy consummation and to pray for God's blessing on the young monarch. David himself fell on his knees, and thanked the Lord who had given him a worthy successor, and vouchsafed to let his aged eyes behold him seated in his place.

Meantime the noise of the tumult in the city and the acclamations of the people reached the ears of Adonijah and his

[1] Gihon is identified with Siloam by some modern authorities and by the Targum of Jonathan and the Syriac Version , but it is highly improbable that David should have directed Solomon to be anointed king at the very place of the rival assembly, thus infallibly provoking a contest between the opposing parties No hint of any such outbreak is given. Most probably there was made in after-years an underground aqueduct between Gihon and Siloam, which led to the identification of the two Comp 2 Chron xxxii 30 , xxxvii 14 The "Speaker's Commentary" suggests that Gihon was the ancient name of the Tyropœon valley

fellow conspirators at Enrogel. Joab was seriously disturbed. What did this commotion portend? Was the uproar favourable to their enterprise or not? While such speculations were rife, suddenly the guests see Jonathan, son of Abiathar, hastening towards them. Knowing that he was a friend, Adonijah at once concluded that he brought good tidings. He was quickly undeceived, and when the true state of affairs was disclosed, and David's energetic action was understood, no attempt at resistance was made, not a blow was struck, the conspirators in abject fear dispersed, each one trying to save himself as best he could. Adonijah himself fled for refuge to the altar raised by his father on Moriah, trusting that the sacredness of the spot would shield him from the consequences of his treason. Here clinging to the horns of the altar in trembling apprehension he waited his fate. Though this use of sanctuary was no part of the law, it was recognized practically,[1] and Adonijah would not be torn from his hold till Solomon promised him his life. This the new king, who, like his father, was loath to follow Eastern customs by inaugurating his rule with bloodshed, granted on condition of his proving himself a worthy man, and Adonijah came and prostrated himself before his royal brother, a submission which was imitated by the other princes who had sided with him in the insurrection.

Shortly after these events David felt his end approaching, and sending for his son Solomon, he proceeded to give him some last instructions and to take leave of him. The youth could not have been more than nineteen or twenty years old on his accession, and the counsel of his father must have been of great value to his inexperience. Recalling by his expressions the Divine address to Joshua, David enjoined upon him strict obedience to the laws, moral, ceremonial, and civil, of the Mosaic code upon due observance of which depended the continuance of God's favour and the preservation of the dynasty. And thus the old man spake: "I go the way of all the earth; be thou strong, therefore, and show thyself a man; and keep the charge of the Lord thy God, to walk in His ways, to keep His statutes and His commandments and His judgments and His testimonies, according to that which is written in the law of Moses, that thou mayest prosper in all that thou doest, and whithersoever thou turnest thyself, that the Lord

[1] Exod. xxi. 14.

may establish His word which He spake concerning me, saying, If thy children take heed to their way, to walk before Me in truth, with all their heart and with all their soul, there shall not fail thee a man on the throne of Israel." No better advice could be given or more befitting a ruler of the theocracy. It was in accordance with the words which he had sung in earlier years (Psa. i):

> "Blessed is the man that walketh not in the counsel of the wicked,
> Nor standeth in the way of sinners,
> Nor sitteth in the seat of the scornful.
> But his delight is in the law of the Lord,
> And in His law doth he meditate day and night."

From these high and noble thoughts David then turned to practical matters, instructing his youthful successor how to consolidate his government and remove some of the dangerous elements which might threaten its dissolution. Among the latter he called special attention to Joab and Shimei. The former, who had taken sanctuary at the altar in Gibeon, had not only forfeited his life by his prominent share in Adonijah's conspiracy, but had twice deserved the penalty of death for the treacherous murders of Abner and Amasa, though on those occasions circumstances had combined to save him from receiving the proper reward of his wickedness. This bloodshed still unatoned called for vengeance, and no righteous ruler, when he had the power, could refrain from wiping this pollution from the land. Looking back on the events of his reign, and regarding them with the clear unbiassed judgment of a dying man, David saw that Joab's influence and ability, governed by no respect for religion or honour, would be a source of continual peril to the throne; therefore he felt himself justified in saying solemnly to his son: "Do according to thy wisdom, and let not his hoar head go down to the grave in peace." It was not in satisfaction of private rancour that this stern injunction was given, nor need we credit David with indulging personal animosity in procuring at another's hands that punishment for an offender which he himself had been unable to inflict. There were reasons enough, religious and political, for the measure; and though to our Christian notions a death-bed should be a scene of forgiveness and reconciliation, yet there are circumstances which sink the individual in the member of the community, when private feeling and sentiment must bow before the public weal. Had David been actuated by personal resentment, he would naturally have put forward Joab's crime in slaying Absalom as a reason for harsh treatment of the offender, but he takes his stand on public grounds, and in his point of view gives advice both wise and just. Similar reasons led to a counsel concerning another man, Shimei the Benjamite, who had endeavoured to atone for his insulting behaviour by abject submission. David had pardoned him at the moment, promising that he should not be visited with death at that time; but his crime against the majesty of the Lord's anointed, his treason, his turbulent disposition, demanded punishment. Speaking as a king who was bound to execute the Law of God, David could only direct his successor to "hold him not guiltless, but to bring his head to the grave with blood." The pardon which a monarch granted to an offender expired with the death of the promiser, and did not bind his successor; so that the fate of this malefactor lay entirely with Solomon. While David gave this stern advice concerning Joab and Shimei, he recognized the fact that their treatment was uncontrolled by any previous engagement, and enjoined his son to use his own wisdom in disposing of them. Their subsequent fate is told in the history of Solomon's reign.

If David was stern in giving these injunctions concerning enemies, he was not in his last moments forgetful of his friends. The loyal assistance rendered by Barzillai in the moment of greatest need lived warmly in his remembrance, and he commended to the care of his successor the family of the old man who was probably by this time deceased. According to Oriental custom they were to eat at the king's table, and thus not only be provided for in a material sense, but displayed to all the people as friends whom the king delighted to honour. There was still one communication to be made ere he was called away. That great object of desire, that project for the execution of which he had made such extensive preparations, had to be so imparted to his son, that without distraction or difficulty he might carry it to completion. With mental powers unimpaired by failing bodily health, he acquainted Solomon with all the details of the Temple which he was to erect. Nothing was forgotten. Such rude plans as the times permitted were exhibited and explained. The buildings, chambers, courts, furniture, utensils, implements, for the future Temple were all sketched out, the patterns of them having been furnished (as those of the tabernacle to Moses) by direct inspiration from God.[1] He had written down these instructions at various times when the hand of the Lord was upon him, and now at the supreme moment delivered them to his successor with a few solemn words: "Thou, Solomon my son, know thou the God of thy father, and serve Him with a perfect heart and with a willing mind; for the Lord searcheth all hearts, and understandeth all the imaginations of the thoughts; if thou seek Him, He will be found of thee, but if thou forsake Him, He will cast thee off for ever. Take heed now; for the Lord hath chosen thee to build an house for the sanctuary . be strong, and do it."

Besides giving private instructions to his son on his duties and responsibilities as a theocratical king, David desired to have him formally acknowledged as his successor. The people indeed at Jerusalem and its neighbourhood had received the new prince with every sign of joy and content, but in the face of the late opposition, and with the knowledge of the jealousies which existed among the tribes, the old king determined on a step which nothing but his great zeal and an overpowering sense of duty enabled him to execute. Round his dying bed he convoked an assembly of the principal men of the country; the heads of tribes, the leaders of the army, the chiefs of the various departments, the veterans who had served him so well in all his trials, together with his own children and attendants —a representative congress whose doings the rest of the nation would certainly confirm and sanction with full approval. Rising from his sick couch with laborious effort he addressed the assembly, calling upon them as his brethren and his people to listen to his last words.[2] He had two subjects on which to speak. First, he reminded them that Jehovah had chosen the tribe of Judah to rule the land, and from that tribe had selected him to hold the place of king; and now that he was about to go the way of all flesh, it was equally God's choice that his son Solomon should sit upon the throne, and that the crown should remain in his descendants, if they were obedient to the Law of God. And secondly, he unfolded his plans for the construction

[1] 1 Chron xxviii 11 ff [2] 1 Chron. xxviii 2 ff

of the Temple, and solemnly adjured the assembled chiefs to assist his son in the accomplishment of this long-cherished project, which had been specially sanctioned by the Lord. All went as he wished. The chiefs willingly and gladly paid homage to the new monarch, and undertook to assist the building of the Temple to the utmost of their ability. With heart elated by the success of his appeal and by perfect confidence in his youthful heir, David uttered a song of thanksgiving and blessed the Lord before all the congregation, owning that all he had was God's gift, and praying to Him to keep his son and the people in the right way. A great feast followed, and amid a profusion of sacrifices, and with much solemn ceremonial, Solomon was a second time anointed king, and received the homage and congratulations of the whole nation.

This was the last public act of the aged king. Soon afterwards he sank calmly to his rest in the seventy-first year of his life, B C. 1018, having reigned forty years, for seven over Judah in Hebron, and for three and thirty over the twelve tribes in Jerusalem. With the work of life happily accomplished, the past forgiven and atoned, the future prudently arranged, with a character chastened by outward circumstances, perfected by suffering, he arrived at the termination of his earthly career. The record of this event is touching in its simplicity "So David slept with his fathers, and was buried in the city of David." The term "slept" thus applied adumbrates for us Christians the resurrection, and doubtless had a similar reference in the minds of the most spiritual among the Israelites. Held in universal veneration, and regarded with a personal affection by the great body of the people, David was buried with the utmost magnificence in a splendid tomb which he had himself erected on Mount Sion, while his arms were preserved and later on deposited as sacred relics in the Temple [1] The exact site of this mausoleum has not yet been ascertained. It was well known till the destruction of Jerusalem : " His tomb is with us unto this day," says St. Peter in his address on the Day of Pentecost, [2] but since then its position has been a matter of conjecture, depending on the meaning affixed to the term "the city of David." Those who regard this as applied to the Temple Mount, appeal to Nehem. iii. 16 and Ezek xliii 7–9, which would seem to imply that the sepulchres of the

[1] 2 Kings xi. 10 , Ewald, iii. 203   [2] Acts ii 29.

kings lay on the west side of Moriah. This may have been the case, and yet David's own tomb may have been elsewhere. Certainly it was not removed when the others were disturbed by Herod on the enlargement of the Temple Court; therefore it could not have been there. And there seems good reason to consider that Sion, Acra, the City of David, and the Lower City, as we have seen above, were names affixed at various periods to the hill north-west of Moriah, on which a site called the Tomb of David is still shown. This monument stands immediately outside the Rotunda of the Church of the Holy Sepulchre. It is said to show even now that it had contained nine bodies deposited in graves beneath the surface of the floor. The kings buried therein were David, Solomon, Rehoboam, Ahijah, Jehoshaphat, Amaziah, Jotham, Hezekiah, and Josiah.[1] In this sepulchre, wherever situated, was buried a mass of treasure the fate of which is detailed by Josephus.[2] When Hyrcanus the high priest was besieged in Jerusalem by Antiochus Sidetes, B.C. 133, he obtained favourable terms from the enemy by promising a large sum of money; and having no funds in his treasury, he opened one of the cells of David's sepulchre, and took from it three thousand talents of silver, presenting Antiochus with one tenth of the riches thus obtained which secured his retreat. Many years afterwards, Herod the Great, being in want of money, and hearing what Hyrcanus had done, determined to recruit his resources in the same manner. Accordingly choosing night for his sacrilegious enterprise, and taking with him only a few of his most trusty friends, he entered the sepulchre. His search was rewarded by finding, not indeed money, but a prodigious store of gold and valuable treasures, all of which he carried away. On endeavouring to penetrate further, even to the shrine where lay the ashes of David and Solomon, he was stopped, so the story goes, by Divine interposition, a flame suddenly darting forth and consuming the foremost of his attendants. To atone for this invasion of the sanctities of the tomb, Herod erected at its entrance a magnificent monument of white marble.

[1] Conder, "Handbook," 341 f.
[2] "Ant." vii. 15. 3, xiii. 8. 4, xvi. 7. 1; "Bell Jud." i. 2. 5.

CHAPTER XIII.

CHARACTER.

David, as man, his mental characteristics—David, as king; results of his reign—David, as psalmist, his influence on psalmody—David as prophet—As type of Christ—Conclusion

It is no easy task to gather into one view the various traits of character which the history of David's life has displayed before us. One feels so petty beside this great man; one's own feebleness is in such marked contrast to his strength, that, however one may strive to appreciate his many excellencies, one is conscious of being unable to do justice to them. Their very number confuses the mind. One has to think of him as shepherd, courtier, soldier, leader, poet, statesman, prophet, king, one has to view him as friend, husband, father, in all relations eminent, blameworthy at times, but in all cases remarkable, and worthy of and requiring the deepest study. We can here only give a few brief reflections which may enable the reader to realize the greatness of this ancestor of Christ.

In estimating the character of David we must endeavour to regard its many sides, and to view it unprejudiced by our modern and more enlightened principles. We have to consider what he was in himself, and what he was in his relation to others; what was the form into which he was moulded by the events of his life and the circumstances of his position, and what were the result, of his public action and government. The failings of his age and country clung to him, that in many important particulars he rose superior to them was owing to his **own inherent strength of mind and the grace of God to which** he willingly submitted. In him as in all men, there were some weaknesses, imperfections, unbridled impulses, but these were counterbalanced by uncommon virtues, and his very failings made his excellencies more startling and significant. If the scoffer sneers at the term "a man after God's own heart" being applied to one who was guilty of David's crimes, we must remember that the expression occurs only as denoting one whom God approved in contradistinction to Saul whom he rejected,[1] one who, speaking generally, conformed his will to God's will; and it cannot be reasonably pressed to connote any further commendation. Taking the darkest view of David's fall, seeing it in the full enormity of all its bearings, we must acknowledge that it had its atonement. It was indeed punished temporarily in this world, but it was forgiven. And why? because it was repented of. Never greater was a fall, never more utter a repentance. Marvellous was the faith which from the abyss of guilt could turn to God in steadfast hope of restoration. We extol his faith on other occasions—when trusting in the God of the armies of Israel he went in his simple shepherd's garb against the giant foe whom none of all the host dare face, we extol his faith in the cave of Adullam, in the stronghold of Engedi, amid the persecutions of Saul and the perplexities of government, when beset by enemies on every side he overcame all by strength and counsel not his own; but greater, more wonderful than all, was the faith which led him to cleave unto God in his grievous lapse, and not let go his love. And this thought leads us to see what he was in himself. Now his great characteristic was faith in God, a deep and abiding realization of the unseen Lord, and an entire dependence upon His guidance. We find this exemplified through his whole chequered career; we read it in the utterances of his heart which he poured forth with such varied, but true, expression. History tells of the outer event; his own words lay bare the secret feelings which else were known only to God. This faith led him to the unequal combat with the giant in early youth, it inspired him in his struggles against the machinations of Saul, it enabled him to wait with patience the development of events, it supported him in all contests with enemies, but, as I have said, it showed itself most living and most potent in his great repentance. It is seen also in his resignation under God's chastening hand, in

[1] 1 Sam. xiii 14, comp Acts xiii 22

his meek endurance of the punishment of his sin, in the humility which caused him to bear reproach and contumely as only a righteous retribution. He has true love of God and devotion to His service. How he yearns to build a temple for His worship, and when refused this honour, how he exerts all his energies to prepare the way for his successor to execute the cherished design! Religion with him is no unreal sentiment, no mere politic instrument for satisfying and governing the superstitious multitude. It is his very life and the life of the nation. If we ask, how a religious man could commit David's crimes, does not our own conscience tell us that our religion has not kept us from falling into sin, that now and again some passion, some worldly affection, has obscured our faith and hidden God from us? Possibilities of transgressions as heinous as those of his belong to us all. Not only the grace of God but early training, the constraint of law, the fiat of society, public opinion, bar us from great crimes. With David many of these hindrances were absent. He was practically irresponsible. Practices like his were common among all Eastern rulers; prosperity had made him for the time selfish and despotic; flatterers told him he could do no wrong, after a life of activity and care he was just now idle and unoccupied, he was slack in prayer, and had ceased to realize his dependence upon God, and so when a sudden and violent temptation assailed him, he yielded, and added sin to sin. But this transgression was the fruit of a transient passion, and when this foul fiend was ejected, and the voice of conscience was heeded, and he saw himself as God saw him, the Divine life awoke in him again, his repentance was as signal as his fall, and left its mark on all his future. His religion, once again quickened, was too thorough to be satisfied with any partial contrition; it constrained him to go heavily the rest of his days. He had been cheerful, lighthearted, joyous, but with the consciousness of his sin the joyance of his life died out, his high spirits, his elastic temper, experienced a marked change. Knowing now the evil of his heart, he felt that he deserved the wrath of the God whom he had offended, and he bore all the afflictions that came upon him as the just punishment of his crimes. In the greatness of his one ever pressing sorrow he forgets all minor griefs, no care, no fear has he save that he may not be accepted of the Lord; in the depths of his heart ever sounds the "Miserere" which makes the tumult of the world echo faint and dull. This is true religion, and shows that in spite of his great fall he is rightly called a religious man.

Another characteristic of David is his tenderness; he is full of feeling and affection. Where in all history is there found a more touching episode than the story of his friendship with the chivalrous Jonathan? He is an attached son, a loving husband, a generous foe. Of all that is beautiful and noble he has a vivid appreciation; his sympathy is always enlisted on the side of uprightness and piety; against evil-doers he is stern and inflexible. A fond and doting father, he failed in his duty to his sons. The love which ought to have taught another lesson, led him to be weakly indulgent, so that it is said of the usurper Adonijah that "his father had not displeased him at any time in saying, Why hast thou done so?" The life of the harem, indeed, with its separate households and petty jealousies, tended to weaken parental control, and to make the training of children in the right way a task of enormous difficulty. With firmness and self-control the difficulty might have been overcome. But David weakly gave way to his excessive affection, and the serious faults and the vicious tendencies of his offspring were either unobserved or left unrebuked. The consequences, as we have seen, were most disastrous.

There is another matter that needs a few words while we are speaking of David's tenderness of heart. How are we to attribute to him this quality in the face of his ferocious treatment of the Ammonites, Moabites, and Edomites? Where was his sympathy with the suffering, his consideration for others, when he tortured defeated enemies, or put two-thirds of the captive soldiers to death, or exterminated all the male inhabitants? These proceedings seem to our minds ruthlessly cruel, and such as no humane man could direct or sanction. But the times were rude; civilization had not conquered barbarism; the treatment of enemies was always rough; natural kindliness was not concerned in the disposal and punishment of such as were fighting against the Lord and His people. The Law countenanced even severer measures than David took; and when a ruler was persuaded that he was the instrument of a Divine decree and was only carrying out superior commands, his softer feelings did not oppose their execution and were not outraged by barbarities which revolt Christian morality. Conscience uttered no protest against them ; they were a simple duty ; and if David had neglected to carry out such measures, he would not have been a man of the time, but a prodigy.

There was nothing little in David's character. His qualities were great and strong, for good or evil. Well was it for him that the circumstances of his life were such as to check and modify his natural propensities. His animal courage and self-reliance, combined with the activity and dexterity of a practised athlete, might have led to arrogance and cruelty, had they not been controlled by the early piety which his training had inspired, and the necessity of self-restraint imposed by outward events. Popular, beloved, the darling of the army, winning affection wherever he turned, he might have easily played the part of a demagogue, a usurper, a tyrant ; but his religion proved his safety ; the prophet's voice directed his course of action, and in patience he possessed his soul.

With vehement human affections not unalloyed by sensual tendencies, he possessed an ambitious and aspiring nature, which lifted him above the seductions of passion, and preserved him from becoming a mere selfish voluptuary. And if the love of men and the applause of the multitude proved too elating and satisfactory, there was always a thorn in the flesh which checked self-congratulation and chastened pride. The presence of one such as Joab, privy to all his master's weaknesses and sins, making his power to be miserably felt, yet too strong to be resisted, was, as it were, an embodiment of conscience, reminding of the past, warning for the future. Writhe as he might under the lash of this pitiless accomplice, David could not deliver himself from the infliction ; but he learned humility, patience, self-abasement ; he could not foster high thoughts of himself while cringing beneath his servant's evil influence. Thus that intense love of approbation, that desire to stand well with all men, which would have led to compromise of principle and neglect of obvious duty, was balanced by a power which lowered his self-respect and tendered to destroy his reputation abroad. We see him constantly reminded of the chain that bound him, chafing against it, yet owning its wholesome restraint. His repeated and pathetic exclamation, " What have I to do with you, ye sons of Zeruiah ? " shows the feeling, recognizes the check and its necessity. This ever-present memorial of weakness and guilt was needed for the perfection of the saint, and was received with submission, and its bitter lesson was learned.

Accustomed to overcome opposition, craving liberty of action, compelling circumstances to bend to his wishes, he might naturally have developed into a cruel despot, had not his respect for law and religion again restrained him. Conscious of great abilities, knowing that he rose above his contemporaries in attainments, views, aspirations, his humility, his profound apprehension of his nothingness in the sight of the Almighty, preserved him from arrogance, inspired him to sing in words which tradition ascribes to his pen:

> "Lord, my heart is not haughty, nor mine eyes lofty;
> Neither do I exercise myself in great matters,
> Or in things too wonderful for me
> Surely I have stilled and quieted my soul,
> Like a weaned child with his mother,
> My soul is with me like a weaned child" (Psa. cxxxi)

How magnanimous is his treatment of those who have deeply injured him! How willing is he to sacrifice himself for the good of others! How loath to profit by their danger in which he has had no share! His passions are strong, he is prone to anger, hasty in determining on revenge. yet is he open to reason, and a firm sense of justice overbears the temporary emotion. In many respects he is remarkably superior to the prejudices of his day and country, he looks beyond the narrow bounds of his isolated fatherland, and would fain see the Gentiles partakers of his privileges.

How many-sided is his character; how varied are his accomplishments! He is contemplative, the man of prayer and meditation; his love of nature is intense, he is an intelligent student of the varying aspects of sky, land, water. He has a passionate affection for his native country. Alone with his harp on the breezy upland he sings of the beauties that surround his daily watch, he tells of the high hopes which fire his breast; his soul leans forth in fervent appeals to Jehovah whose presence he feels, whose inspiration he acknowledges. But he is no less the man of action. Whether in youth defending his flock from the lion and the bear, or taking his part in repelling the attacks of marauding rovers, or, later, joining the army in warlike expeditions, leading the troops to victory, or in mature age heading a kingdom which he had made, and giving to it institutions, military, civil, religious—he is energetic, laborious, unsparing of trouble, fertile in expedients, courageous in danger, self-relying, sufficient, in all transactions competent. He loves liberty ; the hard life of the wilderness is more acceptable than the constraints of a tyrant's court , his own plans, his own conclusions, he will not easily consent to relinquish ; they who oppose them are no friends of his ; freedom of action is with him a passion, and he is generally right in vindicating it for himself Ambitious indeed he is, but his ambition is noble and pure. There is nothing of meanness and self-seeking in it. He will walk worthy of his high vocation ; he will be a true theocratic king , he will teach his subjects to aspire to be the people of Jehovah, not in name only, but in heart and life, by showing himself to be guided by heaven in all his actions, by setting an example of obedience and holiness. The weakness of human nature impaired this high ideal, but such was the standard which he had set before him And with such aspirations he could not but love all that was good and beautiful, morally and physically ; his sympathies always were awakened by what was noble and virtuous , he would shower favours on the deserving, and spend himself in their service The grand aim which he hoped to reach encouraged all the finer qualities of his soul ; it nerved his arm ; it controlled his passions , it dictated his policy ; it brought him back to the right path in times of declension , it enabled him to bear affliction, delay, disappointment, and to leave the guidance of events to God.

Much more might be said of this portion of our subject, so rich and varied, and full of deepest interest. But we must turn to another aspect. If we would rightly appreciate the greatness of David's character as king, we must see tl e general results of his reign of forty years What Moses had commenced and Joshua had for a time and in part completed, what Samuel had lived but to accomplish, and had but half-realized, was established first on a permanent basis by David. He gave to his nation that unity which made combination for national good practicable. Under his rule this united people enjoyed a security which allowed growth and expansion , true religion was cultivated and acknowledged as the foundation of prosperity ; the resources of the country were largely and profitably employed; the arts which add to comfort and convenience, as well as those which beautify and adorn, were fostered and developed; and Israel took an influential position among the nations of earth. This was the more remarkable as the Jews had no mission to conquer and annex distant territories; they were to be content with their own beautiful and fruitful country, and maintain their own limits without coveting the possessions of others. Success unexpected and extensive attended their efforts. Circumstances compelled them to enlarge their borders; in defending their own dominions they could not help carrying the war into the enemies' land, and securing future tranquillity by making foemen into tributaries. Thus northwards into Syria, southwards over Edom and the desert tribes, and far eastwards to the very Euphrates, extended the Israelites' dominion when Solomon ascended his father's throne. We have seen how the army was constituted. The veteran six hundred, the Gibborim, with their thirty skilled officers and the three supreme commanders, formed the nucleus, to which was closely united the body-guard composed chiefly of mercenaries. According to the matured plan invented by David, the nation was the army, and had to take its turn of military service under twelve generals selected from the "mighty men." This force amounted to some 300,000 combatants. Formidable in numbers, as it may appear, its true strength lay in the spirit with which it was animated, and which had been infused into it by its king. David had taught and exemplified that religion was a power; that fealty to Jehovah was the source of national prosperity; that the Lord fought for Israel as long as she was true to Him. He had shown himself not a mere warlike leader or a mighty despot, but a theocratic king, a ruler, that is, who is governed and directed by Divine inspiration, following out not his own crude, self-invented projects; but the course delineated by prophetic voice or heaven-sent impulse. The consciousness of this supernatural guidance led the people to regard the Lord's anointed with reverence, and to obey him with ready fidelity; and the same feeling reacted upon themselves, making them sharers in their monarch's glory, and empowered them to rise to the proud conviction that, as their prince was the vicegerent of Jehovah, so they themselves were the people of Jehovah. This was their consecration; they were the Lord's army; their wars were holy wars, waged against the enemies of God; in this conviction they became a nation of heroes, they felt secure of victory; in spite of inferiority in numbers, in arms, in experience, they entered upon every engagement with a confidence that nothing could destroy. So great was Israel under David's rule.

We have noticed what he did for public worship and the ordinances of religion. His piety was thoroughly practical, and he aimed at making the whole nation of one mind with himself in this important matter. He recognized the necessity of an external side to religion, that without form and ritual and ceremony the reality would perish; hence he elaborated a grand system of worship, arranging details, and providing materials which were employed till the latest ages of the Jewish kingdom. He founded himself on the Mosaic system; his idea of the service of Jehovah was only a development of that which was prescribed in the Pentateuch. Doubtless many portions of the arrangements ascribed to him by the Chroniclers were the product of later times, and came into existence by degrees, but he was the author of the centralization of religious worship at Jerusalem, and to him must be attributed the reorganization of the Levites, which not only secured the regular and decent performance of Divine service, but also obtained for the ministers of religion a recognized position and maintenance which the confusion of the times had greatly impaired. Whether the piety of the people grew and flourished under these careful arrangements we cannot accurately determine. Certainly nothing could have been better calculated for raising and maintaining a high standard, and diffusing Divine knowledge. The priests were not kept at Jerusalem. As soon as their turn of service was expired, they returned to their own homes, thus carrying into the remotest districts the sanctities of religion, and presenting examples of religious households. The Levites too were spread throughout the land in different capacities. Though a large proportion were employed at the sanctuary as porters, singers, guards, a great number filled the offices of magistrates, judges, and teachers in other parts of the country. Some three thousand of these officers were settled among the eastern tribes, which, as being far removed from the centre, needed more careful oversight. To Levites were entrusted the preparation of the public annals; they were the lawyers and registrars of the community; the little acquaintance with medicine and surgery which existed anywhere was found among them. Their labours in the cause of religion were materially assisted by the Schools of the Prophets in which David took the warmest interest, excited thereto originally by his friend and tutor Samuel, and supported by the assistance of the prophets Gad and Nathan. If in spite of the institutions, and notwithstanding the many aids which were provided for the maintenance of true religion, the people were easily seduced to rebel against the Lord s anointed and to side with the godless usurper, we must remember that the best constituted arrangements cannot absolutely secure the intended effect, while men remain such as they are. The Mosaic enactments, sanctioned and confirmed in the most miraculous manner, were never fully carried out. The human element of imperfection and weakness impairs the institutions of fairest promise; the fickleness and inconsistency of the multitude disturb the wisest calculations. The very piety and devotion of David were a cause of offence to many worldlings, and raised up enmity against him. The tacit reproach of a life animated by love of God and ruled by His commandments occasioned a dislike and even animosity which culminated for a time in rebellion. But these untoward circumstances do not lessen the glory of him who first gave life and substance to a great devotional system, who showed such remarkable ability in organizing the ecclesiastical department, and in reducing to method and regularity the scattered forces of the spiritual army. And however temporary hallucinations on some occasions may have obscured loyalty and allegiance, true religion during all this reign was so powerful and so universally acknowledged that idolatry was unknown, and not in the remotest village was any god honoured but Jehovah. This is a great and noble result.

But succeeding ages owe another debt to David, an obligation ever fresh and of incalculable importance. He is the founder of psalmody. Now in estimating David's connection with our existing Psalter, we must beware of falling into two errors: first, that of attributing to him too large a share in its composition, and, secondly, that of refusing him any part whatever. Destructive criticism has reached its lowest depth when it can say that there is no probability that he wrote a single psalm of our present collection, and that he was known by tradition only as the composer of secular drinking-songs, resting this last assertion on an erroneous interpretation of Amos vi 5

The truth, like virtue, lies in the mean. While there are certainly many poems assigned to him which internal evidence indisputably appropriates to other authors and times, there are others where the same evidence as plainly confirms the witness of tradition and title. Agreeing with the writers of the Old and New Testaments in regarding Moses in a general way as the author of the Pentateuch, we are not constrained to see in every allusion to the Mosaic Law a proof of late authorship; rather, appreciating David's intense devotion to the ordinances of the God of his fathers, and his regard for the marvellous history of his nation, we should be astonished not to find continual references to the Book of the Law of Moses, and should consider the omission of such topic a presumption that a composition did not emanate from the son of Jesse. We must also give full weight to the inscriptions both in the Hebrew and the Greek. Some, indeed, are manifestly erroneous; but when we remember that the Greek translators found them in their copies of the original, and that they were so ancient that in many cases their true meaning had perished, we must be cautious of rejecting them at the bidding of a captious criticism which forces facts to suit its theories and seeks truth through the medium of scepticism. Having premised thus much, we may proceed to estimate briefly what part David had in our present collection, and the influence exercised by him on the form and import and genius of the whole Psalter.

In the Hebrew text seventy-three psalms are ascribed to David, and in the Greek eleven others; there are also a few anonymous ones which are also assigned to him by internal evidence. The first Book of the Psalter (Psa. i.-xli.) claims David exclusively as its author, and though this conclusion has been strongly disputed, we are inclined both in this and other cases to allow great weight to the traditional inscription, where the contents are not manifestly repugnant to the title, and where the theory of later interpolations satisfactorily accounts for the introduction of certain phrases and allusions. Taking a liberal view of David's connection with our present Book we may say that the Psalter grew gradually in his hands, reflecting the various circumstances of his life, and the various phases of his mental and religious character. Feeling strongly on this point, the ancient editors and translators have often endeavoured to fix the particular period to which a poem belongs, and we cannot doubt, in spite of the objections of modern critics and sciolists, that they were more often right than wrong in their conjectures. Who does not see the propriety of the heading of Psa. li, "When Nathan the prophet came unto him after he had gone in to Bathsheba"; of Psa. iii. ("Lord, how are they increased that trouble me"), "When he fled from Absalom his son;" of Psa. vii, "Which he sang unto the Lord concerning the words of Cush the Benjamite;" of Psa. xviii. (2 Sam xxii.), "A psalm of David, the servant of the Lord, who spake unto the Lord the words of this song in the day that the Lord delivered him from the hand of all his enemies, and from the hand of Saul;" of Psa. xxxiv., "When he changed his behaviour before Abimelech, who drove him away, and he departed," where the use of the name Abimelech, instead of Achish, shows that the writer of the inscription derived his information from a tradition different from that contained in 1 Sam. xxi.; of Psa. lii, "When Doeg the Edomite came and told Saul, and said unto him, David is come to the house of Abimelech;" Psa lvii., "When he fled from Saul in the cave;" Psa lix., "When Saul sent, and they watched the house to kill him"? In all these instances the contents of the poem, more or less, confirm the authenticity of the heading The subject matter often enables us to determine the circumstances in David's life to which allusion is made. The early shepherd days, which fostered the love of nature and encouraged the contemplation of the wonders of creation, are reflected in Psa. xix. ("The heavens declare the glory of God"), xxix. ("The voice of the Lord is upon the waters"), xxiii. ("The Lord is my Shepherd"), and viii. ("O Lord, our Lord, how excellent is Thy name in all the earth"). The persecutions of Saul and the wanderings in the desert give occasion for many an outburst of song. Psa xi, is his answer to Saul's jealousy: Psa. vii, his appeal against the slanders of envious courtiers; Psa lvi, lviii, lix, xxxiv, refer to his escape from court and his abode at Gath; reference to Adullam is found in Psa. lvii., to Engedi in Psa xxxv, xxxvi; while Psa xxii. gives an ideal representation of all the sufferings which his outlaw life had brought upon him There are no poems which can be assigned exclusively to the reign at Hebron, but the establishment of the kingdom gave occasion to the godly resolutions of Psa. ci., and the high anticipations of Psa ii, to the exultation at the reunion of Israel of Psa. cxxxiii., and the prayer for grace to perform the duties of his station in Psa ci., for the removal of the Ark were composed Psa xxiv, xxix., and perhaps xv.; in connection with foreign wars we have Psa. lx, cx, xx., xxi.; the great sin is marked by Psa xxxii and li., the rebellion of Absalom called forth many precious monuments of piety and faith; to it we are indebted for the Third and Fourth Psalms, the morning and evening hymns of the Church, as they have been called; for the Sixty-third, which speaks of the unquenchable thirst for God and His worship, for the Fifty-fifth, Sixty-second, and Sixty-ninth, which complain of the treachery of Ahithophel and the falsehood of Ziba. To his old age belong the grand odes, Psa lxv, lxxi, and that in 2 Sam xxiii. Thus we see that the harp of David celebrated his triumphs, soothed his sorrows, expressed his repentance, animated his patriotism, declared his faith, gave a vivid representation of his outward and inward life throughout his varied career We cannot doubt that we possess only a portion of the poems which he composed Some that are absent from the Psalter have been preserved in the historical books, *e g*, his last words, his lament over Saul and Jonathan, his dirge over the murdered Abner Such as we have are those which were adapted for and used in public service, and were preserved for that purpose But the existing matter shows how largely he contributed to the Psalter both personally and through his imitators and descendants The impulse given by him thrilled through after-ages; and sons of Asaph, and sons of Korah, taking him as their model, carried on the Divine afflatus, and in strains learned from their great predecessor celebrated the acts of Israel and the praises of Jehovah Two-thirds of our Psalter are attributable to David and his immediate successors. The sweet psalmist of Israel led the way for a band of pupils and followers, who were happy in building on his foundation, and were even enjoined so to do, so that when Hezekiah introduced a reformation in the Temple services, he and his princes "commanded the Levites to sing praise unto the Lord with the words of David and of Asaph the Seer."[1] To him must be ascribed the invention of psalmody, as an integral part of Divine worship. The ritual of Moses made no provision for sacred song, and as far as we know, no form of words was prescribed

[1] 2 Chron. xxix. 30

for any officiant save only the threefold benediction. The great work of introducing orderly music and song into the ritual of the tabernacle was effected by David. As the leader who taught the Church to sing the praises of the Lord he deserves to be held in everlasting remembrance. On the inestimable value of his words to every soul, on their adaptability to every phase of humanity, how the penitent finds herein the voice of his complaint, the sorrowful finds sympathy and comfort; how the tempted, the sick, the timid, the bold, the happy, the young, the old, the oppressed, the favoured, meet herein with vehicles of expression so appropriate, so uniquely suited to their thoughts, that they seem to have been written especially for them—on all this I cannot dilate. It is a blessed thing that his words are familiar to us all, and we need no guide to point us to one who is our dearest friend and brother, whose heart beats in our own breast.

It remains to speak of David as a prophet. This appellation is expressly applied to him by St. Peter in his Pentecostal sermon (Acts ii. 30), "Being a prophet, and knowing that God had sworn with an oath to him, that of the fruit of his loins, according to the flesh, He would raise up Christ to sit upon His throne; he seeing this before spake of the resurrection of Christ." Herein is showed the inspired view of the apostle regarding the psalmist; and the circumstances of his life, and the productions of his pen confirm the verdict Our blessed Lord also Himself testifies (Matt. xxii. 43) that David spake in the Spirit, *i.e.*, as inspired by the Holy Ghost. The Spirit of the Lord that came upon him when he was anointed in his father's house at Bethlehem not only fired his breast with high aims, and prepared him for ruling men, it also inspired him to sing the praises of God, and put words into his mouth, the full import of which should be developed in after-ages. In the Schools of the Prophets he had witnessed bursts of enthusiasm, and had himself yielded to the same Divine impulse; and as he grew up, and more especially in his later years, the spirit within him found utterance, and the hopes of a pious Israelite for a great future were expressed in language which could but have a Messianic interpretation. At the same time, David never assumed the office or character of a prophet; he spake as he was moved; how much he understood of the coming event of which he sung, we cannot tell ; but his forward glance passed beyond earthly thrones and earthly conquests, and rested on a Divine personage who should realize the grand ideal of King. Some of his poems can apply in fulness to no one but the Christ of God. Others, indeed, have a primary sense which suits himself, his circumstances, or his people; but those which cannot be so interpreted are strictly prophetical. We can see one great occasion when the Messianic idea was unfolded to him, and he learned that in his line the great promise should be fulfilled, and that his kingdom foreshadowed, and should pass into that of Messiah. It was after he had expressed his desire to build a house to Jehovah at Jerusalem that Nathan cheered him with this grand promise.[1] He intimated that the chieftain from the house of Judah should rule for ever, and be established in an everlasting kingdom, that his seed should build an everlasting temple to the Lord, and that God would deal with them as His sons in chastisement and mercy. Taking this promise to heart, and meditating upon it with reverence and hope, David in his last recorded utterance looks forward to the Antitype as his greatest comfort, he beholds the righteous ruler shining forth as the dawn, he utters his confidence in the everlasting covenant, his belief that salvation will extend far and wide, that the promise of dominion is not confined to an earthly victor, but appertains to a royal race which culminates in Christ. In Psa. cx., a psalm continually quoted in the New Testament by Christ and the apostles, the prediction of Nathan is further unfolded ; it is " the oracle of Jehovah " to one whom he acknowledges as his Lord and Sovereign, and whom he hears to be enthroned at the right hand of God and victorious over all enemies ; and this monarch is a priest-king like Melchizedek ; in him are combined royalty and priesthood, such an union as was never seen in the history of Israel, such as David could have had no conception of save by supernatural revelation ; for it involves a belief in the exaltation of Messiah and the abrogation of the Mosaic system which no uninspired Jew could have imagined. If the Second Psalm speaks primarily of the utter defeat of enemies who combined against an earthly king, as the singer goes on, he turns his gaze away from such puny foes, and rests his eye upon the Hope of Israel enthroned at the right hand of Jehovah as

[1] 2 Sam. vii , 1 Chron xvii See p. 117 f

his Son, and enjoying all the prerogatives of this glorious position. Here, too, we meet with the names by which the coming Prince is commonly known, "Jehovah's Anointed," "The Lord's Christ," and "The Son of God." Here surely is predictive power exhibited. David, in Psa. xviii., speaks of his many dangers and deliverances, of the final establishment of his throne and the extension of his sway; but these allusions do not exhaust the subject; though they are true of himself, they are much more true of Christ, and could only be considered fulfilled in Him; and the Psalmist was directed so to indite that the words might have a further and higher application, and the apostle with no forced accommodation might find in them mention of the work of Christ among the Gentiles.[1] When he wrote the Twenty-fourth Psalm to celebrate the removal of the Ark to Jerusalem, did not the royal poet have a vision of the Messiah ascending in triumph to heaven after His glorious resurrection? When he penned Psa. viii., recalling his shepherd life on the pastures of Bethlehem, did he not think of the ideal Man who from His humility is exalted to the right hand of God? As in Psa. xvi. he looks to God as his portion and refuge in this world and the next, so his language is explained by apostles[2] to apply to the resurrection of Jesus Christ in whom man first attained to the blessed hope of everlasting life. We cannot pursue this subject further; enough has been said to show that in calling David a prophet, St. Peter not only asserted the Psalmist's claim to inspired utterance of praise and prayer, but also vindicated for him the possession of predictive powers, which an unprejudiced consideration of his genuine compositions proves to be well founded.

Of David as a type of Christ little need be said. This view is one with which every one is familiar; it has prevailed in the Christian Church from the earliest times; it is confirmed by the verdicts of Christ Himself and His apostles; it is the interpretation of many of his acts and words, and often affords the truest clue to their significance. If the Twenty-second Psalm was written by David to express the deep anguish of his soul at some poignant and supreme suffering, and his thanksgiving for deliverance, it is only as fulfilled in the Passion and death of Christ and in the assurance of the joy that His affliction would

[1] Rom. xv. 9.   [2] Acts ii. 27; xiii. 35.

win for the world, that the hyperbolical language can be taken The very details of the psalm are reproduced in the sufferings of Messiah, who Himself appropriated the words to Himself and makes the sufferer His type. Through all the circumstances of his life David has been regarded as typical of His great Son His birth at Bethlehem, his private unction there, his victory over the giant foe who had defied the army of the living God, his sweet music which put to flight the evil spirit, the persecutions that he endured, the compassion and forgiveness that he exhibited, his zeal for the House of God, his wars and triumphs over heathen nations, his rejection by his own people, the treachery of his tried comrade, his final victory over all opposition—all these and such like details have a prophetic and typical import and speak to the Christian of the love and sufferings and triumph of Jesus.

The estimation in which uninspired Jews held David is seen in the Book of Ecclesiasticus where he takes a prominent place among "famous men"[1] "As is the fat," says the son of Sirach, "separated for its excellence from the peace offering, so was David chosen out of the children of Israel . . . He called upon the most high Lord, and God gave him strength in his right hand to slay that mighty warrior, and set up the horn of His people. . . . He destroyed the enemies on every side, and brought to nought the Philistines. . . . In all his works he praised the Holy One most High with words of glory, with his whole heart he sang songs and loved Him that made him He set singers also before the altar, that by their voices they might make sweet melody, and daily sing praises in their songs He beautified their feasts, and set in order the solemn times until the end, that they might praise His holy name, and that the temple might sound from morning The Lord took away his sins and exalted his horn for ever, He gave him a covenant of kings and a throne of glory in Israel."

David is the ideal king of Israel, the standard and model by which all succeeding monarchs are tried As no other "worthy" ever assumed his name, so no one ever occupied his place or usurped his pedestal He is unique, alone, unapproachable. Other monarchs "went not fully after the Lord as David did," their "heart was not perfect with the Lord as was the heart of David;" they were "not as My servant David;" and if one was

[1] Chap. xlvii. 2-11.

righteous and obedient he is still compared with the same example : "Asa did that which was right in the eyes of the Lord as did David his father;" Hezekiah "did that which was right in the sight of the Lord, according to all that his father David did;" Josiah "walked in all the way of David his father."[1] Never has the memory of his pre-eminence been forgotten Time, which casts the mantle of oblivion on most things, only added to his reputation, and gave new impulse to the affection with which he was regarded. Down the ages, in the writings of historians and prophets, in canonical and apocryphal Scriptures, his figure looms large and brilliant, till He of whom he was the type and forerunner, whose character and life he so wonderfully foreshadowed, appeared in the flesh, and Christ the great Son of David visited and redeemed His people Israel. Then the mystery was revealed, the promise of the past was fulfilled when He came of whom it was said . "The Lord God will give unto Him the throne of His servant David, and He shall reign over the house of Judah for ever, and of His kingdom there shall be no end."

[1] Niemeyer, "Charakt. der Bibel," iv. 395.